W9-ARG-095

HISTORY
OF RUSSIA

Sergei Mikhailovich Soloviev

The
Academic International Press
Edition
of
Sergei M. Soloviev

History of Russia From Earliest Times

G. EDWARD ORCHARD
General Editor

Contributing Editors

HUGH F. GRAHAM

JOHN D. WINDHAUSEN

ALEXANDER V. MULLER

K.A. PAPMEHL

RICHARD HANTULA

WALTER J. GLEASON, JR.

WILLIAM H. HILL

G. EDWARD ORCHARD

LINDSEY A.J. HUGHES

NICKOLAS LUPININ

GEORGE E. MUNRO

DANIEL L. SCHLAFLY, JR.

ANTHONY L.H. RHINELANDER

PATRICK J. O'MEARA

PETER C. STUPPLES

T. ALLAN SMITH

MARTHA L. LAHANA

ANTHONY V. KNOWLES

HELEN Y. PROCHAZKA

ALEXANDRA S. KORROS

GARY J. MARKER

SERGEI M. SOLOVIEV

History of Russia

Volume 11

The Reign of Ivan the Terrible
The Struggle against Bathory
Expansion into Siberia

Edited and Translated
By

Alexandra S. Korros

2002
Academic International Press

The Academic International Press Edition of S.M. Soloviev's
History of Russia From Earliest Times in fifty volumes.

Volume 3. *The Reign of Ivan the Terrible, The Struggle against
Bathory, Expansion into Siberia.*
Unabridged translation of the text of Volume 6, Chapters 6-7 as
contained in Volume III of S.M. Soloviev's *Istoria Rossii s
drevneishikh vremen* published in Moscow between 1959-1966, with
added annotation by Alexandra S. Korros.

ISBN: 0-87569-235-4

Composition by Llano F. McCowen

Printed in the United States of America

A list of Academic International Press publications is found at
the end of this volume.

ACADEMIC INTERNATIONAL PRESS
Box 1111 • Gulf Breeze FL 32562-1111 • USA
www.ai-press.com

Errata p. iv, line 3 read *Volume 11*

CONTENTS

WEIGHTS AND MEASURES

Linear and Surface Measure

Arshin: 16 vershoks, 28 in. (diuims) 72.12 cm
Chetvert (quarter): 1/4 arshin, 1/2 desiatina, 1.35 acres (sometimes 1.5 desiatinas or c. 4.1 acres)
Desiatina: 2,400 square sazhens, 2.7 acres, 1.025 hectares
Diuim: 1 inch, 2.54 cm
Fut: 12 diuims, 1 foot, 30.48 cm

Obza (areal): c. 10 chetverts, 13–15 acres
Osmina: 1/4 desiatina, 600 sq. sazhens, .256 hectare
Sazhen: 3 arshins, 7 feet, 2.133 m
Vershok: 1.75 in., 4.445 cm, 1/16 arshin
Verst: 500 sazhens, 1,166 yards and 2 feet, .663 miles, 1.0668 km
Voloka (plowland): 19 desiatinas, 20 hectares, 49 acres

Liquid Measure

Bochka (barrel): 40 vedros, 121 gallons, 492 liters
Chetvert (quarter): 1.4 bochkas, 32.5 gallons
Korchago (wine): Rus, unknown

Kufa: 30 stofy
Stof: Kruzhka (cup), 1/10 vedro, c. 1.3 quarts, 1.23 liters
Vedro (pail): 3.25 gallons, 12.3 liters, 10 stofy

Weights

Berkovets: 361 lbs., 10 puds
Bezmen: c. 1 kg, 2.2 lbs.
Chetverik (grain measure dating from 16th century): 1/8 chetvert, 15.8 lbs.
Chetvert (grain measure): 1/4 rad, 3.5 puds, 126.39 lbs., c. 8 bushels
Funt: 96 zolotniks, .903 lbs., 14.4 oz., 408.24 kg
Grivenka: 205 grams
Kad: 4 chetverts, 14 puds, 505.56 lbs.
Kadka malenkaia: 12th-century, small measure

Kamen (stone): 32 funt
Korob (basket): 7 puds, 252 lbs.
Osmina (eighth): 2 osmina to a chetvert (dry measure)
Polbezmen: c. 500 g, 1 lb.
Polosmina (sixteenth): 1/2 osmina
Pud: 40 funts, 36.113 lbs. (US), 40 lbs. (Russian), 16.38 kg
Rad: 14 puds, 505.58 lbs.
Zolotnik: 1/96 lbs., 4.26 grams

Money

Altyn: 6 Muscovite dengas, 3 copecks
Bel: Rus, pure silver coin
Chervonets (chervonnyi): gold coin of first half of 18th century worth c. 3 rubles
Chetvertak: silver coin equal to 25 copecks or 1/4 ruble (18–19th centuries)
Copeck: two Muscovite dengas
Denga: 1/2 copeck
Grivna: 20 Muscovite dengas, 100 grivnas equals 1 ruble, 10 copecks
Grosh: 10 peniaz
Grosh litovsky (Lithuanian grosh): 5 silver copecks
Kopa grosh: 60 groshas, one Muscovite poltina, 1/2 ruble
Kuna: 12th-century Rus coin comparable to Westerns denarii or Eastern dirhems. Varied in value by region. Replaced late 14th century by the denga or serebro (silver). Also a marten skin.
Moskovka: 1/2 copeck
Muscovite denga: 200 equals 1 ruble
Novgorod denga: 100 equals 1 ruble
Novgorodka: 1 copeck

Peniaz: 10 equals one grosh (Lithuania)
Poltina (poltinnik): 50 copecks, 100 dengas, 1 ruble
Poltora: 1 1/2 rubles
Polupoltina (-nik): 25 copecks, 50 dengas
Rezan: 12th century Rus coin. 50 rezan equals one grivna kuna
Ruble: 100 copecks, 200 dengas
Shiroky grosh (large silver coin): 20 Muscovite copecks
Veksa: 12th-century Rus small coin equal to one squirrel pelt (belka)

Foreign Denominations
Chervonnyi: c. 3 rubles
Ducat: c. 3 rubles
Dutch efimok: "lion dollar" or levok, 1 thaler, 2.5 guilders
Efimok: foreign currency, 1 thaler, .75-1 ruble, 1 chervonets or chervonnyi
Levok: Dutch silver lion dollar
Thaler (Joachimsthaler): c. 1 ruble, 1/3 chervonets or chervonnyi

Note: Weights and measures often changed values over time and sometimes held more than one value at the same time. For details consult Sergei G. Pushkarev, *Dictionary of Russian Historical Terms from the Eleventh Century to 1917* (Yale, 1970).

PREFACE

This volume is an unabridged translation of Volume VI, Chapters VI-VII and appendices of S.M. Soloviev's *Istoriia Rossii s drevneishikh vremen* (History of Russia from Earliest Times), published in Moscow between 1959 and 1966. The text used corresponds to pp. 611-724 of Volume III of the Moscow edition of 1963.

The original edition of Soloviev's text was published in St. Peterburg between 1851 and 1879 in twenty-nine volumes. The two chapters contained in this volume have been divided into four, Chapter I corresponding to pp. 611-671, Chapter II to pp. 671-685, Chapter III to pp. 686-702 and Chapter IV to pp. 702-714 of the Moscow edition of 1963. The Appendices appear on pp. 715-724. The headings, in the original clustered at the beginning of each chapter, to aid the reader have been placed in the most logical locations throughout the body of the text.

Although a great historian, Soloviev was not a graceful writer. His paragraphs are extremely long, often exceeding more than one single-spaced Russian page. In keeping with his paragraph style, Soloviev's sentences also verge on paragraph length. One of the major aims of this series is to render Soloviev's words into readabie, accessible English. In so doing sentences were shortened, the interminable paragraphs divided, and every effort made to transform Soloviev's words into modern twentieth-century scholarly language. Thus while the ideas and the history are Soloviev's, the reader must remember that the writing style is very different from the original. To accomplish these goals technical terms were translated into their English equivalents, particularly when referring to administrative ranks, titles, office and military terms. Russian terms in common English usage, such as boyar, Tatar, and khan, were retained. As translator I am acutely aware of the shortcomings of such translation, yet equally cognizant that a text littered with italicized technical terms is a serious barrier to easy reading.

Soloviev rarely footnoted his sources and the original text contains relatively few such notes and a number of references clustered into each annotation. These bibliographic references are useful to specialists who would be using the original Russian rather than a translation. Except for one or two specific notes supplied by Soloviev in the Appendices, none of his notes are included in this translation. Likewise, the notes supplied by the editors of the 1959-1966 edition also are omitted because they, like Soloviev's notes, are highly specialized, updating bibliographic information contained in Soloviev's original work. These notes too are extremely valuable to specialists since they refer the reader to the post-1917 location of materials Soloviev used, but they would be of little possible use to readers in English.

Throughout the text when Soloviev uses parentheses to explain or clarify unclear references, I have retained them. Similarly, the italics in the text are Soloviev's. Occasionally, notations in brackets were added to help readers keep track of the author of the work cited in particularly long quotations.

In preparing the annotation for the text every effort was made to note prominent individuals at their first mention, explain terms or events that Soloviev assumed his readers would recognize, and interpret events in a broader context than Soloviev might have thought to do. Occasionally a note will correct a minor error of Soloviev's or explain why his terminology differs from common usage. The notes also refer the reader to some sources available in English on the subject under discussion. Since this volume contains large amounts of material pertaining to Muscovite foreign policy, there are many references to books recounting Polish, Swedish and Habsburg history. An important, up-to-date and reliable reference on Russian history readily available in most university libraries, frequently cited in the notes, is the *Modern Encyclopedia of Russian and Soviet History* (MERSH) and its *Supplement*.

We have made every effort to preserve personal names in the form used in each country. Therefore Russian personal names are rendered in their Russian forms, except for such familiar names as Alexis, Peter, Nicholas or Catherine. Lithuanian, Polish and French names have been spelled according to their particular language. This is important particularly when it comes to names such as Henri of Anjou or Henri of Navarre, so as not to confuse these French Henris with the English Henry VIII or a German Heinrich. When a place-name or an individual's name has been anglicized and is commonly known, we have adhered to that spelling, for example "Dnieper" rather than "Dnepr." Most commonly known geographical locations are translated in their anglicized forms, such as Warsaw, Volhynia, Moscow or Transylvania.

When the editors of the 1959-1966 edition added patronymics and other names to Soloviev's original I have retained them without brackets. Patronymics appearing in the original edition also have been kept. To make the translation more readable I have anglicized plural forms, such as "Voguls" rather than "Vogulichi." If a Russian plural form is in common use, it appears in the translation.

To simplify the endings of names for non-Russian readers I have changed feminine personal names from "Mariia" to "Maria" or from "Marfa" to "Martha" and so forth. Usually Slavic surnames indicate gender. Thus feminine surnames most often end in "-a" such as "Anastasia Romanova."

I have used a modified form of the Library of Congress transliteration in preparing this volume, omitting diacritical marks such as ligatures, and rendering the initial letters "Ia-" and "Iu-" as "Ya-" and "Yu-," and occasionally "E-" as "Ye-." Thus Ermak (Timofeevich) is spelled as it is pronounced, "Yermak." The suffixes "-ii" and "-yi" are transliterated "-y" so that "Vasilii Kliuchevskii" becomes "Vasily Kliuchevsky." Similarly the suffix "-oi" appears as "-oy" as in "Donskoy" rather than "Donskoi." The soft sign has been dropped entirely, although on occasion we have replaced it with "-i-", most prominently in "Soloviev" rather than "Solovev."

All dates follow the Julian calendar unless otherwise specified. During the sixteenth century the Julian calendar was ten days behind the new Gregorian calendar, which was not in common use in Catholic Europe until after 1582, not adopted in Protestant Europe until 1700, or in England until fifty years later. Russia remained on the Julian calendar until after the Bolshevik revolution, when the Gregorian calendar was adopted in 1918.

A table of weights and measures is found at the front of the volume for the reader's convenience, although some unusual measures are explained in the notes. The sources of the maps included are noted in each case.

I would like to acknowledge Professor Eve Levin of the Ohio State University for her ongoing intellectual support and critical suggestions, and give special thanks to Nikolaos Chrissidis of Yale University for his constructive criticism, as well as all his help in indentifying and obtaining trying bibliographic references. Finally, without the patience and support of my husband and daughter, none of this work would have been possible. It is to them that I dedicate this book.

Alexandra S. Korros

INTRODUCTION

Every serious student of Russian history spends an obligatory amount of time reading the "classic" nineteenth and early twentieth-century Russian historians in order learn their views of Russia's historical development. The works of V.O. Kliuchevsky, S.F. Platonov, P.N. Miliukov and A.E. Presniakov always top the list. In contrast, the multi-volume *History of Russia* by S.M. Soloviev (1820-1879) often is regarded as a reference, used for its extensive documentation rather than reading for its particular point of view. Yet, as Hugh Graham observed in his introduction to Volume 9 of this series, S.M. Soloviev's work "set a new critical standard for detailed sober analysis, which subsequent historians were quick to emulate. His uncompromising insistence that historical narrative must be based on primary sources won wide acceptance. Anyone who pauses to reflect on the number of common assumptions about Russian history which Soloviev was the first to articulate will soon recognize how influential he was in forming attitudes to Russia's past."[1]

This volume is a particularly apt example of these aspects of Soloviev's work. Soloviev always has been described as the "statist" historian, concerned with the development and growth of the Russian state from Muscovy to Empire. Containing an analysis and description of Moscow's foreign policy during the reign of Ivan IV, this volume serves as an excellent vehicle for displaying Soloviev's primary focus on the central role of the state as he examines Moscow's relations with Poland during the reign of Stefan Bathory. The second chapter contains a brief summary of Russia's relations with other foreign powers. The third chapter "The Stroganovs and Yermak" details the first Russian inroads into Siberia, while the concluding chapter contains Soloviev's analysis of Ivan's reign with a focus on the controversies surrounding its historiography. The final section, consisting of two historiographical appendices, presents a fascinating lesson in Soloviev's methods of textual criticism.

Soloviev's style combined narrative sections interspersed with long quotations and paraphrasing from primary sources. In a sense he permitted the documents to speak for themselves. Although it is possible to argue that subsequent studies of Russian history may have reached higher levels of sophistication and synthesis, very few rely so completely on sources to tell their story. Soloviev often inserts complete documents almost entirely without commentary into the text. Although today we label such writing as awkward and cumbersome, in its own time it was innovative. In the mid-nineteenth century many writers of history distorted facts to make them fit some historical scheme, often omitting the documents on which the argument was based, as well as information tending to weaken the argument itself. In contrast, while Soloviev may make his own observations, the inclusion of the original text permits the reader to evaluate independently, without relying entirely on the author. Soloviev also introduces other points of view. For example, in his discussions of Muscovy's relationship with Poland-Lithuania and the election of a successor to Sigismund Augustus, Soloviev assesses both Russian and Polish motivations, adding texture, substance and nuance to what might otherwise be told as a relatively simple and unilinear story.

In composing his complex narrative Soloviev refers to a wide range of Russian and foreign source materials. Unfortunately, in contrast to this volume and to most twentieth-century scholarship, Soloviev annotates rarely and lops together many references into one note. Nevertheless by examining his notes carefully we can compile a bibliography of Soloviev's sources, even though he does not attribute each quotation precisely. In addition to the extensive materials from the archives of the Ministry of Foreign Affairs, documents that date from Ivan's Chancellery for Foreign Affairs (now housed in the Russian Central State Archive of Ancient Acts in Moscow) pertaining to Moscow's relations with Poland, Sweden, Denmark, Crimea, the Nogay Tatars and the Roman popes,[2] Soloviev also cites many published sources pertaining to Poland and Livonia.[3] The various chronicles recounting Ivan's reign constitute another important source for Soloviev, who based much of his narrative on the Nikon transcription, along with the *Book of the Tsars*, compiled in the Muscovite court during Ivan IV's reign.[4] In his treatment of the visit of the Jesuit Antonio Possevino to Moscow and of the discussions of English trade Soloviev relied heavily on various foreign accounts including Possevino's *Moscovia*,[5] and Hakluyt's *Collection of the Early Voyages, Travels and Discoveries of the English Nation*.[6] When discussing the Stroganovs and Yermak, Soloviev extensively utilized the *Stroganov Chronicle*[7] compiled at the court of the Stroganovs. As he points out in Appendix I, Soloviev accepts the *Stroganov Chronicle* as reliable in the same manner as did his predecessor the historian N.M. Karamzin.[8] In addition Soloviev cited other published histories of Siberia, including that of G.F. Müller dating from the mid-eighteenth century.[9] Through this large variety of documents Soloviev pieced together a detailed, highly opinionated story designed to show the paramount role of the ruler and the centralizing state in determining the course of Russia's complex sixteenth-century path.

The long reign of Ivan IV, the Terrible (1533-1584), spans one of the most complex and controversial periods of Russian history. Yet compared to the other aspects of his reign Ivan's diplomacy is less well known than his military ventures or his domestic policy. By following Moscow's relations with Poland-Lithuania at a crucial moment in its history Soloviev showed how themes central to Ivan's domestic policy were played out in his foreign policy as well.

The death of King Sigismund Augustus in 1574 led to the first "open" election for the Polish-Lithuanian throne. Although technically the Polish king had been "elected" since the accession of Jagailo in 1358, because the childless Sigismund Augustus left no heirs with a logical claim to the throne the Polish-Lithuanian Sejm had its first genuine opportunity to elect an outsider. Judging by the array of candidates, the European powers took this royal vacancy very seriously. Polish accounts tend to emphasize the Western and Central European role in the process, concentrating on the efforts of the Valois dynasty in France and the Habsburgs of Austria to accede to the Polish throne, highlighting the role of Catholic and Protestant politics in decision-making. In addition, most accounts simply tend to describe the events, name the various candidates, then list the faction or factions to whom each was most appealing or most dangerous. Because the lesser Lithuanian nobility were their main advocates, little is said about the candidacies of Ivan IV or one of his sons.

Understandably, Soloviev concentrates on the Russian role in the election process, relating far more than a description of Ivan's failed candidacy, but rather retelling it in great detail. Clearly this is the Russian perspective on the events, which in and of itself should be of great interest to Western historians who might not otherwise have access to this particular side of the story. As is his wont, Soloviev goes far beyond a description, stringing together a long series of quotations from appropriate sources to invest his story with a texture usually missing from later, more sophisticated interpretations. It is here that we can see most clearly his extensive use of the archival materials as well as the published diplomatic documents.

Instead of simply claiming that Ivan's on-again off-again candidacy for the Polish-Lithuanian throne was based on a certain ambivalence and skepticism about whether it was a goal worth pursuing, Soloviev presented the actual documents. We observe Ivan's vacillations, seeing his unwillingness to lower himself by sending representatives to bid for the throne. We read his letters to Maximilian II, the Holy Roman emperor, offering the tsar's support for a Habsburg candidate, and proposing to split the throne, with Poland for the Habsburgs and Lithuania for Muscovy. Such techniques mean that readers never have to take the historian's word on faith, and can decide for themselves whether Soloviev's interpretation is satisfactory.

Soloviev's narrative allows the non-Russian historian to examine the conduct, methods and goals of Muscovite diplomacy in Ivan IV's last years. Beyond learning the details of each diplomatic exchange, a picture of the actual conduct of sixteenth-century diplomacy emerges. At a time when international diplomacy was very much in its infancy, bearing letters of safe conduct ambassadors traveled from one ruler to another to deliver messages or transact specific business. Ambassadors to Moscow were charged with definite missions and often carried limited instructions leaving them unprepared to meet Ivan's extensive demands which regularly exceeded the specific business at hand. Similarly Muscovite emissaries often were equally unprepared and fearful of going beyond their particular missions when challenged by their hosts, who frequently were incensed by the tsar's arrogant attitude.

The ceremonial aspects of diplomatic conduct were as important as the substantive negotiations. If the monarch receiving the tsar's letters did not rise and inquire about Ivan's health, if he did not offer the ambassadors sufficient hospitality, his "insults" were at least as important a determinant of the negotiations' success as any meaningful discussions of the issues. Their outcome also could be hampered by Ivan's vituperative letters, which occasionally verged on the poetic, especially when full of vitriol. The seriousness with which all sides regarded the rituals of diplomacy comes to life in Soloviev's pages, particularly in cases where Ivan urged his ambassadors to bear every insult, even those to his person, in order to accomplish their mission.

Although the first chapter contained in this volume is entitled "Stefan Bathory," its scope goes far beyond its title. For Soloviev, relations with

Bathory are a means to introduce the enigmatic character of the last Jagiellonian ruler Sigismund Augustus, to trace the success and influence of Reformation theology in Poland-Lithuania, to describe some of the efforts of the church to combat the "new religion," and illustrate how theological combat influenced the search for Sigismund Augustus's successor.

Protestantism gained an important foothold in Poland and Lithuania, particularly among some of the most important noble families. Whereas his father regarded the new religion with hostility, Sigismund Augustus was far more tolerant. He was especially close to the Lithuanian magnate Radziwill family of his beloved second wife Barbara, who were the major Protestant leaders in their country. Similarly among the great Polish nobles, important families had converted to Protestantism. Toleration of Protestantism was an important aspect of the *Pacta Conventa,* an agreement to which Sigismund Augustus's successor was forced to subscribe. Yet religious rivalries were an important consideration in the political maneuvering to elect the new king. The Catholic prelates of Poland did not stand passively aside permitting Protestantism's spread. They combatted the new religion through the newly founded Jesuit order which established schools throughout Poland. By exploiting the political rifts that grew among the nobility as the various proponents put forth their candidates for the vacant crown, the bishops were able to pit Protestant against Protestant to assure the election of a Catholic king.

Soloviev's careful descriptions underline the fragmentation of Polish-Lithuanian politics. During the election process Ivan's primary advocates were members of the lesser Lithuanian nobility who were almost as wary of the candidates advanced by the great Lithuanian magnates as they were of those supported by the major Polish nobles and/or the minor Polish nobility, the *szlachta.* Thus candidates had to woo at least four different constituencies in their efforts to gain the Polish throne.

Having established the religious context of Polish-Lithuanian politics and its role in fragmenting the nobility further, Soloviev introduces the diplomatic gymnastics that led first to the election of Henri Valois, duke of Anjou, to the Polish-Lithuanian crown. Following Henri's hurried return to France only months after assuming the throne, Soloviev describes the renewed debates that led to the simultaneous election of Maximilian II, the Habsburg emperor, and the Transylvanian prince Stefan Bathory.[10]

Through his discussions of the negotiations over the Polish-Lithuanian succession we glimpse the relations between Moscow and the Holy Roman empire, and in later sections relations between Moscow and Sweden, as well as Moscow and England.[11] The key issue at hand was who would control Livonia—the Russians, the Poles and Lithuanians, or the Swedes. According to Soloviev, Muscovite aspirations in Livonia were based as much on the need for a secure road to Western military technology as on territorial ambition. Polish and Swedish opposition was grounded both on territorial ambition as well as an effort to deny Muscovy access to Western technology. To Soloviev, Russia's greatest tsars were those who at least understood the need to bring Western technology to the Muscovite military. If Soloviev is correct, what became policy in the seventeenth century clearly had its origins in sixteenth-century Muscovite diplomacy.[12]

Muscovy's difficult relations with its neighbors were intensified further by Ivan's preoccupation with his position. The diplomatic sections reveal that like his fellow rulers Ivan constantly asserted his superior ancestry and was loathe to lower himself to monarchs of lesser status. This may in part explain his ambivalence toward bartering for election to the Polish throne. Throughout his correspondence Ivan tried to establish the superiority of his ancestry to that of his rivals, and used it to win his point even when he lacked the requisite military resources. Soloviev's summary reveals Ivan's reliance on two separate arguments to establish his superior lineage. The legend of Prus, the brother of Augustus Caesar who settled in what is today's East Prussia and sent his relatives to help settle in Kiev, linked the Muscovite dynasty directly to Ancient Rome. By invoking Filofey's doctrine of "Moscow, the third Rome" that whereas two Romes (Rome and Constantinople) have fallen, Moscow, the third, will live, Ivan defined himself as the successor to the Roman and Byzantine emperors.[13]

Ivan's proclamations of superior lineage notwithstanding, the upstart Bathory had the technology and armies to defeat the Russians. Soloviev's discussions of Bathory's military campaigns against Moscow are replete with details describing the Russian defense of their cities against Polish attacks. Bathory emerges as a talented but treacherous enemy with a strong army heavily dependent on mercenary Hungarians, yet lacking support among the minor Lithuanian gentry. As Soloviev puts it, Bathory's victories resulted from an overwhelming technical superiority combined with his ability to concentrate his forces in one place whereas Moscow was forced spread its forces to protect against the Swedes in the North and the Tatars in the South and East, as well as against the invading Poles.

Despite what Soloviev describes as enormous bravery, and even an occasional Muscovite victory, the pressure on all his borders forced Ivan to sue for peace. During the course of their correspondence Ivan not only described Bathory as an interloper of less than estimable lineage, he accused him of being an agent of the Ottoman empire. Consequently Ivan constantly sought international support precisely because of Bathory's ties to the Turks. Unfortunately the Habsburgs, who were too indecisive to accept the offer of the Polish throne, continued to vacillate, and the Swedes were more anxious to stop Muscovy in Livonia by linking their activity to Polish attacks on Russian cities. Finally these factors, along with renewed disturbances in the Crimea, forced Ivan to make peace with Poland and Sweden while unsuccessfully seeking Christian support against the Muslim infidel.

In his anxiety to end the war against Poland and Sweden Ivan utilized the services of the Jesuit Antonio Possevino, a papal emissary who arrived in Moscow to unite the Orthodox and Catholic churches. Using the Jesuit's *Moscovia* extensively, Soloviev details Ivan's conversations with Possevino, which illustrated the unbridgeable gulf between the two churches. Possevino's attempts to gain permission to build a Catholic church in Moscow came to naught, for while Ivan was willing to permit Italian merchants to worship privately, he refused to allow any public Catholic worship in Muscovy. Soloviev relates how during the course of one particularly telling conversation between the tsar and the Jesuit, Ivan asked Possevino if it was true that the Pope was carried about Rome on a litter and that he wore a cross on his shoe. In this respect, he told Possevino, the Roman and Russian Orthodox beliefs differed greatly from one another. "The cross of Christ is a victory over our enemies, we honor it and we do not wear the cross lower than our belt."

Ivan's emphasis on the visual-symbolic aspects of his belief illustrate how he viewed the differences between the two churches. Possevino too was struck by Ivan's preoccupation with external symbols and described the tsar as trivial and ill-informed on religious matters.[14] Despite these differences Ivan, desperate to extricate himself from the war, took advantage of Possevino's presence to employ him to negotiate peace between Moscow and Poland, in exchange for which Moscow relinquished its Livonian conquests.

Soloviev quotes Possevino's rather one-sided descriptions of his debates with Ivan extensively, albeit selectively rather than exhaustively. He also regarded *Moscovia* as a key source for various events during the last years of Ivan's reign, singling out Possevino's description of Ivan's behavior after the death of his son Ivan Ivanovich as probably the most accurate.

Soloviev's interpretation of Ivan's relations with Queen Elizabeth I of England is found in the following chapter. Stymied in his efforts to create a route to Western technology by way of Livonia, Ivan hoped to form an exclusive alliance with England in which he traded access to Russian ports on the White Sea for English military and scientific expertise. To cement this special relationship with Elizabeth, Ivan sought a marital alliance by proposing to make one of the queen's cousins his fifth wife. Although one of the most famous stories pertaining to Ivan's reign was about his proposal to marry Elizabeth Tudor, Soloviev de-emphasizes this aspect of Ivan's relations with England and concentrates on the negotiations related to trade. Evidently Ivan sought a marital alliance with one of Elizabeth's cousins to guarantee Moscow's access to England as a means of reaching Western Europe. Soloviev contends that once access to the Baltic through Livonia became precarious and unpredictable Ivan's desire to get along with Elizabeth was related closely to his need to reach Western European technologies through the English trade route. Whatever his success with the English, the Baltic remained the preferable route and Ivan fought to gain Livonia to make that possible.

As we have seen, the struggle for access to the West in quest of modern technology constitutes one of Soloviev's major themes. He bolsters his arguments by indicating how often Ivan included demands for soldiers, technicians or arms in his diplomatic negotiations. In this context Ivan's quest for control of Livonia, as well as his overtures to England and Sweden, were parts of the same pattern, a trend that continued in the following centuries first under Alexis Mikhailovich and especially under Peter the Great.

Ironically, according to Soloviev, Moscow's expansion into Siberia occurred partly because of Moscow's diplomatic problems in the West. He maintains that Ivan's desire for military technology was rooted in Moscow's need to conquer Asia. Yet just as Moscow's access to the West was cut off, its enemies to the Southeast—the Tatars and the Ottomans—began to rise once more, so it was that Ivan IV's reign marked the beginning of Russian expansion into Siberia.

As in his discussion of Bathory, Soloviev seeks to accomplish more in his chapter on the Stroganovs and Yermak than to recount this particular episode. This chapter becomes a vehicle to explore the process by which Russians moved across the Urals into the vastness of Asia. Indeed, one of Soloviev's recurring themes is Muscovite expansion into Asia beginning with the conquest of Kazan in 1552.[15] Conquering Siberia was largely a private enterprise in which the tsar granted exclusive charters to the Stroganov brothers both to pursue economic development as well as to use all means necessary to defend Russian interests against the tribes living in Siberia. Significantly, the charters were primarily to enable the Stroganovs to develop the natural wealth of the trans-Ural area for the benefit of Moscow. Soloviev stresses that the distances were so great between the Urals and Moscow that the Stroganovs could defend their towns only through private means, since there were no standing armies or commanders to come to their aid.

Based on the charters and letters quoted in the text, Soloviev effectively proves that Ivan was primarily interested in the income he could derive at very low cost from these new areas. Consequently he left it to the Stroganovs to find the appropriate means to defend themselves and their property from the various hostile native peoples of Siberia. This is the key, Soloviev asserts, to understanding the Stroganovs' invitation to the cossack Yermak Timofeev to bring his horde to Siberia to assist in this enormous project.

By and large, this section of the book explains how the Stroganovs settled in the trans-Ural area and in what kinds of trade and manufacture they were involved. Soloviev describes the relationship between the Stroganovs and the cossacks and the military campaigns in which they engaged. When Ivan was informed of the cossacks' victory over the Siberian khan Kuchum, any doubts the tsar might have had about allowing the Stroganovs to bring them to Siberia vanished. He granted the Stroganovs even more land and additional towns in Siberia while bestowing favor and money on the cossacks themselves.

Since Soloviev's discussion of the Stroganovs and Yermak occurs near the end of his account of Ivan the Terrible, the following and final chapter contains his analysis of the character of Ivan's rule. He reviews Ivan's marriages and speculates on the causes of Ivan's death. Characteristically Soloviev reviews the murder of Ivan Ivanovich, the tsar's eldest son, referring not only to the Muscovite versions of their quarrel, yet cites Possevino's discussion as the most reliable, for the Jesuit arrived in Moscow only three months after the actual event.

Ultimately Soloviev regarded Ivan's reign as a battle between the "old" principle of family or genealogy represented by the great boyar families who opposed the increasingly centralized nature of the state, and the "new" service classes who were the creations of this new autocratic entity, identified with the lands granted them. Ivan's "terrible" character was a product of this struggle and in turn he too planted more seeds for Muscovy's destruction, culminating in the Time of Troubles.[16]

To explain the nature of this struggle between "old" and "new" Soloviev turns to the documents, analyzing the titles associated with the old boyar families and how they differed from those of the newer service classes that arose as the center of Rus moved from Kiev to Moscow. He stresses that in Kiev grand-princely and boyar names reflected family background in contrast to the titles of the appanage period where the princely name was associated with a specific geographic location. Soloviev thus illustrates how the building blocks of historical analysis can rest in the most fundamental information historians have at their disposal, the names and titles of their protagonists. Among the most important sources for Soloviev's discussion is the correspondence between Ivan and the boyar Prince A.M. Kurbsky, who fled to Lithuania in 1564. Soloviev often cites Kurbsky's descriptions to explain Polish behavior, and regards him as the main spokesman for "old" ideas of boyar supremacy. Soloviev's extensive discussion of the struggle between centralization and retention of boyar primacy does not try to diminish Ivan's responsibility for his cruelty. On the contrary, Soloviev seeks to paint a full picture of Ivan, giving him credit for those aspects of his reign that brought reform to Muscovy, while making him responsible for the actions that led to the weakening of Muscovy and to the Time of Troubles. Soloviev is anxious to counter the notion that we can understand major historical figures only as "good" or "bad," and he argues convincingly that the true measure of the importance of historical figures lies in their contradictions and complexities. Rather than accept the Kurbsky-based scenario that what went well in Ivan's reign was due to the good advice of wise counselors such as Sylvester and Adashev, whereas the failed policies of the Livonian War and of the oprichnina (crown estates) were based on Ivan's paranoid, miserable character, Soloviev attempts to show that Ivan, from 1547 on, was master of his own fate.

Soloviev's interpretation of Ivan's reign created the framework of the debate that dominates Russian historiography to this day. The very different interpretations of Vasily Kliuchevsky and Sergei Platonov of the significance of Ivan's reign have characterized the dispute which has persisted through the Soviet period and into the present.[17] Kliuchevsky,

Soloviev's most distinguished student, argued that, contrary to Soloviev's interpretation which explained Ivan's reign in terms of the centralizing monarch encountering the opposition of entrenched noble interests, Ivan's personality is the most important factor in understanding his reign. Platonov's interpretation resembles that of Soloviev, stressing the old boyar families' opposition to Ivan's reforms. The terms of the debate changed little over the decades, causing Robert Crummey to note that this controversy "encouraged a rather one-sided approach to the issues in question... the debate over Ivan's intentions has too often distracted historians' attention from the more modest and promising questions. What did Ivan's government actually do and how did its actions affect the main groups in Russian society?"[18] In the past four decades, although Soviet scholars such as A.A. Zimin, N.E. Nosov and R.G. Skrynnikov have moved the debate to ever more sophisticated interpretations of the sources to explain the nature and accomplishments of Ivan's reign, they still begin by asking whether it is possible to determine which specific social groups benefitted from Ivan's activities and even whether such a rational approach is possible.[19]

Western historians have added new dimensions to the debate, questioning the veracity of one of the most important sources pertaining to Ivan's rule. Soloviev and his successors relied heavily on Prince A.M. Kurbsky's correspondence with Ivan as well as on Kurbsky's history of Ivan's reign for primary information on the period. Some twenty-five years ago Edward L. Keenan of Harvard University published a highly controversial study which argued that the correspondence between the tsar and Kurbsky was a seventeenth-century fabrication. Although in the ensuing quarter century the controversy has quieted and the correspondence remains an important source for historians, the extraordinary heat it generated is ample evidence of how Ivan's reign continues to fascinate modern historians.[20] In addition to the translation of Skrynnikov's *Ivan the Terrible*, among the best of the general discussions in English-language versions are George Vernadsky's fourth and fifth volumes of his incomplete *History of Russia*,[21] and Robert Crummey's *The Formation of Muscovy, 1304-1613*.

The final section of this translation, the Appendices, epitomizes the use of sources that Soloviev seeks to teach. In a fascinating discussion of historian P.I. Nebolsin's 1849 essay "The Subjugation of Siberia" Soloviev treats us to a dissection of Nebolsin's methodology as an object lesson in how to judge seemingly contradictory sources. Aside from giving us a glimpse of his own methods, Soloviev provides twentieth-century readers with insight into the development of standards of scholarly verification.

Soloviev attempted to refute Nebolsin for a number of reasons, not the least of which was that Nebolsin minimized the role of the Stroganovs and the central government in his effort to bolster the lot of the legendary popular figure Yermak Timofeev. Indeed, reading contemporary accounts of Yermak's expedition is rather like reading a tale of the American Wild West. The description of Yermak's cossacks sailing down Siberian rivers in their high-sided boats, attacked by Tatars using bows and arrows against musket-wielding cossacks, reminds us of the futile attempts by Native Americans to withstand the invasion of their lands. Moreover Yermak's legendary bravery appealed to Russian peasants as well as native Siberian populations. Small wonder that Soloviev was at such pains to reinstate the importance both of the Stroganovs as well as Muscovy in this great Russian "Eastern."

By quoting extensive sections of Nebolsin's essay Soloviev literally explicates the text in a history lesson of how to evaluate the accuracy of a chronicle. He warns us that to understand historical sources we must suspend our contemporary susceptibilities and imagine the world depicted in the document in hand. Nebolsin's erroneous conclusions stemmed from his inability to divorce himself from his nineteenth-century conceptions of Russia and comprehend the sixteenth-century world of the chronicles he critiqued. Soloviev maintains that Nebolsin, in his anxiety to discredit the Stroganovs' role and exalt the cossacks, misread and misinterpreted the chronicle in question, and misunderstood the correspondence between Ivan and the Stroganov brothers. Not content simply to criticize Nebolsin's methods, Soloviev then shows how later additions to the original manuscript explain the inaccuracies Nebolsin found in the Stroganov Chronicle. In a sense we are treated to a short course in how to read a document and sort out the document's development, an invaluable and fascinating lesson whether the reader is a student of Russian history or any other.

Recent interest in Russia's expansion into Siberia is expressed in several English-language histories as well as in some excellent Russian scholarship. W. Bruce Lincoln's *The Conquest of a Continent*[22] entertainingly recounts the story of Yermak's expedition using extensive primary and secondary sources. Skrynnikov is the most important recent Russian chronicler of early Siberian history. His *The Siberian Expedition of*

Yermak examines every aspect of these events in great detail. Unfortunately it is not yet available in English translation.[23]

Soloviev was determined to demonstrate to students of history that it is the historian's duty not only to present his argument, he also must account for the way in which he arrived at his conclusions. As much as the historian is obligated to show the sources used to build the story, he is equally duty-bound to explain why other sources were rejected or deemed unsuitable. That obligation is crucial not only to explain why some sources were utilized but why others were eliminated. It is equally important for the historian to explain these same things to himself as a means of examining his own prejudices and predilections.

Why bother with such a massive translation project? After all, a professional student of Russian history should be able to read Soloviev and all the others in the original rather than relying on a translation. As for historians and students who are not Russian, so many other more sophisticated and better written books are available. Yet when we assign the later and more sophisticated historians to students we deprive them of the opportunity to learn what the sources were like, for no other classic Russian historian used original documents so extensively. As teachers, we demand that our students learn to use sources yet they rarely get a chance to read the original documents or understand how they are evaluated.

Encountering Soloviev's *History of Russia* is an opportunity for a hands-on lesson in historiography. These are lessons that are as valuable for all of us who study history at the beginning of the twenty-first century as they were one hundred and fifty years ago. By reading Soloviev we learn that which we do not know, and how better to write history ourselves.

HISTORY OF RUSSIA

Volume 11

The Reign of Ivan the Terrible
The Struggle against Bathory
Expansion into Siberia

I

STEFAN BATHORY

SITUATION IN POLAND AND LITHUANIA UNDER THE LAST JAGIELLONIAN
Ivan's relations with the Crimean khan improved thanks to the tenacity
of the Muscovite military commanders[1] on the shores of the Lopasnia.[2]
In Lithuania and Poland, to the west, there occurred a series of events
which exerted great influence both on the fate of the Muscovite realm and
on all Eastern Europe. In July 1572 Sigismund Augustus, the last of the
Jagiellonian dynasty,[3] died. During the reigns of Jagailo's son Casimir[4]
and his descendants there were major changes in the Polish aristocracy,
including the creation of gentry democracy, which in turn had important
consequences for the domestic structure and foreign policy of Poland-
Lithuania.

The reign of Sigismund I (1506-1548) was characterized by antagonism between the magnates and gentry fanned by his Italian queen Bona
who conducted herself by the same rules as her compatriot Catherine de
Medici.[5] The Polish magnates[6] used a variety of methods to distinguish
themselves from the gentry[7] who demanded equal status. In Poland princely titles were unknown because the Piast line was completely extinct.[8]
In Lithuania because of the continuing strength of the clans of Riurik[9] and
Gediminas,[10] the title persisted. In 1518 the powerful magnate Radziwiłł
family received the princely title from the Holy Roman emperor. Their
example prompted many magnates to acquire the title of count of the Holy
Roman empire, while others established mayoralties in their families.

Gentry dissatisfaction came to the fore when because of problems in
Wallachia Sigismund called for a general mobilization.[11] In response a
hundred and fifty thousand gentry assembled by the walls of Lvov and
after mounting a powerful disturbance composed a petition[12] listing all
their demands and grievances. The old king, unable to placate the assembly, was forced to dismiss it. This event received the derisive name "the
rooster war."

Just as the magnates sought to distinguish themselves from the gentry the latter in turn claimed the right of life and death over the village
populations entrusted to them. Following this example, elders and palatines

then used every kind of coercion against urban dwellers, whose representatives were expelled from the Sejm by the gentry which in turn rose up against the clergy.

Such was the confusion as Sigismund Augustus ascended the throne. His mother Queen Bona raised him according to her rules and goals, while sapping his emotional energy by keeping him constantly among women and depriving him of any serious interests. His upbringing affected the king's conduct and during his reign he was nicknamed "King Tomorrow" because of his habitual procrastination and dithering. We have seen how Ivan IV used these habits to his advantage.[13]

Sigismund Augustus married three times. His first and third wives were Habsburgs, and unable to ingratiate themselves with him. Sigismund Augustus was forced strongly to defend his second beloved wife Barbara, widow of Gastold, born a Radziwiłł, against the Senate's and Sejm's demands for their divorce. She died soon after her victory and coronation.[14]

During the last years of his life Sigismund Augustus was surrounded by mistresses who robbed him, and by magicians upon whom he relied to restore the energy lost through his lack of will power. When asked why he did not act on pressing matters, he answered "Because of these falcons (as he called women) I cannot make myself concentrate on anything." Thus when the king died there were no funds left in his treasury to pay for his funeral, nor did a gold chain nor even a ring remain with which to dress the corpse.[15]

Nevertheless Sigismund Augustus's character was not the sole reason for the domestic disarray of his reign and the sloth in crown administration. Cravings for peace, pampering and luxury dominated the aristocracy. Their political calculations, justifying peace and avoiding war, prevented strengthening the monarchy even when such policies led to weakening Poland's position as a continental state, surrounded on all sides by powerful neighbors.

The papal legate Cardinal Commendone[16] tried to incite the Poles to war against the Turks, saying to the Senate "How unlike your ancestors you have become. To enlarge the realm they did not sit at banquets for hours, rather they bestrode horses during difficult military campaigns. They quarreled not about who better drains a glass, but about who excels in military arts."

The Muscovite émigré Prince Kurbsky[17] also criticized the moral decline and material inclinations of the Polish magnates. "The local king," he wrote, "thinks not about how to combat unbelievers, only of balls and masquerades. Similarly, the magnates know only how to drink and eat sweets. When drunk they are very brave. They capture Moscow and Constantinople, and if a Turk appeared in the heavens they would snatch him even from there. Yet, when they lie in bed between fat featherbeds, barely rising at noon, they get up half-alive, with a headache. The magnates and princelings are so shy and exhausted by their wives that upon hearing of a barbarian attack they lock themselves up in fortified cities, and having taken up their weapons they sit, bedecked in armor, at tables playing dice, and jabber with their drunken womenfolk without stepping outside the city gates. If they go out on campaign they keep at a distance from their enemy and, having campaigned for a day or two, return home, consuming and pillaging for themselves whatever property or animals the unfortunate city dwellers who fled to the forest were able to save from the Tatars." Kurbsky omits what contemporary Polish writers reveal, that they did not limit themselves to theft. According to their testimony, when one of the gentry killed a servant he said that he had killed a dog, as if the gentry considered peasants and all village dwellers as dogs.

It was left to the last of the Jagiellonians to complete the dynasty's historical task, the creation of a perpetual union between Lithuania and Poland. Under Sigismund I Lithuanians continued sharply to express their separatist aspirations. For example in 1526 Lithuanian magnate representatives addressed the king on the subject. "The papal legate on the way to Moscow said here that he was going to convince the Muscovite ruler to accept Catholicism, and should the grand prince agree the Pope will confer on him the kingly title. If the holy father wishes to grant kingly dignity to your enemy, it would be better if he gave it to your grace's son, our ruler, the grand prince of Lithuania, for the important services rendered by you and your ancestors to the faith. The emperor and Pope would have conferred the crown on your uncle Vytautas[18] but he died, not having lived to receive the crown delayed by the Poles who still will not release it, unwilling to permit your highness' native nobility to receive such an honor.

"It is amazing to us that our brothers, the Poles, do not wish to allow to us, their brothers, that which they do not forbid to Moscow. They long have pleaded that they desire that your highness' nobles of the grand principality of Lithuania always be subordinate to the Polish crown. We obediently ask your grace not to permit your native-born servants to become subjects of the Polish crown. Your grace must strive to do this for the sake of your descendants. It will be better for you that your high-ranking nobility be separate from the Polish crown. Just recently the Lithuanian nobility eagerly elected your son as its sovereign and swore its loyalty to him,[19] whereas the Polish nobles as yet have been unwilling to do the same. If the grand principality of Lithuania were joined to the Polish crown, your son would still not be grand prince. We humbly beg you to order the Polish senators to send the king's crown originally intended for Vytautas, that your son might be crowned king during your lifetime. When the grand principality of Lithuania becomes a kingdom it may not be combined with the Polish crown, as one crown cannot be included in another. If the Poles do not agree to send the crown here, your grace must attempt to request another from the Pope and emperor and, whatever it costs, we eagerly will pay, and spare nothing."

The lack of an heir to succeed Sigismund Augustus forced a rapid solution to the question of permanent union of Lithuania with Poland, even though the only tie between them was the Jagiellonian dynasty. To bring the matter to a close, great difficulties had to be overcome. In Lithuania an aristocracy was dominant which feared an intimate union with a realm where gentry democracy carried so much weight. Moreover this meant joining two long-rival peoples. The Lithuanians also did not wish to travel to Poland to conclude an agreement of perpetual union, nor did the Poles wish to go to Lithuania. It was only after the death of Mikołaj Radziwiłł "the Black,"[20] the most powerful of the Lithuanian magnates and the leading opponent of union, that in 1569 the Sejm actually was summoned to Lublin.

At first the Lithuanians stubbornly persisted in their views, then later were forced to agree to the union when they saw that it received no support from the Rus[21] population. It made little difference to the Rus whether they were part of a union with Lithuania or Poland, although the Lithuanian magnates' conduct toward the Rus population did not gain them any affection. The union which followed was evidently to Lithuanian detriment because Lithuania was forced to cede Podlasie, Volhynia and the principality of Kiev to Poland. Livonia was declared the common property of the two states. The agreement stipulated that the king be elected at a general Sejm, that representatives of both nations meet in the Senate, and the Sejm hold joint meetings.[22]

As the business of the union of Lithuania with Poland apparently was completed, tying native Rus areas directly to the Polish kingdom, in Poland and Lithuania a movement increasingly gathered strength which led to detaching these Rus areas from Poland. Protestantism spread, arousing a strong Catholic reaction. The Jesuits arrived to aid Catholicism in fanning fanaticism among Catholics, who fought not just Protestants, but also began to struggle against Orthodoxy. Within a century this conflict resulted in the secession of Little Russia and its unification with Great Russia or the Muscovite state.[23] In this manner the struggle in Eastern Europe paralleled the general European movement marking the beginning of a new historical era, the age of the Reformation.

During Sigismund I's reign Protestantism began to spread in Poland and Lithuania. The neighboring countries of Prussia and Livonia, which enjoyed extensive commercial and political relations with Poland and Lithuania, accepted Protestantism rapidly. From there it penetrated quickly into the Polish and Lithuanian urban middle classes. Even the upper strata could not long remain unaffected.[24] Wealthy Polish, Lithuanian and Rus aristocrats traveled throughout Europe, marrying foreigners of Protestant belief. They sent their sons to German schools where they studied "the new learning" and then returned home bringing back books supporting these ideas.

Sigismund I greeted Protestantism with animosity, granting his bishops the right to scrutinize those who fell away from Catholicism, to identify heretics and punish them. He decreed that everyone infected with heresy lose his noble title; he forbade importing teachers from Germany, and prohibited young people from attending German universities or schools.

Matters were entirely different under Sigismund Augustus, who was completely indifferent to matters of faith, or at least to the differences between creeds. This king leaned one way or the other depending on political or other considerations. His second and beloved wife was Barbara, the widow of Gastold, née Radziwiłł. The head of the powerful Radziwiłł family in Lithuania was the queen's cousin, Mikołaj Radziwiłł "the Black," prince of Olitsk and Neshvizisk, governor of Wilno, grand marshal and chancellor of Lithuania. Because of both his immense personal dignity and his relationship to the queen Radziwiłł was the magnate with the greatest influence on Sigismund Augustus.

As a zealous Protestant, Radziwiłł used his enormous wealth and influence to spread the new religion in Lithuania. He introduced the new faith into his vast estates and holdings, bringing from Poland the most famous Protestant evangelists, and welcoming under his wing all those who departed from Catholicism. He enticed the common people with treats and gifts, and the gentry with royal favors, so that almost everyone in the highest stratum accepted Protestantism. He had similar success in the cities. It was only in the countryside that the religion of the majority of the population remained unchanged, especially in Orthodox Rus areas.

Radziwiłł needed to take the decisive step, solemnly demonstrating that the king favored Protestantism. He convinced Sigismund Augustus to journey to Wilno to attend services in a Protestant church built opposite the Catholic church of St. John. Because one strong-willed person could convince Sigismund Augustus to do something, another decisive individual could sway him in yet another direction. Learning that the king planned to attend a Protestant church, the Dominican Cyprian, the Lithopenian bishop and suffragan of Wilno, rode to meet the king. Seizing his horse by the reins, Cyprian said "Your majesty's ancestors did not ride to pray along this road, but along another." Embarrassed, Sigismund Augustus was forced to follow Cyprian into the Catholic church.

The death of Mikolaj Radziwiłł "the Black" in 1569 led to the first major blow suffered by Protestantism in Lithuania. Mikolaj Radziwiłł "the Red," the new head of the Radziwiłł clan and leader of Protestantism, did not enjoy the same prestige as his late first cousin.[25] Protestantism's second misfortune resulted from domestic divisions that arose from the strengthening of Arianism or Socinianism.[26] At some point Pope Pius V, hearing of the strength of the new religion in Poland and Lithuania, dispatched his legate Commendone to the court of Sigismund Augustus. The envoy found Poland and Lithuania's Catholic affairs in a pathetic state. In the struggle with as dangerous an enemy as Protestantism animosity and envy soured the relationship of the two most important Catholic bishops. These two, Jacob Uchanski, archbishop of Gniezno and Philip Padniewski, bishop of Cracow, were openly hostile to one another. In addition Uchanski displayed a proclivity towards Protestantism, hoping that with the triumph of the new religion there would be a break with Rome accompanied by preservation of the hierarchy. As archbishop he emerged as the independent leader of the Polish clergy.[27]

Commendone took stock of the situation, paying particular attention to the character and relationship of the king to the important leading figures. In quiet conversations with Sigismund Augustus he related to the king how much he feared for him and for the fate of the entire realm, claiming that in disorders following the unbelievers' victory they would have no mercy, bringing down all institutions, divine and human, lawful and customary, finally destroying even the throne. Heeding Commendone's examples of contemporary France and Germany, torn apart by religious wars because the rulers did not suppress heretical teachings from the first, the king, fearing civil war above all else, took the envoy's suggestions to heart and cooled towards Protestantism. The king's disillusionment grew because of Protestant efforts to gain favor among the gentry by encouraging opposition to royal demands for the increased requisitions needed to conduct the war with Moscow successfully.

Meanwhile a company arrived to aid Catholicism and assure victory over a divided and thereby weakened Protestantism. This company was the Jesuits. Walerian Protaszewicz, the Wilno bishop, seeking assistance in his struggle against heresy, turned for advice to Cardinal Hosius,[28] bishop of Warmia and Prussia, the famous president of the Council of Trent, considered one of the most important pillars of Catholicism in Poland, and in all Europe. Hosius advised all Polish bishops to introduce the Jesuits into their dioceses, urged Protaszewicz to do likewise, and established a Jesuit college in Wilno under the direction of Stanislaw Warszewicki.[29]

At first the Jesuit schools were poorly enrolled. Protestants and Orthodox did not permit their children to enter the schools. The Wilno Chapter [of Canons] forbade Catholics to give their children to the Jesuits, fearing that its own cathedral school would fail. Warszewicki never lost heart, and persisted in seeking means to obtain respect and strength for his college. He worked tirelessly, taught in the schools, gave sermons, attracted a large number of unbelievers to his house to turn them towards Catholicism, and his ambitions began to come to fruition.[30]

DEATH OF SIGISMUND AUGUSTUS AND ELECTION OF NEW KING

Such was Poland and Lithuania's situation when Sigismund Augustus died and it became necessary to think about selecting his successor. The religious movement's important influence on this matter is easy to understand. Protestants, who were strong in the Senate and among the gentry, wanted to elect a Protestant king, or at least someone who would give them full freedom of worship. Commendone saw this danger to Catholicism and was even more astonished when he discovered that Catholics were entirely indifferent to the matter. Instead of viewing Protestants as heretics, as opponents of the true teaching of the church, they were seen merely as people who wished only to limit the clergy's overwhelming power.

Commendone decided the only way to make sure the new king would be a Catholic elected by Catholics was to exploit personal and clan rivalries among the magnates, thereby decreasing enmity between Catholics while igniting it among Protestants. At the time the most important magnate leaders were Peter Zborowski, governor of Sandomir, and Jan Firlej, grand marshal of the crown and governor of Cracow, both Protestants. Both were candidates for the recently-decided Cracow governorship and their competition made them fierce enemies. Zborowski won the office but Sigismund Augustus preferred Firlej, the candidate favored by his mistress. Commendone took advantage of the hostility between the two, insinuating to Zborowski that the lords were meeting at Firlej's home in order to elect him king. Zborowski believed him. With hate overcoming his attachment to faith, he gave his word that although he was himself a Protestant he nevertheless would not permit a Protestant on the throne.

Among the Catholic magnates the celebrated warrior Adalbert Laski occupied first place, partly because of his popularity among the young. Commendone especially tried to win him to his side by making him along with Andrzej Zborowski and Mikolaj Pac, bishop of Kiev, part of a triumvirate to which Catholics could look for strong support and leadership.

Having resolved matters in Poland, Commendone turned to Lithuania where the strongest families were the rival Radziwiłł and Chodkiewicz clans. The death of Mikolaj Radziwiłł "the Black," despite the succession of his cousin, Mikolaj "the Red," who enjoyed far less prestige, eroded the family's power with an accompanying diminution of the strength of Lithuanian Protestantism. Mikolaj "the Black" left several sons the eldest of whom, Mikolaj Krzystof, nicknamed "the Orphan,"[31] was sent to Germany that the young man might be strengthened in the Protestant faith. Upon his father's death Mikolaj Krzystof went to Italy, to Rome, where he abandoned his German ideas in favor of the Italian and returned home a Catholic. The younger brothers followed the example of the eldest.[32] In contrast, Mikolaj "the Red" and his family remained true to Protestantism, splitting the Radziwiłł clan into distinct Catholic and Protestant lines.[33]

Because of Jesuit activities and Commendone's efforts the former Protestant Jan Chodkiewicz returned to Catholicism. Commendone now only had to reconcile the "Orphan" Radziwiłł with Chodkiewicz, a relatively easy task since there was no personal enmity between them as between Firlej and Zborowski. Having taken strong measures to prepare the way for the election of a Catholic king in Poland and Lithuania Commendone suggested, with Radziwiłł and Chodkiewicz concurring, that it would be best to elect one of Emperor Maximilian's[34] sons king in Lithuania. Radziwiłł agreed because of the long-standing ties between his clan and the Habsburgs, Chodkiewicz because he feared that the Muscovite tsar, against whom he led the Lithuanian armies, might be elected. Yet Radziwiłł and Chodkiewicz by themselves could not prevent the election of the tsar or even the Muscovite heir.

As early as 1564 Commendone informed Rome that the residents of Kiev were seeking the Muscovite tsar's favors for religious reasons. At the death of Sigismund Augustus he reported on Orthodox rural population movements in Lithuania advantageous to the Muscovite tsar. A curious essay has come down to us written by Abbot Giovanini in which he enumerated all the incentives and impediments to the election of the Muscovite tsar. The primary obstacles were first that Ivan was constantly at odds with the Polish crown and had given further offense by conquering two Lithuanian principalities. Second, he professed the Greek faith. Third, his harsh temper, his brutal relations with his boyars worked against him. The Holy Roman emperor and the Turkish sultan also were obstacles since each feared having Ivan as a neighbor. The Turk especially did not wish to have a powerful and warlike neighbor as a ruler, and even more dangerous, a talented one of the Greek faith who might incite the rural Orthodox population to rebellion against the Turks. The final impediment to the Muscovite's election was that the Poles feared that the essence and grandeur of their entire realm would be carried off to Moscow.

In contrast, factors favoring the tsar's election included his strength, his ability to force peace and security on Lithuania, as well as similarity of language and customs. In addition, Poland and Moscow shared common enmities with the Tatars and the Holy Roman empire. Finally, there was the example of Jagailo, the grand prince of Lithuania who, when elected king, transformed himself from a pagan and an enemy of Poland to a friend and Christian.[35] The transformation of very same Jagailo set an example. It raised the hope of the tsar spending more time in Poland than in Moscow, just as Northerners always yearn for southern climes. Moreover the need to expand or defend their borders to the Southwest in the direction of the Turks, or in the direction of the Holy Roman empire, would force the tsar to reside more in Poland. Following Jagailo's example, he could be bound by oath not to violate the laws or rights of the Polish gentry. The Protestants were not concerned about Ivan's Orthodox faith. Besides, the Muscovite ruler at one time wanted to establish ties with the Latin church. Finally, he had at his disposal a great treasury through which he might buy many adherents.

NEGOTIATIONS WITH IVAN OVER SUCCESSION

Although at first the Poles thought in this manner subsequently they preferred to elect Tsarevich Fedor instead of the tsar. In so choosing they would satisfy the Orthodox rural population with someone who also would not oppose Protestants. Lithuania would gain security from Muscovy while dispensing with direct relations with Ivan, whose character deficiencies, though well known in Poland, were even more feared in Lithuania.[36] When notified of Sigismund Augustus's death by the courier Voropay, Ivan also received word from the Polish and Lithuanian assembly of its desire to see Tsarevich Fedor as king of Poland and grand prince of Lithuania. As was his wont, Ivan replied to Voropay with a long speech.

"You have come to me from your Polish and Lithuanian nobles and have brought me word that my brother Sigismund Augustus has died. I already have heard this news, yet disbelieved it because although we Christian rulers are often killed off, still by God's will we continue to live on.

"Now, however, I believe and regret my brother's death. I particularly regret that he departed to God leaving behind neither brother nor son to look after his body and soul as befits a king. Your Polish and Lithuanian nobles are now without a leader. Though in the Polish crown and the grand principality of Lithuania there are many leaders, there is no one good enough to rule you all and to whom all of you might come running as streams or floods converge towards the sea.

"For a long time we quarreled with our brother Sigismund Augustus, afterwards matters began to lean towards friendliness between us, then before we could establish this friendship God took Sigismund unto Himself. Because of our disagreement the Muslim hand still hangs over us, whereas the Christian hand is lowered and blood pours out. If your nobles who are now without a ruler want to take me as your sovereign they will see what a good master and defender they will find. Pagan forces will not torment us, neither will Rome nor any other kingdom rise up against us when your lands are one with ours. In your land many say that I am wicked. It is true that I am wicked and temperamental, I am not boasting. Yet, ask me, against whom do I bear malice? 'I hate those who bear malice against me,' I answer, 'but to those who are good I give the chain from about my neck, and my robe.'"

At this point Maliuta Skuratov[37] interrupted him. "Tsar and most glorious ruler!" he said. "Your treasury is not poverty stricken, in it you will find something to give."

"The Polish and Lithuanian nobility," Ivan continued, "knows how wealthy my grandfather and father were, but my treasury and land holdings are twice that size. It is not surprising that your nobles love their people because they, in turn, love their nobles. Yet, my people led me against the Crimean Tatars, of whom there were forty thousand, while I had only six thousand. Was this fair? Moreover, I knew nothing about this except that ahead of me there went six commanders with great forces, but they did not inform me about the Tatars. Had it been difficult for my commanders to overcome such a large enemy, even allowing for the loss of several thousand of their men, they could have brought to me either a Tatar whip or lash. I would have accepted it with thanks. I did not fear Tatar power, but I saw the treason of my people and thus sent some aside, away from the Tatars. At that time the Tatars raided Moscow.[38] Had there been thousands of men there the city could have been defended, but when the great servitors refused to defend it, what could the lesser nobles do? Moscow already was burned, and I knew nothing of it. Just think what the treason of my people has been against me! If anyone has been punished as a consequence, the punishment is his own fault.

"I ask you, do you punish or do you have mercy upon your traitors? I think you punish them. In Wilno there lived Victorine who wrote to me, but whom I did not answer. They laid the fault at my door, as though I inspired this Victorine to do away with my brother. As God is my witness, I did not think of this and I did not order Victorine to do this, and even if he did write to me on this matter his letter never reached me. Victorine was seized and punished. You see, in your lands traitors are not granted mercy.

"So, say this to the Polish and Lithuanian nobility, that they consult with one another on all matters and, once they have made a decision, send ambassadors as soon as possible. If God wishes that I be their ruler, I promise God and the Polish and Lithuanian nobility beforehand that I will maintain all their rights and privileges, and under certain circumstances will grant even greater rights. I do not wish to discuss my goodness or wickedness. Should the Polish and Lithuanian nobles send to me or to my children their sons for service they will discover whether I am good or wicked. Let them not heed what traitors say about me, for they have the habit of speaking foolishly about their rulers. No matter how I refute them, they will not stop speaking ill of me. There are men who have passed from my lands to yours who of necessity fear for themselves. They may yet try to flee to another land, to the Horde or to Turkey, if they imagine that the Polish and Lithuanian nobility wish to elect me their king. Let your nobles try to detain them, and I swear to God that I will not take revenge upon them.

"Kurbsky has come to you, he who has deprived him (pointing to his older son) of his mother and me of my wife.[39] As God is my witness, I did not think to imprison him. I only wished to deprive him of rank, seize his villages and then to have mercy on him, but he took fright and fled to Lithuania. Let your nobles deprive him of his villages and watch that he not flee somewhere else.

"Regarding Livonia, when I become your sovereign then Livonia, Moscow, Novgorod and Pskov shall be as one. Should they decide not to elect me sovereign, let them send illustrious ambassadors for talks in goodwill. I will not continue my claim on Polotsk and will desist in my claims to all its surroundings, in exchange for which let them cede to Moscow Livonia along the Dvina, and we will conclude a perpetual peace with Lithuania. I will make my children swear not to make war with Lithuania until our line becomes extinct. If the nobles wish to elect as their king one of my sons, even though I only have two, just as I have two eyes in my head, giving one of them up is the same thing as cutting out one's heart.

"There are Polish and Lithuanian people who follow the faith of Martin Luther and destroy images, who do not want me as their sovereign. I will say nothing about them because the holy writings were given not for enmity or abuse, rather for peace and submissiveness. Do not forget to tell your Polish and Lithuanian nobles immediately to send ambassadors who are good people, that there be no foolish outcome from goodwill talks."

Judging from these words, Ivan did indeed wish to be elected king, thus he sought to avoid the reproach of having fled from the khan while justifying his cruelty to the boyars. In Poland and Lithuania even during Sigismund Augustus's lifetime and immediately upon his death many desired Ivan's election as king. They discussed the positive and negative consequences of such an election, weighing the factors. They concluded that, given Ivan's more important character deficiencies and the difficulties of joining the interests of the two independent states under the administration of one ruler, it would be preferable to elect one of Ivan's sons. Nevertheless they did ignore an important point, the impossibility of reconciling the needs of both states in this union. In their discussions about electing Ivan or one of his sons they either regarded Muscovy and Lithuania as realms that had not clashed with one another until this time, or they thought that Ivan, tempted by the vision of himself or one of his sons on the Polish throne would make concessions to Lithuania's advantage.

Naturally at first Ivan personally was likely to look upon the matter in much the same way. He saw his character and conduct towards the boyars as one of the main obstacles to his election. His behavior towards his nobles inevitably caused discomfort among the Polish and Lithuanian magnates, who were accustomed to an entirely different order of things. He thought that through his promise to guarantee and even to expand noble and gentry rights and privileges, accompanied by the excuse of his anger at boyar treason, he might avoid the most important obstacles to his election. He thus permitted an important condition to slip from sight, agreement on objectives common to Moscow and Lithuania. Perhaps he thought Poland and Lithuania were so anxious to have as their king a powerful ruler such as he that they would agree to his demands, especially because he tried as best he could to moderate them. It was soon evident that disputed lands whose number increased with the inclusion of Livonia were the main obstacle to election just as they were the obstacle to the conclusion of a perpetual peace between Moscow and Lithuania.

Ivan wanted to be king himself. He was enticed by the possibility of a perpetual close union among the three powers. Then, when the Polish and Lithuanian senates indicated their preference for one of his sons, Ivan was not tempted, for after his death he envisioned war between brothers fiercer than between rulers who were strangers to one another.

During the six-month interval from Voropay's arrival in Moscow until the arrival of the new Lithuanian ambassador Haraburda,[40] Ivan had time to rethink the matter, which by then appeared to him in a totally different light. While his son's election seemed as disadvantageous as before, his own election presented new complications. He would have to rule two independent states, traveling from one to the other. He who in Moscow feared boyar treason, who in his own realm had surrounded himself with the oprichnina [crown estates],[41] would travel to Poland, handing himself over to unruly nobles and gentry. At the end of his life he would be shackled to something contradicting all he tried to achieve. Consequently he envisioned election just as grand prince of Lithuania, as distinct from Poland. Thereby he eliminated the main obstacle arising from the conjunction of two states, neither of which was willing to concede priority to the other. Lithuania was accustomed to second place after Poland and it easily could take the same place in a union with Muscovy, especially because the dominant element in Lithuania was Rus. A large part of the grand principality was composed of lands Ivan considered his patrimony, chiefly populated by Orthodox peasants easily making the Orthodox church dominant. Because of Lithuania's proximity and second rank it would be easier to govern and get on with its nobles.

In Lithuania and Poland the desire to see Ivan elected king failed to gain support just at the time Ivan perceived the matter of election in a new light. Other rulers anxious for election sent ambassadors to Poland to support their claims. We have seen how Commendone worked for the election of a Catholic king. Yet Ivan expected the Polish and Lithuanian ambassadors to visit him, for he did not wish to demean himself by seeking or asking favors. Although the Lithuanian Orthodox population desired Ivan's election it lacked influence in the Sejm since no one at the time considered the religion of the Orthodox rural population of any importance. Other interests dominated.

Ivan told Voropay to have the Polish-Lithuanian Senate send him plenipotentiaries empowered to conduct conclusive negotiations. The Lithuanian Senate immediately informed its Polish counterpart of the tsar's demand, requesting that he be satisfied as quickly as possible, fearing delay might endanger Lithuania. As 1572 ended the Polish plenipotentiaries had not appeared, forcing the Lithuanian Council, at the beginning of 1573, to send Ivan its own ambassador, Michal Haraburda. He explained that the nobles' slow response was due to their inability to meet because of an epidemic spreading throughout Poland and Lithuania. Announcing that the Lithuanian nobles wished either Ivan's election or that of his son Fedor, and that the Polish magnates would agree to either, Haraburda requested Ivan's definitive answer as to whether he wanted the crown or wanted it for his son.

In either case there must be a pledge that the rights and privileges of the nobility would remain untouched. When the boundaries between the realms were set Ivan would cede four cities to Lithuania, namely Smolensk, Polotsk, Usviat and Ozerishche. If Prince Fedor was elected king, his father was to give him several more cities and rural districts.

Haraburda's speech did not please Ivan, who replied "You said that the lords of the council did not send ambassadors for so long a time because of a pestilence. This is the will of God. It would have been worthwhile for the nobles to consider how to complete this business more rapidly, because it is not good for a country to be without a ruler. If the lords of the Lithuanian council do not wish to elect a ruler for themselves without the Polish crown, that is their decision. You spoke of confirming rights and privileges. It is obvious that in a land where certain customs exist it is inappropriate to revoke them. You said that we should return Smolensk, Polotsk, Usviat and Ozerishche to Lithuania. This is a meaningless request. Why should we decrease the size of our realm? It is good to expand a realm, not decrease its size. Why should I give you my son, Prince Fedor, at a loss to my own realm? They wish me to give even more cities and districts to my son, yet even without our cities and districts the Polish kingdom and Lithuanian grand principality possess many cities and districts with income sufficient to support my son's court and ours. Nor does it reward us to do this, because upon the death of the king the kingdom does not belong to his children. Thus, the kingdom of Poland and the grand principality of Lithuania would not be joined to Muscovy. It cannot be done in this way, and we will not give our son Fedor.

"We know that the [Holy Roman] emperor and the French king applied to you. They cannot be considered an example because, apart from ourselves and the Turkish sultan, there are no rulers in any kingdom whose family has ruled without interruption for two hundred years. This is why they request this honor for themselves, yet as everybody knows among all kingdoms we have been sovereigns[42] since the time of Emperor Augustus at the beginning of the centuries. The Polish kingdom and the Lithuanian grand principality are not destitute, it is possible to dwell there for some time. Moreover our son is not a bride for whom we must supply a dowry.

"If the lords of the Lithuanian and Polish councils desire our acknowledgment, let them first write our title in full, because we received our imperial name from our ancestors and did not take it from strangers. Secondly, should God take our son Fedor from this earth and should he leave any descendants, let the Polish kingdom and the grand principality of Lithuania not seek a new ruler from among others, only from among them. If our son leaves no children, Poland and Lithuania shall not cut themselves off from our family kin. Should one of our family die, his body shall be brought here for burial. They may curtail neither the rights nor the privileges of our children or their descendants who sit upon the Polish and Lithuanian throne. Let Poland and Lithuania unite with our kingdom, and then in our title we will write the Muscovite tsardom first, then the Polish kingdom and grand principality of Lithuania. Let us stand and defend ourselves from all enemies as one, and let Kiev be ceded to our domains. Although in the past our patrimony ended on the Berezina river, this we are willing to concede to you for the sake of Christian peace, but Polotsk with all its surrounding areas and the entire Livonian land will go to our side, the Muscovite realm. Unless these conditions are met we cannot release our son Fedor to your realm. Moreover, he is a minor and cannot stand alone against enemies.

"We desire eternal peace only under the following conditions. Polotsk with all its surroundings, as well as Courland, shall be ceded to Lithuania, and Livonia to Moscow. Although the Dvina shall be the border, Polotsk and its by-towns shall be the border with our lands in accordance with the ancient surveys. May all three realms act as one against all enemies. If they elect the emperor's son, let him live in brotherhood with us and confirm a lasting peace. We are prepared to live with the emperor's son in the exact same manner as we would have lived with our own son Fedor, had we given him to you as a ruler. I am aware that several Poles and your Lithuanian nobles wish me rather than my son elected king. Indeed, it would be much better were I to become your ruler."

"The nobles and magnates," Haraburda replied, "would be pleased to elect him as their ruler, but he must explain how it would come about. He must constantly travel from one realm to the other and because of the long distances he would be unable to defend his kingdoms properly. Great difficulties would arise in the judicial aspects of the kingship, and, lastly, without accepting the Roman faith he could not be crowned."

Ivan ordered Haraburda to return for his answer the next day. When the ambassador appeared the tsar again said to him "We who rule over the Muscovite kingdom wish to be sovereign of Poland and Lithuania and administer all these realms by traveling to each and spending some time there. The issues you raised will not interfere with matters of state. As to our title, the Muscovite kingdom[43] occupies first place, then that of Poland and Lithuania. As to patrimonies, Moscow shall have Kiev alone without its by-towns, Polotsk with its by-towns and Courland shall be for Lithuania, and Livonia shall be part of our Muscovite realm. Our full title shall be: By the grace of God, Sovereign Tsar and Grand Prince Ivan Vasilievich of All Rus—Kiev, Vladimir, and Moscow, King of Poland, Grand Prince of Lithuania, Grand Prince of Russia and of Great Novgorod, Tsar of Kazan, Tsar of Astrakhan, then a list by seniority of all our Russian, Polish, and Lithuanian regions.

"Our religion shall receive the highest honor. We will build stone and wood churches in our castles, villages and courtyards as we see fit. We will honor the metropolitans and prelates as is our custom. We will expand rather than disturb the rights and privileges of the magnates and gentry. Should we see fit to retire to a monastery in our old age, let the lords and the entire land elect as their ruler whomever they prefer from among our sons, and I personally will raise no objections. Were the grand principality of Lithuania to desire us to govern alone, without the Polish crown, it would be even more agreeable to us. We desire to become the grand prince of Lithuania, ruling the Muscovite and Lithuanian grand principalities as one, just as Poland and Lithuania were ruled. Our title shall be as stated earlier. We shall restore to Lithuania those lands ceded to the Polish crown with the exception of Kiev, which shall be returned to Muscovy. It is also necessary to agree on the courtiers (oprichnina),[44] who are not many, but without whom I cannot travel either to Poland or Lithuania. I also wish to make known that I will not travel to Poland or Lithuania alone, but accompanied by my children who are too young to be left behind. Rumors are coming to us from your side that Poles and Lithuanians want to seize one of our sons to hand him over to the Turk. I do not know whether or not this is true, or if evil people have invented it. Nevertheless I must inform you of it, because I want to lay everything out.

"I especially want you to know that I am aging rapidly, and it is difficult for me to travel between three such extensive realms. Thus it would be better if Poland and Lithuania took as their ruler the emperor's son and entered into an eternal peace with us in accordance with the terms I have stated. This would be more reassuring for us, as it would for these lands.

"Should Poland and Lithuania not wish an archduke but prefer us, we are willing to become their sovereign. The nobles have only to give their oath and a document that they will cause no harm to our rule or that of our children, set no ruler against us, nor betray us to any other realm nor invent any stratagem to prevent us or our children from traveling as safely on matters of the throne to Poland and Lithuania as we do in our own land. The more gratifying would it be, were only the grand principality of Lithuania, without Poland, to desire us as its lord.

"Tell the lords of the council not to elect a Frenchman king because he may well desire the good of the Turk more than that of Christianity.[45] Should you elect a Frenchman then know you, Lithuania, that I will deal harshly with you. Once more I give you notice that many have written to me from your lands asking that I march against Polotsk with my armies. Then you will petition me to be your ruler to prevent laying the land to waste. Others have written on this matter, some asking money and sables in exchange for which they promise to promote our son's election as king. Convey this to the lords of the council."

As Haraburda was about to set out on his return journey the lord-in-waiting[46] Umnoy-Kolychev, the conciliar noble Pleshcheev, and the crown secretaries[47] Andrei and Vasily Shchelkalov spoke in Ivan's name. "If the grand principality of Lithuania," they said, "wishes to see him as their ruler, he is agreeable. Be assured and do not fear Poland, for the sovereign[48] will reconcile it with Lithuania."

Subsequently Novgorod contributed a number of demands unacceptable to Haraburda. (1) The coronation and placing of the crown of Poland and of the grand principality of Lithuania on our sovereign according to Christian [meaning Orthodox] custom by the archbishops and bishops. Let bishops ordained by Roman law not officiate during that time, rather act as lords of the council of episcopal rank. (2) By God's judgment his majesty the tsar and his son Prince Ivan Ivanovich are without spouses, and Prince Fedor Ivanovich is nearing the age when marriage is necessary. Accordingly the lords of the council shall permit his royal majesty to appraise and select from among his [female] subjects in the Russian realm, the Polish kingdom and grand principality of Lithuania, whosoever is most suitable to the royal rank. It does not befit his royal majesty to marry among other royal houses, for such a match does not accord with custom and for this reason it is inappropriate to contemplate the future otherwise. Perhaps an opportunity will occur permitting marriage to a sovereign's daughter. If so, his royal majesty will discuss the matter with the lords of the council. Our rulers from time immemorial have selected wives from among their subjects. (3) When the sovereign visits with his children in the kingdom of Poland and there is a difference which we cannot adjudicate, the nobles shall permit the tsar and his children to depart without any interference.

HENRI OF ANJOU ELECTED

As his conversations with Haraburda indicate, Ivan was ambivalent about taking the Polish crown. His vacillation, conditions for election, and unwillingness to give his son the crown further weakened Muscovy's supporters in the Sejm. Since the Muscovite ambassadors brought neither flattering words, promises nor gifts for the nobles, it was easy for Chodkiewicz to muffle the tsar's advocates.

Those advocating the election of Emperor Maximilian or his son Ernst[49] also failed to gain strength. Their failure was attributable to Maximilian's hesitation. He expected the Poles to ask him to take the crown, not the other way around. By the time he sent his ambassadors Rosenberg and Perstein they could not change matters. Moreover they did not wish to do so. Both ambassadors and their retinues were Czech. In befriending the Poles at frequent gatherings the Czechs recalled that they too had enjoyed the very same freedoms as existed in Poland. These they were deprived of by the Austrian house, which increased their obligations and sought to destroy their language. As brothers they warned the Poles to beware of the Austrian yoke. Similarly the ambassadors from the imperial princes, while apparently advocating the cause of Ernst, Maximilian's son, secretly advised the Poles to do quite differently. Inasmuch as the Poles already entertained perpetual suspicion of the Habsburgs, it was not difficult for the French ambassador Montluc[50] to fashion a strong, popular case on behalf of Henri of Anjou,[51] brother of the French king Charles IX and son of Catherine de Medici.

In his public speech Montluc did not spare the Poles any flattery, calling their realm the guardian of Christianity, praising their customs, and confirming how the lives of Poles and Frenchmen were more alike than those of any other peoples. Nor was he modest in his promises. In Montluc's words, Henri would build up the fleet, thus quickly accelerating the growth of Narva's trade. He would transform the Cracow Academy into Europe's leading institution by recruiting learned scholars. He would send one hundred members of the Polish nobility to Paris to study science at his own cost, and he would recruit a hundred Gascon archers for Polish service.

Meetings began, opinions were heard about electing one of their own, but the elder of Bielz, the learned Jan Zamoyski,[52] an adherent of noble democracy and a supporter of the French prince, spoke out eloquently against such solutions. The majority[53] voted for Henri, and Montluc hurried to swear the oath for him so as to keep intact the conditions of the election, the famous Pacta Conventa.[54] Firlej led the Protestant protest. Apparently, they did not want the brother of Charles IX as king, fearing a repetition of the St. Bartholomew massacre[55] in Cracow or Warsaw. Montluc reassured even the Protestants, swearing to them on Henri's behalf to safeguard all their rights and privileges.

In August 1573 twenty Polish ambassadors escorted by a hundred and fifty members of the petty nobility arrived in Paris to fetch Henri.[56] They spoke of conditions for his assumption of the kingship. The Poles demanded that Henri reconfirm the rights of Polish Protestants and that French Huguenots also receive freedom of religion as Montluc promised.

They asked Montluc how he could make such a promise without direct instructions. Montluc replied that he really had no order to this effect. He was compelled to make this pledge in order to silence France's enemies and to satisfy Protestants disturbed by the news of the St. Bartholomew's massacre. Other ambassadors desirous of undermining the election were spreading rumors that Prince Henri had participated in the killings. This Montluc denied, reassuring them that the massacre had occurred by chance. "If it took place without the support of the monarchy the king is obligated to punish the offenders and grant French Protestants guarantees of their rights," replied the Polish Protestants. "I did not know how to answer them," said Montluc, "and fearful that this situation might interfere with the election, gave the promise demanded. Since it did not apply to Poland, the king is not required to fulfill the promise."

The Polish ambassadors did not stop demanding fulfillment of the promise. Then Laureo, the papal nuncio, took it upon himself to reconcile the parties. In the dark of night and in shabby dress he betook himself to the Polish Catholic delegates, to the bishop of Poznan, and to Adalbert Laski. At first they were not inclined to agree to his demands. Finally after threats against the Catholics and promises to the Protestants Laureo managed to convince the envoys to desist from demanding fulfillment of Montluc's promises. These events demonstrated the strength of Protestantism in Poland and Lithuania, and that even among Catholics there was not yet religious tolerance.

HENRI FLEES POLAND

At the beginning of 1574 Henri arrived in Poland. The Protestants demanded that he repeat his oath protecting their rights. The king declined. Protestants disrupted the coronation ceremony, disturbing the Sejm with their shouts.[57] The parties fought on. Henri's display of an evident predilection for Zborowski further inflamed the conflict. On one side there were cries against the king, libels, and quarrels with the French. Rarely did a day pass without a murder on one side or the other. Finally someone evidently threatened that Henri would be toppled from his throne should he not fulfill his obligations appropriately.[58]

In France Henri was not accustomed to such obligations and complained that the Poles wanted to depose him prior to calling the parliamentary court.

Aside from laziness and a passion for empty amusements it was difficult for Henri to occupy himself with affairs of state inasmuch as he knew neither Polish nor Latin. Other than his native tongue he spoke only a little Italian and so sat like a mute spending his time in the Senate thinking about how most quickly to escape it. He went entire nights without sleep, playing cards and carousing, spending all his time with his Frenchmen, avoiding the Poles. Although his generosity and extravagance knew no limits, such poverty existed in the palace that on occasion there was nothing to prepare for dinner, and nothing with which to set the table.[59]

This was Henri's situation when he received news of the death of his brother Charles IX, in light of which his mother, Catherine de Medici, demanded that he return to France as quickly as possible. Unable to keep his news secret, the king announced his mother's request to the senators, who replied they must call a meeting of the Sejm, which had sole authority to allow him to leave the realm. Henri knew how slowly the Sejm assembled. Without hope even of receiving its agreement to his departure, after hearing about movements against him in France he secretly fled at night across the border.[60]

At Henri's departure from Poland the nobles were at a loss of what to do. Should they declare an interregnum or not? Rather than this they informed Henri that should he not return to Poland within nine months the Sejm would elect a new king.[61]

Along with Henri's envoys bearing news of his accession to the throne, word was sent posthaste to Moscow of Henri's departure for France, which suggested that he had authorized the lords of the council to conduct conversations with foreign rulers. Ivan replied that he had sent his courier Yelchaninov to Poland to request safe conduct for his envoys to visit Henri to congratulate him on his accession to the throne. While Yelchaninov awaited the king's return he could not present himself to the lords of the council because a ruler has dealings only with rulers, and nobles only with boyars.

The prior negotiations between Ivan and the nobles occurred because Poland had no king, and they petitioned for him or one of his sons to rule. Now that they had a king it was unbecoming to negotiate without him. Yelchaninov waited a long time for Henri. One night while waiting for the Sejm to convene a Lithuanian noble, the elder of Samogitia, visited him secretly saying "[Your] sovereign should send his trusted envoy to Lithuania bearing separate letters with words of favor: a letter to the commander of Wilno, another to me, a third to the lord of Troki, a fourth

Conquests during Ivan IV.   Losses during Ivan IV

TERRITORIAL CHANGES UNDER IVAN IV

to the Sierotka Radziwiłł,[62] a fifth to all the knights. He must send his envoy immediately without delay, for King Henri will not come back.

"Through my own fault, in the sovereign's view, I am of no consequence. The sovereign does not reply to me formally on any matters, nor does he command me to serve him. It is infinitely annoying to us that despite our wishes the Poles want to invite a king to rule over us. Our faith coincides better with the Muscovites', and all of us in Lithuania want our own sovereign as king. If we beseech God, and entreat for [your] sovereign to rule over us in Lithuania, all Poles will come before [your] sovereign with their heads humbly bowed. [Your] sovereign knows that formerly we had our own king, Vytautas, who always lived in Wilno. Now we desire the same thing, that our king reside in Wilno and travel to Cracow periodically, but it appears that [your] master does things his own way."[63]

Further the elder related that the Lithuanians, in accordance with the tsar's desires, wished to elect the archduke, whereas the Poles wanted to elect the friend of the sultan. He said that it was difficult for the Poles to accept Ivan's condition that his descendants inherit the crown. Yet once they experienced Ivan's kindness and tenderness never would they desert his descendants, even if another people objected. Moreover, it seemed cruel that the tsar referred to Kiev and Volhynia as belonging to him, and wished the Muscovite metropolitan to crown him.

On behalf of the Poles Bishop Jakub Uchanski of Gniezno sent to Yelchaninov examples of the kind of letters that the tsar might send to the clergy, the great nobles, all the knights and to each noble individually. In his general letters Ivan was to request his election, and point out that he was not a heretic but rather a Christian baptized in the name of the Holy Trinity. Since Poles and Russians were descended from the same tribes, whether Slavic or Sarmatian, as brothers they should have a single ruler.

Remarkable examples of letters to several magnates exist. For instance in one the tsar wrote "You know me and I know you and that you have a great sum (purse). I do not want your bag of money, I want you for a friend because you are skilled in all matters, you know how to give advice so that there will be not merely a purse, but trunks of money."

Ivan found himself in a difficult position. He considered it demeaning to try to ingratiate himself. He was uncertain of success. And, a much more complicated situation probably would have developed had he succeeded. In contrast, not being elected could be equally unpleasant, especially if the choice fell on an undesirable against whom it might again be necessary to begin war over Livonia.

After Yelchaninov's report the tsar decided to send the courier Bastanov to the lords, demanding letters of safe conduct for his high ambassadors. Bastanov reported that according to all rumors the Lithuanian council wanted to elect the Muscovite sovereign. The papal nuncio had reported to Rome that although the great magnates did not wish the Muscovite tsar under any circumstances, the people were strongly inclined towards him. In another letter he reported that the entire Polish and Lithuanian gentry desired the election of the Muscovite tsar, hoping that in this manner they would free themselves from the power of the magnates.

Having learned from Bastanov the possibility of success Ivan commanded the immediate dispatch to Poland of his emissary Novosiltsev, with letters to Uchanski, the archbishop of Cracow, and to the secular lords. In his letter to Uchanski Ivan assured him that he would not interfere with the beliefs and honors of the clergy. To Uchanski himself Ivan promised great rewards if by his efforts he were elected to the crown. "We will reward you with honors and treasure for your services. Let us know the kind of payments you desire, and we will bestow great favor upon you." Individual promises to private persons were insufficient. Ivan did not utter one word about whether he would retract his previous conditions, while the Sejm would not hear of any conditions save those according to which Henri was elected earlier. Besides, Novosiltsev was a impotent ambassador who lacked authority to behave in a manner comparable to that of the other competitors' representatives.

These circumstances again created a situation, especially among the Poles, which caused the pro-Muscovites to despair, and forced two other sides into prominence. These were the magnates wishing to elect Emperor Maximilian,[64] and the petty nobility wishing to elect a candidate not favored by the magnates, a Piast, meaning any descendant of the Polish kings, or at the very least someone who was not an Austrian.

NEW ELECTIONS

In November 1575 the electoral Sejm began by first hearing the foreign ambassadors. In the name of their master the Holy Roman emperor's emissaries offered his son Archduke Ernst as a candidate for the crown. They extolled the prince's qualities, arguing that because of his frequent dealings with the Czechs he understood their language, and thus easily could learn Polish as well. While he was learning Polish he would use Latin, which he spoke fluently, and which was in general use among the Poles. In listing the advantages of Ernst's election they pointed out that Poland would enter into alliances with the house of Austria, the lords of German and Italian domains, the Spanish crown, and finally even with the Muscovite tsar.

Following the imperial emissaries the ambassadors of Maximilian's brother Archduke Ferdinand[65] similarly extolled their master's qualities, namely his military prowess and knowledge of the Czech language, promising that Ferdinand would bring to Poland the greater portion of his income, one hundred and fifty thousand thalers per year, and an additional fifty thousand for building and repairing border fortresses. He would bring strong German infantry regiments with him to repel enemy forces.

The Swedish ambassador began his speech by exhorting the Sejm to employ all its forces to war against Muscovy, promising that the Swedish king would commit one third of his tax revenues to such an endeavor. To expedite resolution of disputes between Sweden and Poland over Livonia, he suggested that the Poles cede to Sweden their portion of Livonia, in exchange for which the Swedish king would drop all claims for funds received by the Polish government as loans against his wife's dowry. During her fourteen years on the throne the Poles neither repaid the loans nor returned the moneys and lands to which she was entitled by inheritance. He also offered the alternative of permitting Poland permanently to transfer its part of Livonia as a fief to the Swedish crown prince Sigismund, to whom his father also would give his part of the country.

Then the ambassador came to the main issue, suggesting election of either his king John,[66] or the equally acceptable alternative of electing as queen Anna, sister of the late Sigismund Augustus. Citing as an example how by giving the crown to Queen Elizabeth England achieved its greatest prosperity, he said that only through such approaches might matters between Poland, Sweden, Livonia and Muscovy be resolved. A strong tie between the two neighboring countries would ensue, they would have peace with the Turks, Tatars and Germany, and the Muscovites would be banished from Livonia. The Narva trade, so detrimental to Polish interests and so beneficial to the Muscovites, would cease. Queen Anna, knowing the language and popular customs, would listen to every one, showing fairness to all and supporting all rights and privileges. She would not be among those who sit deafly and mutely on the throne, displaying contempt for Polish customs (an allusion to Henri). Moreover should the very same Sejm name as Anna's successor the only son of the Swedish king they would be designating, through his mother, Sigismund, the sole descendant of the Jagiellonian line. By the time he reached adulthood Sigismund would know Polish and Swedish, along with sufficient Latin, Italian and German. The king and queen of Sweden would spare nothing for their son, who would come to Poland with a substantial sum of money for the gentry.

ELECTION OF STEFAN BATHORY

Earlier in 1574, after Henri's flight, the sultan sent a letter demanding that the Poles not elect an Austrian who of necessity must involve them in a war with the Porte. He suggested they elect someone from among themselves, for example Jan Kosta, governor of Sandomir. Should they desire someone foreign, he suggested the king of Sweden or Stefan Bathory,[67] prince of Transylvania. Bathory's emissary visited the Sejm and after the usual enumeration of his prince's good qualities he began to make promises: to keep intact the rights of the lords and gentry, conforming to their will; to repay all the king's debts; to bring with him his army to reconquer all lands lost to Muscovy; to maintain peace with the Turks and Tatars; to lead his armies personally; to send eight hundred thousand zlotys for military expenses and for ransom of imprisoned gentry seized from the Russian lands in the last Tatar invasion.

Finally, the emissary of Alfonso II, duke of Ferrara, made his presentation, promising among other things to supplement the faculty of the Cracow Academy, to bring to Poland artists whom he would support from his own funds, and to educate at his own expense in Italy fifty young members of the Polish gentry.[68] There were no Muscovite emissaries. No one praised Ivan's virtues, no one spoke of his promises.

The Sejm's proceedings were dominated by the split among the magnates and the Polish gentry. On December 12 the Austrian party, consisting primarily of the magnates, proclaimed Emperor Maximilian king, but fourteen members of the gentry proclaimed Anna queen so that she might marry Stefan Bathory. The Austrian side held great hopes of triumphing over the opposition since Lithuania and Prussia largely supported Maximilian, yet from the very outset the emperor's hesitation doomed his chances. When the Polish emissaries favoring him brought news of his election he suggested altering the conditions governing his election to include the same conditions as Henri, namely that at least two words be inserted, "as he is able."[69] Since several of the clauses related not to himself alone, rather to the empire as a whole, and since the dual election meant he could not become king of Poland without armed assistance, Maximilian could not make the decision himself. To reconcile both sides he proposed that Anna remain queen while instead of Bathory his own son Archduke Ernst become her husband and king.

It was evident to everyone that the elderly Maximilian, who even as a youth was not regarded as a particularly energetic individual, cooled in his ardor to accept the Polish throne when he found that he must attain it by force of arms. He conducted his negotiations with Muscovy, whose interests now were linked closely to Austria's, from a similar point of view.

The alliances concluded between Muscovy and Austria against Poland under Ivan III[70] and his son Vasily[71] came to naught. Under Ivan IV negotiations resumed on the subject of Livonia when in 1559 Emperor Ferdinand I wrote to Ivan suggesting that he not fight in Livonia, which belonged to the Holy Roman empire, and that he return conquered areas. Ivan replied that should the emperor wish amicable and brotherly relations with him he was to send high ambassadors to begin negotiations on all matters.

The high ambassadors never arrived, yet nevertheless Ivan demanded that the Poles and Lithuanians elect the archduke to the crown. The tsar's demand explains the sultan's call to elect neither the emperor nor his son. To the Muscovite crown, the enmity between Austria and the Ottomans guaranteed that Poland and the Turks would conclude no alliance. A Polish king from the Austrian house, always fearful of the Turk, would be forced to seek a Muscovite alliance in exchange for which he would not begrudge Livonia.

In July 1573 an imperial courier called Paul Magnus arrived in Moscow bearing a letter from Maximilian II suggesting to Ivan a unification of forces opposing the French Henri's accession to the Polish throne. The herald recounted the St. Bartholomew's Eve massacre, which very much grieved his master. "The French king," he said, "battled with the king of Navarre[72] and designed a villainous subterfuge to reconcile with him. They reconciled and agreed that the king's sister would marry the king of Navarre, who arrived for the wedding accompanied by many important dignitaries.The French king seized the king of Navarre, his brother-in-law, and put him in prison where he still languishes, while murdering everyone in his entourage, including wives and children, on that same night, claiming that he killed them in the name of religion, for they were not of his faith. He even murdered those of his own people who professed the same religious belief as the king of Navarre. In total he murdered as many as a hundred thousand. Every Christian king is driven to pity and anguish over this event, and not to associate with this evil Frenchman. Now the French king releases his brother for the Polish kingship with the consent of the Turkish sultan, thus creating anguish for the Holy Roman emperor, whose wish is that either his own son or the Muscovite ruler ascend the Polish throne to restore their past amity and brotherhood. The emperor offers to divide the realm, the Polish kingdom to the emperor and the grand principality of Lithuania to Muscovy. They would stand together against the Turks and all the Tatar rulers. Should the French prince assume the Polish crown an alliance with the Turks would result, and Christianity face great adversity and ruin."

Ivan's courier Skobeltsyn was dispatched to Vienna to express to the emperor Ivan's readiness to prevent the alienation of Poland and Lithuania from Muscovy or Austria. In regard to the Saint Bartholomew's Eve event Ivan wrote "You, our dearest brother, grieve over the bloodletting that occurred in the French kingdom, killing several thousand people, including babes in arms. A Christian ruler must feel anguish at the French king's display of such inhumanity towards so many people and for mindlessly spilling so much blood."[73]

Skobeltsyn returned without so much as a reply, complaining of his bad treatment at the hands of the imperial envoy Paul Magnus, who soon arrived with complaints about Skobeltsyn, accusing him of not wishing to accept the emperor's letters, of speaking impolitely, remarking "his tongue is sweet, but his heart is bitter," and of conducting himself inappropriately.

The tsar ordered Skobeltsyn to answer the charges. The messenger confessed to not accepting the imperial letter because it did not refer to Ivan as tsar. Ivan sent the emperor a reply noting that because of the complaints he had put Skobeltsyn into disgrace, yet simultaneously let it be known that in his eyes Skobeltsyn's blameworthiness and Paul Magnus's innocence was not at all demonstrated. "We ordered our trusted servant Skobeltsyn to be questioned in the presence of your envoy Paul. Skobeltsyn said that Paul borrowed four hundred Joachimsthalers[74] from him, but returned only 138, and dealt disgracefully with him, for which he accuses him of this behavior. Our envoys on both sides must be obliged in advance not to undertake any such activities as would bring us anguish, or bring grief upon us, lest their meaningless nonsense cause strain on our brotherly love."

Afterwards other messengers arrived in Moscow with apologies stating that Maximilian because of severe lack of time was unable to reach agreement with the tsar on Polish matters. These excuses greatly angered Ivan, and he grew even more furious for instead of diplomats the emperor sent merchants seeking to expedite trade with Moscow.

Finally in December 1575 the high ambassadors arrived, Johann Kobenzl[75] and Daniel Prinz.[76] Their escort reported to the tsar regarding his conversations with the embassy's interpreters who were hired in Poland. "The Lithuanian people did not want to allow the embassy to pass through their land, but acquiesced out of fear of the emperor. Nevertheless in Lithuania it was rumored that the emperor's emissaries were to consult the Muscovite ruler that together they might gain control of Lithuania and divide it between them."

Ivan wanted to make the emissaries understand how late was their arrival, and how inappropriate it was for the emperor, in light of their important mutual interests, to prolong negotiations by sending mere couriers and merchants. He ordered the embassy's detention at Dorogobuzh where Boyar Nikita Romanovich-Yuriev, Prince Sitsky and Crown Secretary Andrei Shchelkalov appeared bearing the following order from Ivan. "Having arrived in Dorogobuzh, you will arrange a meeting place, confer with the imperial emissaries there and inquire of them, in the tsar's name, on what business the emperor sent them. If the ambassadors decline to reveal their mission, force them to do so by meeting with them frequently, saying 'Do not be surprised that our ruler ordered us to question you while still enroute, without admitting you to his presence. Everything exists by chance. Previously it was not customary to question emissaries on the road as to their business, but previously it was also not customary that members of the ruler's own court rode so far to speak to ambassadors regarding their business. This incident has occurred because your lord Emperor Maximilian sent traders to our lord, claiming to be his ambassadors and couriers. Our ruler wished to accord them the honor due ambassadors and couriers, but it was evident that they were merely merchants and traders! Now our lord has sent us, the closest of his servants, to ask the nature of your service to your emperor and if you have arrived with the same dignity as your predecessors.'"

The ambassadors answered that they deplored these words and that they were unable to transmit the emperor's words to anyone save his majesty the tsar. If traders called themselves ambassadors or couriers, the emperor would authorize their punishment. They, the ambassadors, were the emperor's privy councillors, arriving to confirm the previous alliance of their sovereigns, and to agree about the Lithuania matter and the spread of Christianity.

Previously Maximilian wrote that he could not begin negotiations with Muscovy for lack of time. Once Ivan heard the reply of Kobenzl and Prinz he sent them the following letter. "Do not be insulted," he wrote, "that we did not admit you to our presence more quickly. We are very busy and had departed the city. As soon as we arrive in Mozhaisk we will summon you to our presence immediately."

The ambassadors' speeches contained two demands. Ivan must cooperate in the election of Archduke Ernst as king of Poland and grand prince of Lithuania, and leave Livonia in peace. "The election of Ernst as king," said the ambassadors, "will be very useful to your highness, since you, Ernst, the emperor, the king of Spain, the Pope and other Christian rulers together, by land and sea may attack your foremost enemy the Turkish sultan, whereupon you can drive the infidels back into Asia. Then by the will of the emperor, the Pope, the king of Spain, Grand Duke Ernst, the imperial princes and orders, the entire Eastern Greek empire [the former Byzantine empire] shall be ceded to your highness, and your majesty will be proclaimed the Eastern emperor." Ivan commanded that the ambassadors be reminded that, according to the emperor's previous proposals, Archduke Ernst was to be raised to the Polish throne, and Lithuania was to fall to Muscovy.

The envoys replied that these demands would never come to fruition. The link between the Polish kingdom and the grand principality of Lithuania was too strong, one could not be parted from the other, and must remain under one ruler. When Grand Duke Ernst was elected king, in the name brotherly love he would agree to cede Kiev along with several other cities to the tsar, for the emperor was also aware that Kiev was part of the tsar's patrimony. "The emperor instructed us only to make passing mention of Livonia, not to speak of it in great detail. We ask only that your lord not order an attack on Livonia until the arrival of great imperial envoys, appanage princes[77] and distinguished servitors."

Ivan instructed his representatives to respond to the ambassadors by suggesting his doubts of the emperor's promises. "If between rulers a matter of this nature begins with an alliance, perpetual brotherhood and friendship, it must be strong and unmovable. According to our master's custom, whoever gives his word in brotherhood and love must hold it firmly and immovably, for otherwise his word has no meaning. Was that not what happened to Ladislas the Hungarian king who seeking to oppose the Turkish sultan concluded an alliance with the emperor and with many German lords? Yet when the Turkish sultan attacked him the emperor and the German lords did not come to his aid. They betrayed him instead, permitting the Turkish host to defeat and then kill him.[78] Let Maximilian's allies, the Pope, the kings of Spain and Denmark, dukes, counts, and various nobles, send to our ruler ambassadors together with those of the emperor to affirm that all stand united as one against all enemies to the finish."

The emperor would rather see blood on his hands or lose all his territories than break his word said the envoys in reply. Following these negotiations Ivan dismissed the ambassadors with a message to the emperor. "We wish that our most beloved brother's son Ernst, the Austrian prince, become king of Poland, and that the grand principality of Lithuania with Kiev become part of our Muscovite realm. From the beginning the Livonian lands have been our patrimony, and the Livonian Germans paid tribute to our ancestors. Having forgotten the law, they withdrew from us, thus their circumstances have become those of today. The Livonian and Courland lands must be a part of our realm in their entirety, and because the Livonian land must necessarily be favorable to us, we have placed a king, our own vassal Magnus,[79] on their throne. Thus let our most beloved brother Emperor Maximilian demonstrate his affection for us by not entering the Livonian lands. As for us, with the Livonian lands in hand we shall proceed further. We will send word to the Polish nobility to elect Ernst their king, and to the Lithuanians that they choose us. Should Lithuania not agree to part from Poland, let it also elect Ernst. If Poland and Lithuania do not agree to have either Ernst or ourselves as their kings, we with Emperor Maximilian will deal with them and compel their cooperation." Prince Sugorsky, the tsar's ambassador to Maximilian, was obliged to repeat the message word for word, adding in regard to Livonia "The tsar has no alternative but to uphold his Livonian patrimony."

As Kobenzl and Prinz negotiated with the Muscovite boyars the Jagellonian lands already were divided, though not between Ivan and Ernst, but between Maximilian and Bathory. The Muscovite courier Bastanov arrived from Lithuania with news of the elections of Bathory and Maximilian. He reported that in Lithuania many were unsure that either of them would be confirmed on the throne and believed that the tsar still might gain the advantage of them.

It was for this reason that the Minsk castellan Jan Hlebowicz approached Bastanov, saying "Why does the sovereign not send word first of all, without delay, to the lords of the council and the knights? If he does so, neither one will sit on the throne, for the whole country wants the tsar as its ruler." The young Radziwiłł, son of the Wilno commandant, said the same.

The Lithuanian council dispatched an embassy to Ivan announcing that in accordance with the tsar's command Maximilian had been elected. Novosiltsev returned [to Ivan's court] also reporting that the tsar could succeed if he acted more quickly and decisively. He explained that when he presented the tsar's letter to Jan Chodkiewicz, the latter said to him "Had your lord sent such letters to us earlier, he would have been elected a long time ago. The tsar requested letters of safe conduct for his emissaries, but I asked the tsar, through Yelchaninov, to send his envoys more quickly, even without safe conduct. Letters of safe conduct were not sent because all the lords of the council must append their signatures. Of the nobles, some serve your master, the others do not desire him and delay safe conduct by refusing their signatures. When I heard about the courier Bastanov I thought he was travelling to us with letters that included the desired words and instructions, but he arrived with nothing. We had already, involuntarily, elected Maximilian, who is old and ill. We hold to you while we await messages from the emperor. We think that he will decline the throne. The Polaks[80] are picking Bathory for the kingship, and they are sending word yet once again that we elect him, but not under no circumstances will we accept Bathory as our ruler. Bathory is a Turkish vassal. How can we hand a Christian realm into Muslim hands? You are on your way to the Poles where you will see for yourself the truth about them. They will not send letters of safe conduct for the tsar's ambassadors with you under any circumstances. I am happy to serve the tsar with all my soul if only he does not deprive us of our freedoms, for we are free people."

At a secret meeting with Novosiltsev Mikolaj Radziwill spoke the same words. The noble Holub added "Because of all the various promises the great nobles are selecting the emperor and Bathory, yet the knights of the whole land do not want them, and prefer the tsar. The lords of the council are all entangled by promises, and they themselves know not what to do."

Having elected two kings, the lords did indeed find themselves in a difficult position. Maximilian hesitated while Bathory rapidly moved to confirm all conditions offered him, solving their dilemma. On April 18, 1576 Bathory made his grand entry into Cracow and was crowned on May 1.

In April 1576 Maximilian wrote to the tsar. "We think that you already know that last December we were elected with great glory and honor as king of the Polish kingdom and the grand principality of Lithuania. We believe that your majesty will not regret this."

"We were pleased at your election," Ivan replied, "but we later discovered that in addition to you the nobles also elected Stefan Bathory, governor of Transylvania. Already he has arrived in Cracow, been crowned and wed to Queen Anna. All the nobles, except for three, paid homage to him. We are amazed at the nobles' inconstancy. Whom can you believe if you cannot believe someone's word or soul? You must make haste to decide this matter, our dearest brother, before Stefan Bathory has established fully his hold on these realms. Write us and send by a swift and light courier what is to be done concerning our common interests in Poland and Lithuania, lest these realms slip through our hands and Bathory's sway is established over them. You know better than anyone that if Bathory can establish himself in these lands as a gift from Muslim hands all we Christian rulers will suffer a great loss."

Instead of pursuing his claim to Poland along with the tsar, Maximilian grew angry at Ivan's requests not to trouble wretched Livonia. Ivan, to the contrary, seeing that the situation in Poland was not settled according to his wishes, decided that come what may he would finish with Livonia.

IVAN'S RELATIONS WITH SWEDEN

In addition to the Poles Ivan also had to combat the Swedes occupying Reval. After unsuccessfully besieging this city, at the end of 1571 Ivan arrived in Novgorod, ordering his regiments to gather in Oreshek and Dorpat for war against the Swedes in Estonia and Finland. Prior to the attack he wanted to learn whether the Swedes, frightened by his preparations, might not agree to relinquish Estonia without fighting. To this end, he summoned the Swedish envoys and proposed to delay fighting until the spring of the following year on condition King John dispatched ambassadors to Novgorod with ten thousand thaler [Joachimsthalers or efimki] as compensation for the insult inflicted on Muscovite ambassadors who during uprising against Erik[81] were robbed by two hundred cavalrymen dressed in German style. Ivan further asked the Swedish king to send men acquainted with mineralogy, requesting the king's promise to permit the free flow into Russia of copper, tin, lead and oil, as well as physicians, artists, and soldiers.

The ambassadors signed the agreement, saying that the king would make amends for everything and submit to Ivan's requests. Ivan stipulated that the necessary condition for peace was the king's abdication of his rights to Estonia. In addition, he demanded that the king make an alliance with him against Lithuania and Denmark, and in the event of war give him one thousand cavalry and five hundred infantry. Finally he demanded from the king the insertion of a Swedish rank in the tsar's title, and that he send his coat of arms so it could be included in the Muscovite seal.

The tsar congratulated himself in front of the ambassadors in regard to his demand to Erik for Queen Catherine's hand. "Of Erik," he said, "we requested Catherine, the sister of the Polish king, to gain advantage over our enemy, the Polish king. Through her we wished to initiate good relations with him. As for John, we were told that he had died and left no surviving children."[82]

In those days such demands with regard to title and seal were not considered unusual. The recipient of such a request easily declined with greater or lesser severity, depending on the petitioner. Their tone apparently corresponded to the status of the states at which the requests were directed. We have seen that there were several acceptable forms allowed by the established relations with Sweden and Denmark among them *petitions, grants*, and so forth. These long had vexed Swedish kings. It is understandable, in view of his strong personal animosity toward Ivan because of the matter of Catherine, that King John was likely to be outraged by the tsar's requests. He did not dispatch new ambassadors to conclude a peace treaty. Moreover the vicegerent of Oreshek, Prince Putiatin, reported to the tsar that the king's lieutenant in Vyborg wrote to him that an agreement was unseemly, as if the tsar personally were asking for peace from the Swedish envoys. Ivan replied to the king with this letter.

"He who holds the scepter of the Russian tsardom received his awesome injunction by a great and mighty commandment. Your envoys violated the dignity of our majesty in a repulsive manner. Because of your [domestic] confusion, had I wished I could have taken out my wrath on your land, but I laid my anger aside for a time, and we sent you our request as a way for you to ameliorate your insult. We thought that by now you and the Swedish realm would have realized your foolishness, but you have lost your senses for as of now there has been no reply from you. Yet your Vyborg governor writes as if we, in our high estate, besought peace from your envoys! You will witness the high measure of our forgiveness this winter and it will not be as it was the preceding winter! Or do you think that you can steal the Swedish land as your father did when he continued to fight during the Truce of Oreshek?[83] What ripened then in the Swedish land? Your brother tried to deceive us by offering to give us your wife, but was himself banished from the kingship! In the fall they said you were dead, yet in the spring they said that you were forced from government. Now they claim that you are imprisoned in Stockholm and that your brother Erik assails you. As for your larceny, it is apparent to all. With glee you plunge hastily into various guises. Your lands and your people have no value, you depend on money for wealth.

"We do not wish to write very much, we have placed our great hopes in God. As to what happened to our military commanders without us in the Crimea, ask about it and you will learn. We are now returning to our kingdom in Moscow and will again hold court in our principality of Novgorod in December. You will observe then how we and our people will request peace from you."

WAR OVER ESTONIA AND LIVONIA

The king's reply to Ivan's abusive letter was anything but cordial. At the end of 1572 Ivan attacked Estonia with an army of eighty thousand. Wittenstein was captured by storm during the campaign in which the tsar's favorite Maliuta Skuratov-Belsky fell in battle. According to Livonian chroniclers the Swedish and German prisoners were burned.

After the capture of Wittenstein Ivan returned to Novgorod and sent the Swedish king a new letter. "As to the abusive content of your letter," he wrote, "more on that later. Now we reply humbly and at length regarding the honor of our imperial dignity. In the first place, you write your name before ours. This is unbecoming because the Holy Roman emperor is our brother, as are other great rulers. For you to call them brothers is impossible because the Swedish realm has less honor than these other states. You say that the Swedish land is the family property of your father. Inform us whose son was your Gustav, by what title your grandfather was addressed, whether he was crowned, and to which rulers he pledged his friendship and brotherhood. Tell us of this and send us documents containing this information. The truth is that you are of peasant ancestry. We asked for your wife Catherine because we wished to return her to her brother, the Polish king, and in exchange obtain Livonia from him without shedding blood. We were told that you had died and left no children to succeed you. Had we not believed your lies, we would not have asked for your wife. We have informed you of this, so it is pointless to discuss it further. Your wife is in your hands and no one is trying to seize her, yet because of one word about your wife you spilled the blood of many in vain. In the future it will not be necessary to speak of this unprecedented event and if you do, we will not listen. It is amusing that you wrote us with accusations of fighting against you on your brother Erik's behalf inasmuch as we do not need your brother Erik. You know that we instructed no one about him, neither did we negotiate on his behalf with anyone. You write and speak in vain, for no one is interfering over your wife or your brother. Conduct yourself with them as you wish. There was no arrogance on our side, it was appropriate that we wrote to you with regard to our autocratic rights."

Ivan cited a passage from the treaties with Gustav Vasa,[84] "the Archbishop of Uppsala offered his hand to the whole kingdom of Sweden." He then continued, "If your kingship was absolute then your father would not have to include the archbishop and councillors and all the people [in the treaty]. Great lords do not have land registered to them. The envoys represent the entire Swedish kingdom not your father alone, for your father is its head, much in the same manner as the elder of a rural district.

"We wrote to you with respect to the seal for should you wish to communicate with us through lieutenants you will have to pay to see it. If as a result you wish to spill blood, you already know how to do that. We do not wish to have your title and seal without due ceremony. If you wish to treat with us through lieutenants you must submit to us, yield to us and pay homage to us as is the more appropriate. Then we will grant you favor and excuse you from dealing with our vicegerents.[85] It is useless for you to communicate with us in an inappropriate manner, both as to our government and our heritage. Without your submission we desire neither your titles nor your seals. In early chronicles and annals it is written that there were Varangians at many battles with the grand prince and autocrat, Georgii-Yaroslav [Yaroslav Mudryi or Yaroslav the Wise].[86] The Varangians, who were Swedes,[87] obeyed him and were his subjects. It is incomprehensible that you request our title and seal, that you wish our subjugation. Even were you to call yourself lord of the whole universe, who would obey you?!"

The Russian commanders continued their military activities in Estonia, taking Neuhof and Karkus. Yet, almost always, because they lacked military training, in the open field they could not beat the Swedes easily even when they outnumbered them. Near Loda they suffered defeat at the hand of the Swedish General Klas Akeson Tot. News of this defeat and of the uprising of the Cheremiss in the Kazan region forced Ivan once again to offer peace to the Swedish king. The messenger Chikhachev was sent with a proposal which the king refused to take from him, thinking that the tsar's latest letter was written in the same tone as the previous one. He ordered Chikhachev to take it to his magnates and read it to them. Because the envoy was instructed to present the letter to the king himself, bitter arguments between Chikhachev and the Swedes ensued. "You have come to our lord's land," said the Swedes, "thus you must fulfill our will as we wish it." "I came to your lord's land," Chikhachev replied, "but I must fulfill the instructions of my lord, his majesty the tsar, not yours."

The Swedes threatened to deny him food. "Let me die of starvation," replied the messenger. "It will make no difference to my master, with me or without me." "You were incautious," said the Swedes to him, "for you came without the king's safe conduct. You yourself know that your master is a great enemy of ours, there has never been another like him. He wished to bring down our lord the king and take our queen for himself. He warred upon our land seizing two cities, he dishonored our ambassadors and, what is more, addressed such an indecent letter to our master that even a commoner cannot listen to it. Our lord will treat you in the same manner if you will not hand over your master's letter."

Chikhachev did not give in to them. Then one of the Swedes hit the messenger in the chest, waving the butt of his axe at his neck and while shouting abuse yelled "Chop off his head!" "If I, the slave of his majesty the tsar," said Chikhachev, "were sitting on my horse at this moment, you would not have so dishonored me, peasant. I could have answered you, but I did not come here to fight."

They searched the courier and his entourage, undressing them, removing their shoes, looking for the tsar's letter, but it could not be found. They searched through all their things, breaking into their chests of icons, scattering the icons on the benches. Upon leaving they threatened the envoy, saying "You might as well be on the fire if you do not give up the letters."

The threats were to no avail and the king finally received Chikhachev, personally taking the letter from him. After this reception the magnates arrived to treat with the courier saying "Your lord did not write the present letter in the previous manner, and it will be possible to begin dealings between our lords. The king thought that the letter would be like the earlier ones."

Chikhachev was detained. The king wrote to Ivan that he was holding his courier and would not free him until the two Swedish interpreters from the previous embassy held by Ivan were released. His note stated that he would not dispatch high ambassadors for fear their treatment would be as inappropriate as that of the earlier ones. Rather, the envoys of both rulers must meet at the border to seek a peaceful resolution. Ivan replied that the king must send his high ambassadors because a border meeting would be futile. "You had no need to detain our herald," he wrote. "We kept the interpreters in our country to teach students. One died, but the other is teaching two students the Swedish language, and lives without need. Previously your interpreters studied Russian reading and writing in our country. As soon as your interpreter completes his task, we will release him to you."

The king replied as before. "We do not wish to dispatch high ambassadors, for despite their letters of safe conduct you acquitted yourself poorly with our emissaries. You disturbed the peace and now you must send us envoys. Should you not wish to do so, send them to the frontier. You write that the interpreters are teaching your Russian boys, whereas we sent them with our envoys for our business and at our command, not to teach your subjects' children. If you want to teach Russian children the Swedish language, when there is peace, negotiate with our Vyborg vicegerents, but do not hold our servants in violation of the law."

The interpreter was sent off for exchange and Prince Sitsky headed for the border, the Sestra river, where Admiral Fleming represented the Swedes. They quarreled about the site of the negotiations. Fleming demanded that they hold them on the bridge in tents. Sitsky replied that vital matters are not discussed on a bridge and insisted that the Swede cross to the Russian side of the river.

They failed to conclude a peace. The tsar demanded Estonia and that Sweden send two hundred artillerymen for war against the Crimea, in exchange for which he conceded to the king the privilege of communicating directly with him. The king demanded direct communications without any concessions of his own. They concluded a truce of only two years' duration (from July 20, 1575 to July 20, 1577) between Finland and the Novgorod region. The matter of Estonia was to be settled by arms if the king did not hasten to send his high ambassadors to Moscow to conclude peace. The letter of agreement employed bygone wording, saying that the king petitioned the tsar.[88]

This extraordinary truce is explained by Ivan's desire to concentrate all his forces in Livonia without distraction by war on other fronts. In giving his niece Maria Vladimirovna[89] as bride to Magnus, Ivan did not abandon his prior plan to make Livonia a vassal kingdom. He granted Magnus only the small town of Karkus, and withheld part of the moneys of Maria's dowry because the treason of four foreigners in Russian service, who enjoyed Ivan's particular favor, Taube, Kruse,[90] Fahrensbach and Wachtmeister, aroused the tsar's suspicions. He feared that Magnus would use the money to raise an army to oppose the Russians.

Immediately upon the conclusion of peace with the Swedes Muscovite armies appeared near Pernau, seizing it and, according to the Livonian chroniclers, losing seven thousand men in the assault. The commander, Nikita Romanovich Yuriev, treated the residents of Pernau very kindly, with good will permitting them to leave the city and allowing them to return later for whatever they were unable to take with them at that time. Helmed, Ermes, Ruen and Purkel became Russian immediately after the seizure of Pernau.

In the beginning of 1576 six thousand Russians pushed into Estonia once again taking Leal, Loda, Fikkel and Hapsal without a shot. On the evening after its capture the people of Hapsal prepared feasts and dances. The Russians, astounded by this, said "What a strange people are these Germans! Had we, Russians, unnecessarily surrendered such a city, we would not have dared raise our eyes to an honorable person, and our tsar would not have known which punishment to lay upon us." Øsel was devastated and Padis surrendered after a one-day siege although the Swedes vainly attempted to recapture it.

In January 1577 a Russian army fifty thousand strong appeared near Reval and divided into five encampments. The besieging force used three artillery pieces shooting balls from fifty-two to fifty-five pounds and six cannon shooting balls of twenty to thirty pounds. Four pieces of siege artillery threw stones of up to two hundred and twenty-five pounds, and from fifteen cannon they shot balls of six to twelve pounds. For every piece there were seven hundred balls. Although that was considered substantial weaponry for those times, Reval possessed five times more. Moreover, the besieged took every measure against the fires erupting from enemy volleys. All easily flammable objects were removed. In addition to the requirement that each resident guard his house day and night, detachments constantly patrolled at night searching for stray shots. Each detachment consisted of four hundred peasants under the leadership of Ivo Schenckenberg, nicknamed Hannibal, the son of Reval's coiner. These brave men, along with the Swedish and German landsknechts, made constant daily and nightly sorties. After an unsuccessful six-week long barrage, the Russians lifted the siege and left. As the Muscovite armies departed Reval the Swedes proclaimed the freedom of the military to ravage all Russian holdings in Livonia. All the street vagabonds and even the cripples rose up to search for booty. Even the peasants who were robbed themselves joined the raiding parties in order to rob their brothers.

During the summer the tsar personally went on campaign from Novgorod but instead of moving on Reval, as it was thought he would, he turned towards Polish Livonia. Chodkiewicz, governor of Livonia, decided not to oppose Ivan with his small army and retreated. City after city surrendered to the tsar and his commanders attacking from one direction, or to King Magnus from the other.

Soon disagreements arose between them. Magnus demanded that the time had come for him, the designated Livonian king, to take control of all places occupied by the Russians. But Ivan had heard news of Magnus's contacts with the Polish king and the duke of Courland. "If you wish to take the cities from us," he answered Magnus's demand, "go ahead. We are here, close to you. Do not trouble yourself over these cities, they are safeguarded without you. We will send as many bailiffs to your cities as we can with God's help, for we have the money and rations for whatever may occur. If you do not wish to obey, we are prepared. We have no need to deprive you of our property. If you have nothing to live on at Kes [Wenden], go to your land beyond the sea, or it will be better to transport you to Kazan. If you go to the sea, we will clean out our Livonian principality without you."

Having ordered his commanders to occupy the cities under Magnus's control, as he approached Wenden, the Livonian king's seat, Ivan commanded him to present himself before the tsar. At first Magnus sent Ivan two emissaries, whom Ivan ordered mutilated and sent back to Wenden. The residents of the city begged Magnus not to anger the tsar further through useless opposition, and asked that he go to him personally to beseech mercy for himself as well as for them. Magnus went to the tsar's camp after allowing the Russian army into the city, but the citadel did not surrender. Upon seeing Ivan, Magnus fell to his knees before him and asked for mercy. "If you were not the son of a king," Ivan replied, "I would have taught you a lesson for opposing me and taking my cities." Magnus was put under guard. At that moment the Germans taking shelter in the Wenden citadel began to shoot, one missile almost hitting the tsar himself. Ivan swore not to leave even one of the Germans in Wenden alive.

The siege of the citadel lasted three days. The besieged saw that further defense was impossible and decided to blow themselves to bits to avoid witnessing the Tatars dishonoring their wives and daughters prior to their own death by torture. The clergy approved their decision and three hundred people, mostly of noble birth, locked themselves in a room under which they placed three barrels of gunpowder. Having received last rites, they lit the powder and blew themselves to pieces. The residents of the city verified that the besieged in the citadel had chosen suicide.

Having regained control of several other places, Ivan completed the campaign. In Dorpat he pardoned Magnus and again gave him several cities in Livonia as well as the right to call himself its king. Magnus went off to Karkus to his wife, while Ivan returned by way of Pskov to Alexandrov Village. With the tsar's departure matters were reversed in Livonia. The Swedes attacked Narva, the Poles appeared in southern Livonia and seized city after city there, even taking Wenden, despite the Russians' heroic resistance. Magnus turned himself over to the Poles.

In the fall of 1578 Russian commanders besieged Wenden, but after three unsuccessful assaults they lifted the siege when they heard of the approach of enemy armies. The Poles attacked them along with the Swedes. The Tatar cavalry could not withstand the attack and fled. The Russians retreated to their camp and returned fire until that night. Four commanders—Prince Ivan Golitsyn, Fedor Sheremetev, Prince Andrei Paletsky and Crown Secretary[91] Andrei Shchelkalov—took advantage of the dark of night and escaped with the cavalry from the encampment. The commanders to whom the artillery was entrusted did not wish to abandon it and were seized by the enemy the next morning. The gunners did not give themselves up as prisoners. Seeing the enemy was already in the camp, they hanged themselves on their weapons. In this battle four commanders lost their lives, four were taken prisoner. In total, according to the Livonian chroniclers, the Russians lost 6,022 men out of eighteen thousand.

The next year, 1579, was to have been decisive for Livonia. Ivan prepared for a new campaign. The heavy artillery was moved to Pskov intended for the siege of Reval. This artillery then was assigned a new task. The enemy was on Russian soil.

We have noted how through his quick actions Stefan Bathory thwarted the slower Maximilian and was crowned in Cracow. Although Lithuania and Prussia supported Maximilian, not seeing the least movement from his side, they were forced to acknowledge Stefan as king. Only Danzig, for specific reasons, held out for Maximilian. At the end of Sigismund Augustus's reign the residents of Danzig were outraged by Polish government policies violating their rights and privileges. Those most responsible for these policies were also Bathory's strongest supporters, thus explaining Danzig's strong animosity toward Stefan from whom the citizens expected nothing good. They announced that they would not recognize Stefan as king until their rights were assured and until some kind of agreement was signed with the emperor, the news of whose death presented them with great difficulties. Relying on the Sejm's procrastination, this time in the name of their distinctive rights they decided to continue their struggle by attacking the gentry lands mingled with theirs and destroying Catholic churches.[92]

The matter could be settled only through force of arms, and Bathory besieged Danzig. The opposition's agitation, unpleasantness in the Sejm, and the siege of Danzig finally forced Bathory to postpone his fight with Moscow for the time being. In July 1576 he sent Ivan emissaries, Gródenski and Buchowecki, with a proposal not to disturb their truce and to send letters of safe conduct for high ambassadors. The lords of the council wrote to the boyars in the same vein.

"We were surprised," replied the boyars, "that your sovereign does not refer to our sovereign as tsar and grand prince of Smolensk and Polotsk and refers to our sovereign's inheritance, Livonia, as a part of his own title. Your sovereign came to the Polish throne as the governor of Transylvania, a rather small place, subservient to the Hungarian realm. All our master's brothers, great sovereigns, the heads of their kingdoms, refer to him as tsar. It would be appropriate that you lords so advise your King Stefan that in the future he not undertake ventures that might lead to the shedding of Christian blood." Because they had not acknowledged Bathory's [inferior] heritage the envoys were not invited to dine, yet the letters of safe conduct for the high ambassadors were issued.

BATHORY'S ONSLAUGHT

When he heard about Ivan's attack on Livonia in 1577 and his seizure of Polish-controlled cities Bathory wrote to Ivan reproaching him for having sent letters of safe conduct and seizing cities from him without having declared war. "By God's will," Ivan answered, "we liberated our principality of Livonia, and you should lay your annoyance aside. It would have been inappropriate for you to intervene in Livonia because you were taken from the principality Transylvania to rule the Polish crown and the grand principality of Lithuania, but not Livonia. As for Livonia, what occurred happened before your time. It would be unsuitable to take on yourself such matters as preceded your taking the throne. Our letter of safe conduct was not violated by our attack on Livonia. We did you no harm. We sought what was ours, not your Lithuanian grand principality, and we captured no Lithuanians. Accordingly you may put aside any anguish and anger, and send ambassadors to us immediately."

These ambassadors, Stanislaw Krynski, governor of Mazovia, and Mikolaj Sapieha, governor of Minsk, arrived in Moscow in January 1578. Although they spoke of signing perpetual peace, both sides proposed conditions that precluded any such peace. In addition to Livonia, Courland and Polotsk the tsar demanded Kiev, Kanev and Vitebsk. To bolster his claims Ivan cited the heritage of the Lithuanian princes descended from Rogvolod of Polotsk.[93] "These princes (sons of Gediminas)," he said, "were renowned as great rulers, and were our brothers, in all established records and by birth (by generation) they were our brothers. This is why the Polish kingdom and the grand principality of Lithuania are our ancestral lands, even though no one of this princely family remains, and a king's sister cannot succeed by patrimonial right. The princes and kings of Poland were equal in their friendship and love with the princes of Galich and others in the Ukraine. Of the Transylvanian domain they had never heard. Since it is unsuitable for your ruler Stefan to receive status equal to ours, he must do us honor."

The ambassadors took offense and referred to the biblical king David, who was chosen from among the lower ranks. Ivan sent reply to them, saying "David was chosen as king by God, not by men. Hear the words of Solomon inspired by the Holy Spirit, 'Woe to the house that lets the wife rule. Woe to the city if the majority rules.' That is your affair. Through a popular uprising you elected someone of inferior descent, and he is your sovereign. As for us, we are brothers only with those meet for us as brothers. If he not meet, he is not our brother. We heard rumors that you wished to place Jan Kostka on the throne and that the governor of Wilno, Mikolaj Radziwiłł, also wanted to be sovereign. How can you think that we could consider these or any others you have chosen? You claim that we insult your sovereign but we do not insult him, we write only the truth about him. We could have written even worse things about him, to the point that we do not acknowledge him as a Christian. Your sovereign insults himself and you also insult him. You write in every letter that God in His infinite mercy had blessed him, praising yourselves that you elected him, and that God in his great mercy loved him. It is clear that he was unworthy of such a great realm, however God had mercy on him and also how you favored him, though not because of his worthiness."[94]

They agreed to extend the truce for another three years from March 25, 1578. In the treaty, signed on the tsar's behalf, a condition was inserted. "Stefan, our *neighbor* (not brother), as king of your estates in Livonia and Courland, you may not enter into our cities, homesteads, anchorages, islands or other places, or make war against them. You shall not besiege cities, create new cities or accept Livonian and Courland nobles into your service until the expiry of the truce." In the Polish treaty, written by the envoys in the name of Stefan, this condition was not included. The Muscovite emissaries Karpov and Golovin rode to Stefan to be present at his oath to observe the truce. By this time Bathory no longer wished to make peace.

At the end of 1577 the residents of Danzig swore Bathory their allegiance under conditions they found sufficiently favorable. The king made concessions because his entire attention was turned to the East. In February 1578 the Sejm assembled in Warsaw to debate with which of its two enemies it should begin war, the Crimean khan or the Muscovite tsar? At the time of the campaign against Danzig the Tatars had attacked Poland's borders. They had to be taught a lesson, yet how much booty could be gained from such a poor, nomadic people? Moreover a war against the Tatars might provoke the Turks against the Poles, since the khan was a Turkish vassal.[95]

Whereas Muscovy's strength was enormous, the stronger the enemy, how much more glorious the victory! The prize was Livonia, a wealthy region whose access to the sea offered great advantages. The Poles decided on a war of conquest. After calculating the size of the army and the sums needed, they authorized the requisitions.

All these preparations required time. In March 1578 Bathory wrote to the tsar asking Muscovy to avoid any military activities in Livonia until Ivan's envoys returned from Lithuania, where Polish nobles were to conduct negotiations regarding Livonia's future. The tsar held Bathory's messenger for nearly an entire year, and delayed his answer while awaiting the

results of his commanders' attack on Livonia. Bathory behaved similarly
with the Muscovite emissaries. The Poles delayed them on the way, argued with them about the rulers' titles, and finally presented them to the
king in Cracow.

When he received the Muscovite emissaries Bathory neither stood in
Ivan's honor nor inquired about the tsar's health as was the custom heretofore. The ambassadors, in view of this violation of custom, refused to
continue the embassy. It was then that Wolowicz, the Lithuanian deputy
chancellor said "You did not arrive in the customary manner. No one here
will listen to your instructions. You shall do as you are told. If there is
business concerning you, you must kneel to the hand of the king and
conduct your embassy. Our sovereign King Stefan will not rise because
your lord did not rise in response to his greeting." The ambassadors replied that because the king was not equal in status to Ivan, the tsar did
not rise, nor was it apparent at that time what the king wanted, peace or
war, although now a truce prevailed. The Poles responded that the ambassadors might depart. They turned back to Moscow with nothing; moreover, they were detained in Lithuania.

Ivan was disturbed by the ill turn of his efforts in Livonia and the
detention of his ambassadors in Lithuania. "Despite past custom," he
wrote to Stefan, "you, our neighbor, have detained our ambassadors. The
matter for which your ambassadors solemnly kissed the cross is not yet
completed. Nothing of this sort ever has occurred before between such
sovereigns. Such things cannot happen in Christian countries. Our emissaries have nothing to say to your nobles about Livonia because they
have no instructions in this regard. This is a separate matter, and you must
send your high ambassadors to us immediately."

Meanwhile, as far back as December 1578, pleading for God's mercy,
the tsar determined with his boyars how he would travel in his realm and
deal with affairs in the German and Lithuanian lands. Having formed his
regiments, in July 1579 he set out for Novgorod, where the ambassadors
Karpov and Golovin appeared with the news that Bathory was advancing on Muscovy's borders. They also reported that Bathory was accompanied by a few Lithuanian gentry who had volunteered to join him, at
their own expense. Those not wishing to join his campaign were not
compelled to do so. None of the Polish nobility or petty nobility had
joined him, only mercenaries.

The king insisted to the nobles and gentry that all the land must accompany him to Smolensk or Polotsk. Nevertheless the great nobles of

the council tried to dissuade him from starting a war over Lithuania's borders. "If you do not wish to go with me yourselves," said the king to them, "give me the men, and I will go without you." The nobles sought to convince him not to attack Smolensk or Polotsk, rather to hold on to Livonia. The king informed the nobles heeding his call that he wanted to attack all of Livonia and recapture the cities Moscow had seized. The nobles attempted to convince him not to attack Livonia himself, to send mercenaries to defend the cities favoring him, and to negotiate with the others. The great nobles promised men whereas the gentry demurred, saying "The money for mercenaries already has been taken from us!" The great nobles, in an effort to satisfy the king, sought to convince the gentry to follow him to Livonia, yet few volunteered. To this point it remained unclear to the king where he would attack.

Throughout Poland and Lithuania it was the general opinion among the petty nobility and the common people that they did not want Stefan on the throne and as long as Stefan remained king no good would come of it. Among the many kings they might have chosen, other than the sons of the Muscovite ruler or the Danish king, there was no one they favored. Above all else, people across the land wished that their lord could have been the son of the Muscovite ruler.

The ambassadors' reports were correct. Bathory found himself in an unenviable situation at the outset of the Muscovite war because, as we have seen, the Poles and Lithuanians had long expressed their aversion to war, putting their particular needs above the general good. The Lithuanians feared exposing their borders to danger and demanded that the king shift the war to Livonia. Bathory's greatness lay precisely in his success in overcoming these obstacles.

REASONS FOR BATHORY'S SUCCESS

Bathory's greatness as a commander was due to the fact that he was responsible for transforming warfare in the East by using methods well known to the West. Poland and Lithuania, like Muscovy, had practically no standing army. The service or noble estate gathered by order under their lords' banners. We have a clear understanding of the composition of the Polish infantry from Hetman Chodkiewicz's description of the siege of Ulla.[96] Accordingly we can conclude that Eastern European armies still retained an earlier, medieval, or better still, Asiatic, character. In Eastern Europe the cavalry still dominated whereas in the West it had yielded its primacy to the infantry, and rulers long were convinced of the need to maintain a standing army consisting primarily of paid soldiers.

Previous volumes have described the character of Muscovy's wars through the reigns of Ivan III, and especially those of Ivan III, his son and his grandson with Lithuania. The military invaded enemy territory, ravaged it, rarely conquered the cities, and came back boasting how they had returned in strength with quantities of booty. The Lithuanians followed suit, although their activities grew weaker and weaker for reasons described above, and thus Moscow regularly prevailed in its wars with Lithuania. Yet despite these losses even in the Lithuanian army, or more precisely, among the Lithuanian commanders, not even to mention the Swedes, a higher level of military technique was evident than in the Muscovite armies or among its commanders. This backwardness became particularly clear when in almost every significant encounter with Western enemies on a battlefield Muscovite armies sustained defeat. It was so in battles at Orsha, Ulla, Loda and Wenden. Moscow's enemies grasped this very well and thus endeavored to prevent the transfer to Moscow of all technology, ordnance, military specialists or master artisans whose help would have made it invincible. The Muscovites understood this situation equally well, it accounts for their commanders' caution, and their reluctance to enter into battle against armies possessing a higher level of technology. Muscovite commanders deserve credit for not relying on the numerical superiority of their armies because they recognized the importance of quality over quantity, and the superiority of technology over material strength.

Tsar Ivan understood this problem very well, if not better than anyone else. This accounted for his overwhelming desire to possess Livonia and thus control the routes leading to educated [Western] societies. For similar reasons he wanted foreigners talented in the military arts such as Fahrensbach and others in his service. So it was that he requested the Swedish king to send a military detachment trained and armed according to European standards. Absent any hope for military success without sheer good fortune, Ivan followed the example of his ancestors by adopting their caution, evasiveness, and even diffidence in military matters.

At the very moment the Muscovite government so thoroughly recognized its limitations in military arts and had so little hope for success in a decisive war against a talented, energetic general, that very general appeared on the Polish-Lithuanian throne. Bathory was an energetic, glory-loving, talented general who understood how to triumph over a rival having greater but only material means. Bathory's skilled, battle-hardened mercenary Hungarian and German infantry, with well-maintained artillery, attacked in rapid movements. This gave him an enormous advantage over his opponents who were forced to spread their forces along their borders awaiting an enemy whose direction of attack they could not predict. These were the major causes of Bathory's successes, as well as the reasons for Ivan's hesitancy and the Muscovite commanders' inactivity.

We cannot agree with Kurbsky and the writers who blindly followed his lead that Ivan's behavior in liquidating his brave and talented commanders was the sole reason for Moscow's lack of military success. It is futile to speak of talent among the Muscovite commanders who were appointed not for their military talents but because of the place they occupied in the council [the Boyar Duma]. When an important boyar was also a military commander it was because he was a boyar, it did not matter whether he possessed the least bit of military talent. After all, where could such talent be identified? In the battles against Kazan and the Crimean Tatars? Prince Peter Shuisky was regarded as a famous commander, but what did he do at the battle at Ulla (the second battle of Orsha)?[97] Ivan's father did not slay his commanders, yet how did they acquit themselves against the attack mounted by Sigismund I's forces at the conclusion of the first battle at Orsha?[98] We note the same retreat, the same appalling failure as in the war with Bathory. The difference lay only in that Sigismund I and Prince Ostrogorski did not have the means at their disposal to exploit their success while Bathory with Zamoyski's help was prepared for such an eventuality. Finally, we have become accustomed to thinking that Ivan had at his disposal huge armies which remained inactive because of his cowardice. No trustworthy evidence exists on the size of the Muscovite army at the time of the war with Bathory, and the least reliable testimony in this regard is that of the Pskov chroniclers.

BATHORY'S CONQUESTS

Now that he was prepared, in June 1579 Bathory sent a herald to Moscow to declare war. He blamed the break in relations on Ivan's attack on Livonia in disregard of the truce with Lithuania. In July, having gathered his forces by the Svir, the king held council to discuss the best direction to commence the campaign. As before, the Lithuanian nobles counseled going through Livonia to Pskov, reasoning that taking this rich city would repay the army for its efforts. Seizing the city would not be difficult because it was so distant from the theatre of war that it was unlikely to have received any recent attention. They assumed that the city's original walls must be decrepit.

The king was of the opposite opinion. Because the purpose of the war was to liberate Livonia, he said, it would be odd to take war into a region already devastated. Moreover, Livonia was bristling with cities and castles whose sieges would lead to great delays. Finally, transferring the entire army to Livonia would leave Lithuania undefended. Rather than by way of Livonia, Pskov could be reached through enemy territory although many unfriendly fortresses must remain in the rear. Having advanced so deeply into enemy territory it would be difficult to turn back and to receive reinforcements. Best to take Polotsk first, thus securing both Livonia and Lithuania. The location of Polotsk, on the Dvina, was the key to both countries and the army would not be too distant from either border. In addition, taking Polotsk secured navigation on the Dvina, important both to Lithuania and Livonia, especially for the city of Riga.

Unaware of Bathory's opinion, Ivan thought that the war for Livonia would be waged in Livonia, knowing that to be the majority opinion in Poland and Lithuania. Therefore he sent his largest army across the Dvina into Courland. According to custom this army limited itself to looting the country and was expected to return soon. Then the enemy appeared in an unexpected place when early in August Bathory besieged Polotsk.

The besieged city's commanders, Prince Vasily Teliatevsky, Peter Volynsky, Prince Dmitry Shcherbaty and Crown Secretary Rzhevsky held the wooden citadel for more than three weeks with unusual courage. The residents, old people and women alike, rushed everywhere a fire broke out and extinguished it. They lowered themselves down the walls by rope to get water to bring to the citadel to put out fires. Most were killed by enemy shots, but new workers immediately appeared in their places. Neither was it easy for the besieging forces, who had great difficulty in supplementing their food and forage in an underpopulated forest-filled land, recently ravaged by war.

When the tsar learned of the siege of Polotsk he dispatched his advanced detachments towards the city under the command of the lords-in-waiting Boris Shein and Fedor Sheremetev. The commanders seeing all the roads to Polotsk blocked by Bathory's armies, occupied the fortress at Sokol and tried to block food supplies from reaching the besiegers. They avoided conflict in the open field with the regiments sent against them commanded by Krzystof Radziwiłł and Jan Hlebowicz. In addition, the weather turned rainy, spoiling the roads. Transport horses fell, soldiers could not find a dry spot in their tents. The Germans suffered especially, accustomed as they were to waging war in wealthy, heavily populated lands. In contrast the Hungarians proved outstanding for their forbearance and indefatigability.

In these difficult circumstances the king called a council of war. The majority of the commanders recommended an assault, but the king disagreed. "If the assault is unsuccessful," he said, "what will there be left to do? We could only retreat in shame!" Promising them great rewards, he convinced the Hungarians to advance on the citadel walls and set fire to them from all sides.

Selecting a clear day, August 29, the Hungarians rushed the walls and set them on fire. The flames quickly spread and the besieged population was unable to extinguish the fires the entire day. Meanwhile the king, with the bigger part of his army, stood on the road to Sokol fearing that, seeing the glow of the fires the Muscovite commanders would come to the aid of Polotsk. Assistance did not appear, and the besieged began to think of surrender.

Ten Russians lowered themselves down the walls to negotiate with the besiegers, but the Hungarians murdered them. They wanted no negotiations, desiring to take the city by assault and have the right to plunder. They were especially tempted by the church of Holy Wisdom, about whose wealth they had heard. With this goal in mind the Hungarians, without orders from the king, rushed into the city through its charred walls with the Polish infantry following close behind. The besieged had managed to dig a moat where the walls had burned, and they met the attackers with a musket volley and chased them off.

The next day the fire and the pressure on the besieged resumed. Then the musketeers with their commander Volynsky sent out negotiators surrendering the city under the condition of free exit for all the military. Several of the soldiers entered the king's service, but the majority preferred to return home. Bishop Cyprian and the other commanders, excluding Volynsky, refused to agree to the surrender. They decided long before to blow up the citadel, which the soldiers had not permitted them to do. When the musketeers surrendered the city the bishop and the commander barricaded themselves in the Holy Wisdom church and announced that only force could remove them. This is exactly what the enemy did. The expected plunder in Polotsk betrayed the attackers' expectations. The most valuable part of the booty was the library whose holdings included many chronicles and commentaries by the holy Greek fathers in Slavic translations. All were destroyed.

Bathory did not offer generous rewards to the Russians who joined the Lithuanians. His letter to the Lithuanian court equerry contained the following comment. "Many musketeers and other Muscovite servitors have become our subjects after the taking of Polotsk and the nearby Russian forts. We have granted them empty plots of land in the Gródno district, although they have nothing with which to cultivate these lands. You are instructed to obtain a selection of a hundred and fifty of the most worthless and small items from our Lithuanian subjects and divide them among the Muscovites."

On September 25 Bathory's army took Sokol and burned it, producing terrible carnage. An old colonel, Beier, serving under Bathory, said that though he had participated in many battles nowhere had he seen so many corpses lying in one place. Several other nearby fortresses also were taken. Attacking from the other direction, Prince Konstantin Ostrogski plundered the Seversk region from Starodub to Pochep, and Kmita, the elder of Orsha, plundered the Smolensk region. The Swedes devastated Karelia and the land of Izhora, but when they besieged Narva they were turned away.

BATHORY'S SECOND CAMPAIGN

When Bathory completed the campaign of 1579 he returned to Wilno. As early as mid-September he sent the tsar a letter stating that upon ascending the throne he succeeded almost everywhere in his primary desire of achieving peace with all his neighbors save with the tsar, whose arrogant letter demanded Livonia and Courland. "Since there was little advantage to us to fulfill these demands," the king concluded, "we mounted our horses and moved on our hereditary city of Polotsk, which God returned to us. Consequently the Christian blood spilled is your responsibility."

"Other rulers, your neighbors," replied Ivan, "agreed to live in peace with you because it served their purposes, whereas we acted in a manner beneficial to us, apparently not to your liking. We did not send you haughty letters, nor did we do you any harm. Regarding Livonia, or your seizure of Polotsk, now there is nothing to be said. If you wish to learn our response, in the name of Christian peace send us your high ambassadors empowered to conclude matters in good faith between ourselves as necessary. We desire to have good relations and live in brotherhood with you. Therefore we have forbidden warfare along all our borders.

IVAN THE TERRIBLE

M.M. Antolsky, 1871
Russian Museum, St. Petersburg

Conduct yourself in the same way on all your borders until our ambassadors create friendship and brotherhood between us. Our boyars petitioned us not to allow the shedding of Christian blood, and to permit negotiations with your nobles. We agreed to their request."

The tsar, acceding to Bathory's request, released his messenger Lopatinski, who was detained because he brought the declaration of war. Upon release the tsar instructed that he be told "You came before us with a letter from your lord in which King Stefan wrote many reproachful words and sent back our truce proposal. Everywhere people who bring such letters are executed, but we, a Christian ruler, do not wish your blood, and following Christian custom, release you."

In January 1580, accompanying Lopatinski, Ivan sent a special messenger charged to demand the release of prisoners for exchange and ransom. "We have sent you our ambassadors," replied Stefan in March, "yet you sent them away in an unusual manner not conducive to friendship, and your ambassadors proposed nothing worthwhile during their stay with us. In view of these events it is inappropriate for us now to send you ambassadors. Send yours to me and send them immediately. As to what you write about freeing prisoners, consider for yourself, is it opportune to do so at this time? Still, we have no need of them."

The Polish nobles sent the boyars letters of safe conduct for Muscovite ambassadors. The tsar decided to reply to the Polish nobles through his boyars stating that the letter of safe conduct was unsuitable; above all in gross violation of previous customs. Better that they had insisted their ruler send his ambassadors to Moscow immediately.

Ivan sent his reply to Bathory with the boyar Nashchokin. "We accepted your ambassadors," the tsar wrote, "and dismissed them according to previous custom. They did nothing unwillingly, they were not dishonored nor did they lack anything. Our ambassadors resolved nothing because you did not wish to confirm what was decided by your ambassadors to us. You raised new issues, you dishonored our ambassadors. You did not receive them according to past custom, rather you returned them to us without having accomplished anything. Then afterwards you sent us the messenger Lopatinski with a letter, the contents of which you are well aware.

"Were we now to enumerate all the dealings between us, we would never achieve Christian peace. Thus it is better for us to forget the words that passed between us in grief and rage. As a Christian ruler, you should leave acrimonious matters behind and wish for brotherly goodwill and affection. We, on our side, already have set aside all matters provoking anger and you, according to custom, are obliged to send us your ambassadors."

In the event of need Nashchokin was authorized to agree to sending the tsar's ambassadors to Lithuania. The Muscovites received these instructions to guide their conduct. "Should something be needed, speak softly to the bailiff [escort] about the matter without abuse or threats. If they permit the purchase of food supplies, buy them. Should they not, bear with it. If the king does not ask about the tsar's health and does not rise before the tsar's compliments, allow it to pass without calling it to attention, and say nothing. Should they dishonor, crowd, annoy, or scold, then complain to the bailiff politely. Do not speak of these matters in an ill-tempered manner, bear with them."

Bathory responded that he had already taken to horse to lead his armies on whatever path God showed him and that he would await the Muscovite ambassadors for five weeks beginning June 14. Ivan replied that he had named his ambassadors, the table attendant[99] Prince Ivan Sitsky-Yaroslavsky, and the conciliar noble Roman Pivov. Yet the short time specified by the king barely allowed them to reach the border, let alone Wilno. Bathory answered that all these delays merely led to the loss of a favorable moment for war, that he was about to leave on campaign, that even so his departure should not bar the Muscovite ambassadors from negotiating with him at the Polish army's encampments.

It was clear that Bathory had corresponded with the tsar only to gain time to organize sufficient forces for a successful campaign. For this he had needed almost an entire year. Nevertheless, instead of thanking him, many met him with complaints which the talented and eloquent Chancellor Zamoyski then refuted in the Sejm. It was impossible to act quickly, because of lack of money and the slow pace at which the army assembled. The king somehow managed to gather the funds, some of which he contributed himself, or obtained from private individuals, and Zamoyski gave considerable assistance. Bathory's brother, the prince of Transylvania, sent a substantial force of Hungarians once again, but nevertheless there was insufficient infantry. The lesser nobility refused to serve in it under any circumstances. Townsmen therefore had to be recruited but they were unaccustomed to military service, pampered by living peacefully in the cities. Then, to supply the infantry with strong men capable of enduring hard labor and privations, it was proposed that one in twenty serfs from the king's domains be selected for service. Once he had served the appointed time, the conscript and all his descendants was freed forever from all seigneurial obligations.

In Moscow no time was lost in gathering funds and an army, although with no foreigners skilled in military arts or regimental commanders to rival Bathory. Ignorant of Bathory's intentions, once again Ivan had to disperse his armies by sending regiments to both Novgorod and Pskov, to Kokenhausen and Smolensk. In the event the khan appeared, strong detachments also remained on the southern borders, and precautions were necessary against the Swedes in the Northwest. Ivan sent the convert Tatar prince Semeon Bekbulatovich[100] and the boyar Prince Ivan Fedorovich Mstislavsky[101] with an army to the Lithuanian border, declaring that "the tsar has placed this matter in the hands of God and in hands of the grand prince Semeon and the boyar I.F. Mstislavsky and their companions to defend Muscovy, to do as God sees fit, and as will be best for the lords and the people." Letters were dispatched to all the monasteries. "Now our enemy the Lithuanian king," they read, "is upon us with great force. We humbly treated with him on the subject of peace, yet he did not want to make peace with us and invades our land with his armies. Please pray to our Lord God and all the saints and the Immaculate Virgin Mary, that our Lord God release His dreadful wrath against those moving against us, keeping his Orthodox Christian tsardom in peace and in its entirety, untouched and unmoved, and that he grant victory to Orthodox Christianity over all its visible and invisible enemies."

Bathory decided to move against Velikie Luki. To disguise this move he ordered the army to gather at Chasniki, on the Ulla river, a spot equidistant from Velikie Luki and Smolensk. In this way it would be unclear until the last minute to which of these cities the king would direct his path. He set out for Velikie Luki with fifty thousand men, of whom twenty-one thousand were infantry. The wooden fortress of Velizh went up in flames from the red-hot cannonballs, and surrendered. Usviat followed its example. Bathory was already at Velikie Luki when the Muscovite envoys Princes Sitsky and Pivov arrived. They were met at the border and subjected to unpleasant and even rude treatment by the envoy of the Orsha commander, Filon Kmita. The envoy referred to Kmita as the military governor of Smolensk. The envoys responded to this. "Filon brings unpleasantness by calling himself commander of Smolensk. He is not yet that Philon who was a close friend to Alexander of Macedonia.[102] Smolensk is the patrimony of our sovereign and there have been many Filons displayed on the gates of our forts."

When the ambassadors rode to the king's encampment from their posts the guards shot at the Muscovites' horses and wads from the muskets fell on them. In receiving them the king neither stood for the tsar's name or title, nor removed his cap nor inquired about the tsar's health. The ambassadors demanded that Bathory lift the siege of Velikie Luki before they could begin their embassy, even though they were ordered to conduct the embassy on the king's territory, not near their master's cities. To this the Polish nobles replied "Get out!" and the Wilno commander said to them as they left "Get out! You came with nothing, and you will leave with nothing!"

The ambassadors' request that the king at least withdraw from Velikie Luki during their embassy was refused. They asked that during the negotiations Bathory cease attacking the city, but neither did he agree to this. The ambassadors began to conduct their business, ceding Polotsk, Courland and twenty-four Livonian cities to the king who, in turn, demanded all of Livonia, Velikie Luki, Smolensk, Pskov and Novgorod. The ambassadors then asked permission to send a messenger to Moscow for new instructions. The courier was sent but Bathory did not wait for his return.

After extended efforts Zamoyski managed to burn the fortress, and the besieged began surrender negotiations. The Hungarians, fearing loss of their booty, raided the city, killing everyone they chanced to find. The Poles followed their example, allowing Zamoyski to save only the two commanders.

Prince Zbarazski with Polish, Hungarian and German cavalry defeated Prince Khilkov at Toropets. Nevel was burned and surrendered. Ozerishche surrendered even prior to its fire. The mighty Zavolochie turned back the first attempt against it, then later it too was forced to surrender to Zamoyski.

The commander from Orsha, Filon Kmita, was not as fortunate. Leading nine thousand Lithuanians he moved on Smolensk with the aim of burning its outlying areas. In the village of Nastasyin the tsar's commander Ivan Mikhailovich Buturlin and his companions attacked and ran him out of his camp. That evening Kmita pitched camp in a strong position, then abandoned it during the night. The next day Buturlin caught up with his enemy some forty versts from Smolensk at Spassk Meadow and defeated him, capturing his colors, his tents, ten cannon, fifty defensive[103] muskets and three hundred and seventy prisoners.

Having captured Velikie Luki, Bathory completed his 1580 campaign, although this time military activities continued into winter. In February

1581 the Lithuanians attacked Kholm at night, seized it and reserved it for themselves. They burned Staraia Rusa. In Livonia they seized the Schmilten castle, and with Magnus they devastated the Dorpat region from Neuhausen to the Russian border.

From the other direction the Swedish commander Pontus de la Gardie[104] entered Karelia and in November 1580 seized Kexholm where, according to Livonian chronicles, two thousand Russians were slaughtered. In Estonia the Swedes besieged Padis (within six miles of Reval). The besieged under the leadership of the commander Chikhachev suffered terrible starvation. For thirteen weeks they tasted no bread, consumed all their horses, dogs, cats, hay, straw, skins and some, it is written, even tasted human flesh. Finally in December the enemy took the city on the second try.

At the beginning of 1581 De la Gardie left Karelia and unexpectedly appeared in Livonia at Wesenberg. In March Wesenberg surrendered after a huge barrage and under the condition of free exit for the besieged. That same month Muscovite commanders, according to long-standing custom, left Mozhaisk to raid Lithuanian lands, attacking Dubrovna, Orsha and Mogilev. At Shklov they fought a successful battle with Lithuanian forces and returned safely to Smolensk.

In the meantime Bathory petitioned for a third campaign, having obtained funds from the Prussian duke and the electors of Saxony and Brandenburg. At the Sejm assembled in February of 1581 he announced that there was little to be happy about in the army's successes, let alone in making use of them. If the Sejm did not wish or hope for the subjugation of the entire Muscovite realm, at least it still did not have to think about arms for such an effort until the whole of Livonia was seized. He then explained how damaging it was to tear himself away from the army every year and hurry to the Sejm to request money, weakening his own forces while giving the enemy time to reconstitute its strength. Since delay in collecting funds forced him to lose the most suitable time for military activities, the only means to hasten the solution to these problems would be a two-year allocation. At first the Sejm objected to the king's request, then in the end agreed. When the Sejm concluded the deputies requested that in his next campaign, his third, the king make every effort to end the war. The lesser nobility and especially its peasantry were exhausted from monetary exactions, which would be impossible to continue.

The king responded through Zamoyski that he was not purposely prolonging the war, which was undertaken for the sake of peace as well as the common good. The enemy's situation now was such that it would be easy to bring him to the final extremity by continuing the war just a bit longer. In accordance with the people's desire he declared he would not be an obstacle to peace once he compelled the enemy to cede all Livonia to him.

Meanwhile the peace negotiations continued. Sitsky and Pivov followed Bathory from Velikie Luki to Warsaw. The bailiffs who for so long detained the ambassadors, now escorted them, following the king to Polotsk. Along the road the Lithuanians dishonored the emissaries, beat the ambassadors' servants, robbed them, deprived them food for themselves and their animals, causing the loss of many of their horses. Afterwards, they apologized and explained to the envoys that food was short. Bathory tried to compensate the ambassadors for their deprivations by giving them imported wines and aged mead. Later the ambassadors again experienced deprivations. "Why," the bailiff replied to their complaints, "should we give you all the food?! This cannot be for a good cause. The money allotted to you for your food is now needed for other things."

In Warsaw the Polish lords of the council addressed the emissaries with provocative, grand speeches filled with inappropriate words. Even in council session they spoke similarly, not one saying anything in a placating spirit of compromise. The emissaries said nothing in the face of these discussions. They tried to dissuade the senators without scolding, speaking softly as the tsar had ordered. The ambassadors offered peace on condition that each remain in possession of what he had, which proposal the lords did not even bring to the king.

The tsar sent a courier to the king asking for letters of safe conduct for new ambassadors. "These ambassadors," wrote Ivan, "have received instructions for detailed negotiations about Livonia exclusively, since the matter might become relevant. According to an agreement, at that time we will order the removal of our troops from Livonia but until then you, our brother, shall not gather forces and incur loss to your treasury." The messenger received orders stating "If the king does not ask about the tsar's health and does not rise out of respect to the tsar's greeting, say nothing."

The conciliar secretaries Pushkin[105] and Pisemsky[106] were dispatched as ambassadors with these instructions. "The ambassadors are not to give their letters of accreditation to anyone other than the king. They must demand that they be presented without fail to Bathory. If anyone reproaches, dishonors, scolds or beats them, they must respond to the reproaches, dishonor, scoldings or beatings, by doing what is appropriate to the matter, and as God lets them understand it, but gently and without abuse. They must put up with the beatings and stand firm until allowed to see the king, and until presented to the king they must not give anyone their letters nor conduct their embassy with anyone else. If the king does not stand or order the nobles to inquire about their sovereign's health, they are not to hesitate to speak of their master's health, present the letter entrusted to them, or conduct the embassy. Even if abused and beaten during their mission they are to seek only to fulfill their embassy, undeterred by anything, nor may they hector or say impolite words to the king.

"If the [Polish] lords say that they [the Muscovite envoys] may not write their master as tsar, and on account of this negotiations are delayed, the ambassadors are to answer 'Our master received the title of tsar from God, and who then may deprive him of it? Our lords have not been sovereigns since just yesterday, they have been lords forever and if your master did not permit our sovereign to call himself tsar, our master for the sake of Christian peace, will permit himself not to be inscribed as tsar. It makes no difference, no matter how you address him, for in all the lands it is known what kind of a ruler he is.' If they ask 'Who is this who has been ruler only since yesterday?' Answer, 'We speak of the fact that he who is our sovereign is not our ruler since yesterday, but he who has been ruler for only a day knows who he is.'

"Should they refuse to address the tsar as the king's brother, you shall answer 'Our sovereigns are rulers for all time. Our ruler's brothers are the Turkish emperor and other great rulers. Although it is unimportant to our sovereign to be addressed as brother to your ruler, and your sovereign does not desire this, we will simply address him without brotherhood as long as he accepts peace from ruler to ruler.' They may say that in the peace treaty you must write thus in the name of the king. 'We committed ourselves to you (the tsar) in brotherhood, and in friendship and in love.' Even if this occurs do not allow the matter at hand to lapse. Should the king not agree to address the tsar as ruler of Smolensk, acquiesce also to this." Curiously, although Ivan agreed to everything, and even ordered his ambassadors to tolerate any insult, he was unable to deprive himself of the pleasure of needling Bathory as an upstart ruler.

The ambassadors arrived with a proposition offering the king all of Livonia excluding only four cities. The king not only demanded all of Livonia as previously, he added new demands for the cession of Sebezh and the payment of four hundred thousand gold Hungarian coins for military expenses. These new demands exhausted Ivan's patience. The ambassadors declined to continue the negotiations, asking permission to send for new instructions from their master. Apparently, the ambassadors informed Ivan that due to the loss of his brother, the prince of Transylvania,[107] Bathory found himself in difficulties which in this instance might draw him into major troubles.

When Bathory's messenger arrived asking for new instructions for the ambassadors the tsar did not rise in response to the king's name, nor did he inquire as to the king's health because the king had not accorded a similar courtesy to the tsar. They did not place a bench for the courier, nor did they accept his gifts, nor did they ask him to dine because King Stefan stood for the continual shedding of Christian blood. Ivan sent a letter to Stefan by courier, beginning it with the words "We, humble Ivan, tsar and grand prince of all Russia, *by God's will, and not by rebellious human desire....*" Laying out the conditions for peace proposed by the ambassadors, the tsar wrote "We have never heard such extraordinary praise anywhere and conclude that you wish to make peace, yet your nobles mouth such excesses. They told our ambassadors that the latter came to bargain over Livonia. Our ambassadors are haggling over Livonia and this is not good. Is it well that your nobles are playing with us and our lands? Because of their pride they want that which cannot be yielded. This is not bargaining but small talk!

"In the past your country's Christian rulers were honorable and spared Christian bloodshed. In those days the lords of your council conducted negotiations and agreed to many treaties with our ambassadors, and there was satisfaction on both sides. It takes not an hour but much time to meet together frequently to advance arguments and then to compromise. Yet now we see and hear that the peasantry in your land is diminishing, and that as a result your senators, having no desire to shed Christian blood, wish to make peace quickly."

Having accused Bathory of violating the truce made by his ambassadors in Moscow, Ivan continued. "A thing such as this has never occurred before. If you regard the former kings of Poland as your ancestors, why do you not abide by their laws? You attacked with many allies and with our traitors Kurbsky, Zabolotsky, Teterin and others. Our commanders and defenders fought badly and gave up Polotsk to you by treason. When you entered Polotsk you wrote to all our servants, urging them to betray us and enter your service along with their cities, and you praised our traitors to chastise us, relying on treason rather than armed valor!

"Because of our oath, seeking to avoid war with you we did not personally go against you, neither did we send our great nobles against you, instead we sent some men to Sokol to learn about your activities. Yet your Wilno commander, coming upon Sokol with many followers, burned the city with a new determination, attacked the people and mutilated the dead in an unlawful manner, unheard of even among non-believers. You call yourself a Christian king, yet under your rule matters are not conducted according to Christian custom! Whether or not it is a Christian matter your nobles do not spare Christian blood, rather they begrudge their expenditures. If you have sustained losses [of land] how was it that you did not seize Zavolochie, which petitioned your favor? What kind of peace is this? Our treasury has been seized, you are enriched at our expense, you mutilate us, you hire troops with our money, our Livonian lands have been seized and you have filled them with your servitors. Moreover, you have not waited long before gathering an even larger force than before to fight us and to take the remainder![108] It is clear that you wish to make war unceasingly, and seek not peace. We would have ceded all of Livonia to you but we could not satisfy you with that, and afterwards you will spill blood anyway. Even now you ask one thing of the first ambassadors and yet another of the second! As for Sebezh, if we give you this place you will ask for more, and in no measure will you be deterred. We seek something to stop the spilling of Christian blood, and you seek to continue to make war. What is the use of making peace with you? The same situation will persist even without it."

The ambassadors were sent instructions to concede to the king the Russian cities that he had conquered, but to demand Livonia, Narva, Yuriev and thirty-six other strong points, and to conclude a truce on these conditions only for six or seven years. The [Polish] nobles complained that these were new conditions, in turn the ambassadors replied that the king changed the previous conditions in the same manner thus the tsar merely followed his lead. Since they had no other instructions, they rode off to their lodging.

The negotiations ended. Bathory went on campaign and sent a letter laden with insults to Ivan, calling him the Muscovite Pharaoh, a wolf let loose among the sheep, a man full of venom, an insignificant, rude and vulgar man. Among other things, Bathory wrote "Why is it that you personally did not accompany your armies, why did you not defend your subjects? Even a poor chicken covers its chicks when attacked by a hawk or an eagle whereas you, the two-headed eagle (at least on your crest), hide!" In the end Bathory challenged Ivan to single combat. The tsar refused the courtesy of dinner to the courier bringing the letter, and refused to send him food in place of what he would have had at the table.

SIEGE OF PSKOV

Before setting out on campaign Bathory called together his war council and asked where to direct the attack. Almost everybody was of the same opinion. Because the war was being fought to gain Livonia it was best to attack and gain control of Pskov thereby gathering all of Livonia into the king's hands. The king, and several of his commanders, were tempted to go on straight to Novgorod for they had information that the service class there was prepared to renounce Ivan. Yet it would be dangerous to attack Novgorod leaving as strong a city as Pskov intact in the rear, where almost all the enemy forces were concentrated. This consideration forced Bathory to agree with the majority and attack Pskov.

The stone walls of Ostrov could not withstand his barrages, and the fortress surrendered. On August 26 Polish forces reached Pskov, whose garrison was under the command of two boyars, Princes Vasily Fedorovich Skopin-Shuisky[109] and Ivan Petrovich Shuisky,[110] the son of the prominent commander Peter, and the grandson of Ivan, the famous regent during Ivan's minority.[111] Pskov was renowned as the foremost fortress in the Muscovite realm. Over entire centuries the citizens' main concern was strengthening their city, a victim of unceasing German attacks. Now its dilapidated fortifications were improved and the city supplied with much artillery. The army stationed at Pskov, according to foreign estimates, included up to seven thousand cavalry and fifty thousand infantry. By including citizens who had completed military service, the number of the besieged rose to a hundred thousand.

Once he had reconnoitered the city and learned from prisoners about its strength Bathory recognized his error, realizing that he had received false information about the situation in Pskov. He understood that first of all he had too few infantry. A successful assault would require twice as many as he had at hand. He also had insufficient gunpowder supplies for besieging such a city. On September 1 the besiegers began their labors by digging trenches. On September 7 they opened fire, and on the eighth they breached the walls and launched what became an initially successful assault. The enemy forces rushed into the breach and occupied the Intercession and Lead towers and displayed their banners from them.

The defenders lost spirit and began to retreat when their commander Prince Ivan Petrovich Shuisky, first in courage though second in command, was able to hold them through threats, pleas and tears, and Abbot Tikhon of the Caves monastery came to their support bearing icons and relics. Their resistance rekindled with renewed strength, the besieged retook the Lead tower occupied by the Poles, and chased the Hungarians from the Intercession. The assault was turned back, Pskov lost 863 dead and 1,626 wounded whereas Bathory's forces lost more than five thousand dead, including Gavril Bekesh, the crafty Hungarian commander.

In the aftermath the besiegers could do nothing more, for there was no gunpowder. They sent for additional supplies to the duke of Courland in Riga, but even after the powder arrived renewed attempts to conquer the city were in vain. Not even the attempt to conquer the Caves monastery was successful. Cold weather now began in earnest. The army, suffering great deprivations and distress, demanded curtailment of the war.

Raising the siege of Pskov and returning home for the winter meant abandoning the campaign, consequently Bathory decided to have the army winter at Pskov whatever the outcome. The situation was extremely difficult, but the king had Zamoyski! The latter's most important task was disciplining the army, which meant overcoming a most serious obstacle, the young lords and petty noblemen who were accustomed to having their own way. Zamoyski excused no infraction. The more prominent the criminal, the more serious in his view was his obligation to punish him. He held one of the king's nobles in fetters for violating military regulations, refusing to release him despite the pleas of the entire army. He humiliated unruly petty noblemen before the entire army. When necessary he meted out corporal punishment, hanged criminals, and even severely punished women for daring to infiltrate the wagon train.

It is easy to understand how Zamoyski's conduct aroused hatred against him. "From his youth," they cried, "he knows only what he learned from books or studied in Italian schools. He does not understand military affairs yet advises the king to hold at Pskov, and with this advice he will destroy the entire army!" The thoughtless lesser nobility reproached Zamoyski for his learning. Indeed, Zamoyski acknowledged that learning made him what he was, repeating bravely "Padua made me a man."[112] They complained that Zamoyski would abandon the army at Pskov to be sacrificed to hunger and cold while he departed with the king for the Sejm, with the excuse of fulfilling the chancellor's obligations. The king left, but Zamoyski remained with the army.

In addition to Pskov there were military activities on the upper Volga, in Livonia, and in the Novgorod region. Krzystof Radziwiłł, Filon Kmita and Haraburda attacked on the Volga, but could not go very far, fearing the tsar's mighty regiments. Of greater importance were the hostile activities of the Swedes who captured Lode, Fikkel, Leal, Hapsal, and Wittenstein as well as Narva, where seven thousand Russians fell. Finally De la Gardie carried the war across to Russian soil to capture Ivangorod, Yama and Koporie. Such was the situation when the tsar decided to renew peace negotiations with Bathory at which moment the papal envoy, the Jesuit Antonio Possevino,[113] appeared as mediator.

THE JESUIT POSSEVINO

In 1550 Schlitte,[114] whom Ivan sent to Germany to bring back scholars and artists, took it upon himself to rouse the hopes of the Pope and Holy Roman emperor of joining Muscovy to the Roman church. Pope Julius III[115] had named an embassy to the tsar with the proposal of a kingly title, in exchange for which the tsar was to swear obedience to the apostolic throne. In 1561 Pope Pius IV[116] invited Ivan to send his delegation to the Council of Trent. No one had paid any attention to these proposals in Moscow, but when Bathory began to threaten dangerous war Ivan sent Pope Gregory XIII[117] an ambassador[118] with a letter complaining that Bathory was the sultan's *proxy*[119] and announced his desire to share, in harmony and love, common enemies with the Pope and the Holy Roman emperor. Gregory took advantage of the situation and dispatched the Jesuit Antonio Possevino to Moscow with orders stating "Once you have acquired the favorable disposition and trust of the Muscovite ruler, proceed to business and suggest as cleverly as possible the idea of the necessity to accept the Catholic religion, and to recognize the Roman church as the primary church as recognized by all Christian monarchs. Guide the tsar to the idea that it is indecent for such a great ruler to recognize the metropolitan of Constantinople, who is not a lawful pastor, rather a slave and simoniac of the Turk.[120] It would be much better and more glorious for him were he, along with the other Christian sovereigns to recognize as head of the church the Roman pontiff. In reaching this goal, take with you in Greek translation the statement of faith composed at the Council of Trent.

"It is possible that among the monks and the other Muscovite clergy there will be some who in ignorance have an aversion to the Latin church, and still others who, fearing loss of their position, will be opposed to our honorable purposes and will make every effort to prevent their sovereign from abandoning his Greek faith. You must nevertheless try with all your strength to acquire their favorable disposition. More than anything else, seek to acquire information about everything regarding the faith of this people. Suggest to their sovereign what great purpose the union of Christian rulers against the Turk can achieve, that as a neighboring and powerful ruler it is his duty to play a glorious and valuable role in winning many Turkish lands. You must learn exactly the numbers and quality of the Muscovite military forces, how many infantry, cavalry, and from which position the Muscovite ruler thinks it is better to attack the Turk, and whether there is some neighboring people with whom we might enter into alliance. Nevertheless, after all these discussions igniting the tsar's desire to glorious exploits, you must return again to the main goal, spiritual union.

"If you meet with difficulties, do not be discouraged. Employ every means to gain at least some fruit from your embassy. You must ask permission for construction of one or several churches in Moscow for Catholics visiting on commercial business. Explain that otherwise there cannot be commercial relations with Catholic countries."

In contrast, the bailiff sent to the border to meet and escort Possevino received an entirely different kind of order. "If the ambassador starts to hector and speak of faith, either Greek or Roman, the bailiff is to answer that he has no learning, and is not to speak of religion."

On August 18 Possevino came to see Ivan at Staritsa. One of the Pope's gifts to Ivan was a book about the Council of Florence about which he wrote "I am sending your majesty a printed book about the Council of Florence. I ask that you read it yourself and that you instruct your scholars to read it. You will receive God's mercy and wisdom from it as well as knowledge. For my own sake, I desire from you only that the Holy Apostolic Church be one in faith with you. Thereafter all other matters between your highness and ourselves and all Christian rulers will be at hand."

Possevino, who had visited Bathory, announced that the king wished no peace without all Livonia. He transmitted Bathory's own words. "If the Muscovite ruler does not wish to cede the small Livonian cities to me, I will attack a large city of his, such as Pskov or Novgorod, and the moment I conquer a large city all the German cities will be mine."

"Whatever speeches," said Possevino, "I heard from the king, those I relay to the tsar, and those which the tsar will let be known to me, I will transmit to King Stefan. I wish to give my life and soul for the tsar's mercy." In keeping with his instructions Possevino asked for permission to build a Catholic church in Moscow for Venetian merchants. He spoke of the necessity of a union of all Christian rulers against the Turks, then let it be known that such a union could not be strong unless all the rulers shared one faith.

In his efforts to convince Ivan of the need to unite with Rome, Possevino said "To the realms and riches of which you have many, to the glories which you have brought to your expansive lands, add the glory of unity with the apostolic faith, and you will receive a great multitude of divine blessings."

"We never wished," replied the tsar, "nor do we want bloodshed in Christendom. Because of God's mercy, for many years since our infancy there was no bloodshed in Christendom but despising the good, an enemy with its vessels introduced into Lithuania a new religion which calls itself after one Martin Luther. As these teachings have gained strength, spreading strongly in your lands, so has bloodshed begun in Christendom. How, by what means and why enmity began between us and King Stefan we will tell you another time. Now we will relate to you how we can live in friendship and love with the Pope and Emperor Rudolph.

"It pleases us and we look with favor on the most exalted Pope Gregory's wish to establish peace among all Christian rulers. We are sending his holiness a letter of safe conduct so that his ambassadors may come and go as they please. Our children are also of the same mind. Our son Ivan is not yet honored with an official title. Fedor is not as yet of age competent to rule the realm with us and therefore it is unnecessary to write them into the safe conduct, even more so since our word will not be misinterpreted by anyone. Our realm is unlike others, where children, brothers and great nobles can alter their ruler's words.

"Venetians may travel freely to our country with their priests and with every variety of goods, although it is inappropriate to build Roman churches in our domains because this is against our custom. We wish to rule according to the old ways."

Then Ivan came to the main item of discussion, permitting Possevino to act as mediator between himself and Bathory. Ivan informed him of the Muscovite conditions for peace with Poland. The tsar would cede to Bathory sixty-six towns in Livonia as well as the Russian cities of Velikie Luki, Zavolochie, Nevel, Velizh and Kholm, retaining for himself thirty-five Livonian towns. In explaining his claims to Livonia, Ivan said "The lords of the council say that if Livonia were ours from ancient times, our predecessors would not have concluded a peace treaty with it. This land was separate, but we held the land in hereditary tenure by force of arms. Only Germans lived there, and in compliance with our wishes they made peaceful agreements with our hereditary cities of Novgorod and Pskov exactly as local peasants write their documents on how to trade among themselves, not in the manner that rulers write peace treaties between themselves. Livonia has been our hereditary property in the same way that Stefan claims Prussia. He styles himself as lord of Prussia, but Prussia has its own prince.

"You say that we must turn all our energies on the Turk, but how can we do this before there is peace between us and King Stefan? We ordered our ambassadors to make concessions, yet he is immoderate in everything. He demands monetary compensation for his losses. He wars against us, yet demands that we pay him compensation! Even Muslim nations do not conduct themselves in this manner! Who made him so obstinate? We are surprised how King Stefan does things not done in any other kingdom. He catches on to some matter, and he wants it to go only his own way.

"King Stefan told you that he does not want to make peace until we have given him the pledged lands, but how are we to rely on this? Suppose we ceded Livonia to him without making peace beforehand!

"He also has raised all of Italy (meaning all of Western Europe) against us. Not too long ago a French prisoner was brought to us. It is clear that Stefan has raised all Italy against us. What is the point of concluding an unequal peace? That peace which is good is when both sides are equal. This is why we cannot concede all Livonia to the king. Were we to concede it, we would have no access to the Pope, the emperor, nor to any other Italian (European) rulers or any outlet to the sea except when the Polish king desires to allow our emissaries to pass. The king calls me a Pharaoh and demands four hundred thousand chervontsy, yet the Egyptian pharaoh never gave tribute to anyone."

As to union with the Roman church, Ivan replied "We are releasing you to King Stefan on immediate important matters. When you return we will let you know in regard to religion." To Possevino the most important matter was the union of the churches. Because he received such an unsatisfactory answer, especially following Ivan's decisive rejection of the construction of a Catholic church, he had little hope for a future meeting and negotiations with the tsar. Possevino could hardly be an impartial mediator in peace negotiations. He saw that it would be to the advantage of the Roman church if all Livonia were part of the Polish crown since with its help it would be easy to restore declining Catholicism there. In one of his notes preserved in the Vatican archive Possevino wrote "There is hope that with God's help directed at the Catholic king all Livonia will soon belong to Poland. Then it will be important not to lose the chance for the restoration there of the Catholic religion under a king who even in time of war does not forget the holy teachings supporting and spreading the true belief. In addition, in Rus,[121] Podolia, Volhynia, Lithuania and Samogitia the populations strongly hold the Greek belief, but at least they have Catholics for rulers. The Senate [upper house of the Polish Sejm] and especially the king, doubting their loyalty, wish to convert them to Catholicism. The residents of these areas are devoted to their co-religionists the Muscovites, and publicly pray for their victory over the Poles."

Thus Possevino's primary aim in visiting the king was to convince Ivan that Stefan, despite his failure at Pskov, had decided to do whatever was necessary to conquer the city should the tsar not make peace quickly by ceding all Livonia. Ivan with his sons and boyars announced "Because at this moment the Lithuanian king with his many lands stands as one with the Swedish king, it is with extreme reluctance that we declare it would be possible to make peace with Lithuania only in the following manner. The Livonian towns that are for the ruler [Ivan] would be ceded to the king, but Velikie Luki and the other towns which the king conquered are to be ceded to the tsar. Peace made with King Stefan, we propose to the Swedish king that the towns he conquered, including Reval, not be named in the peace treaty with King Stefan."

Prince Eletsky and the keeper of the seal Alferiev were appointed as negotiators, receiving instructions to hold onto Livonia at all costs. To influence Possevino to their side they were to say "What kind of peace is this if our master concedes all of Livonia so that he no longer has any ports, and is unable to communicate with the Pope, the emperor and other foreign rulers, or enter into alliances against the Muslim nations." The ambassadors were to conclude a truce for twelve years. Should the Lithuanian ambassadors not agree to a truce, they were to conclude a perpetual peace.

TRUCE OF YAM ZAPOLSKY

The peace negotiations began in December 1581 in the village of Kirerova Hill, fifteen versts from Yam Zapolsky. The king's plenipotentiaries were Janusz Zbarazski, Prince Albrycht Radziwiłł and Haraburda, secretary of the grand principality of Lithuania. When the Muscovite ambassadors began by demanding part of Livonia the nobles answered them "Whatever you say, our master will not make peace without Livonia. You, it appears, were sent to talk, not to act. We do not want to bargain over Livonia. Our master ordered us to finish in three days, and that is why you spoke with us earlier, but we cannot make peace without all of Livonia, we will not give an inch."

The [Muscovite] ambassadors wrote that they wanted to leave and end the peace talks. Possevino persuaded them to stay and subsequently turned them around more than once. They concluded a truce for ten years beginning January 6, 1582 according to the conditions the tsar had decided in counsel with his son and the boyars. Having completed their major business, they began to quarrel over titles and expressions used in the treaty. The Muscovite ambassadors wanted to call their sovereign tsar. Possevino objected, claiming the king could not grant him this title without the Pope's permission. "Convincing the lords and Antonio was impossible," wrote the ambassadors. "Antonio sides with the Polish nobles." As a consequence they inscribed Ivan as tsar, ruler of Livonia and Smolensk, only in the Muscovite copy of the treaty. In the agreement Possevino was referred to simply as the ambassador of Pope Gregory XIII. When Possevino heard about this description of Pope Gregory XIII, he uttered a heart-felt cry. "Your master writes as though the Pope were a plain priest, whereas the Holy Roman emperor and all Christian rulers call the Pope the Vicar of Christ and the Teacher of all Christendom."

When the Muscovite ambassadors wanted to write that the tsar cedes Courland and Livonia to the king, again Possevino exclaimed "You come as thieves, not ambassadors!" He tore the treaty from Alferiev's hands, and threw it at the doors. He took Prince Eletsky by the collar of his fur coat, turned him around, tore the buttons off and yelled "Leave me, leave this hut, I cannot stand talking to you." In the aftermath of this scene the ambassadors were informed that the negotiations had ended and they were to return home. Then they very unwillingly agreed to write that the tsar yielded those towns in Livonia still under his control, but not those already conquered by the Poles.

On hearing of the signing of the truce the tsar ordered the release of the king's herald who brought the reproving letter discussed previously. At first he was given a reply written in the same scolding manner, then they chose not to use this tone and gave him another more conciliatory in tone, in which the tsar wrote "You sent us a letter in which you wrote many scolding and insulting words. Reproving words between us took place earlier but now we have a peaceful situation between us, and it is no longer appropriate for us as great rulers to write about such insulting matters, which only evoke anger."

In June 1582 the Lithuanian ambassadors Prince Zbarazski and his companions arrived in Moscow to confirm the truce agreement, with the new condition that the tsar not make war in Estonia for ten years. The ambassadors' bailiff received the following order. "Should the ambassadors boast how the king seized many towns from the tsar, that the king's servitors fought in many places on the tsar's land, yet the king and his people never met the tsar on the field of battle, answer 'Do not regard the number of towns our master yielded to Stefan of his property, Livonia, as a concession. You have no reason to brag about this matter, for it is God's business. On one hand, it is not rewarding, for God subdues those who are proud and greedy, but he praises the humble. There is no use speaking to us about this, for everything is in God's hands. It would be more appropriate for us to speak of the need for brotherhood, harmony and Christian peace between rulers, and to leave behind such meaningless discussions.'"

In the meantime hostile activities along the borders continued. Pats, the governor of Vitebsk, built a town at the mouth of the Mezh river in the Velizh district, a strategic location along the ancient water route from Smolensk and Belaia to Velikie Luki and Toropets. The tsar sent messages of complaint to the king, instructing his envoys that should the king wish to tear up the peace treaty because of the Velizh district they must stand their ground, only as a last resort ceding all of the Velizh district to the king.

The king ordered the town built by Pats destroyed, and in general received the Muscovite ambassadors very pleasantly. His behavior was motivated by various disputes he encountered in the Sejm, unfriendly skirmishes with Sweden over Estonia, and threats from the Crimean khan and sultan, who were enraged at attacks by Ukrainian cossacks.

Arriving in Moscow upon conclusion of the peace Antonio Possevino said to Ivan "King Stefan instructed me to tell you that he wishes the Muscovite land to increase, and does not wish to dominate it. He wants Muscovite merchants to have free passage through his lands with the same for Lithuanian merchants crossing Muscovite lands, that both countries benefit from every kind of growth.

"King Stefan wishes to attack Perekop so that in the future [the Crimeans] spill no more Christian blood. He says that Perekop takes money from both us rulers and makes war on our lands incessantly. King Stefan will attack from one side and either the Muscovite ruler or the army sent on his behalf shall attack from the other. When the king personally attacked Perekop the tsar was to send to his ally an observer, a good man, to see how he would attack Perekop to avenge Christian blood. Since we both give Perekop money, would it not be better to give these sums to our servitors to protect Christendom from the Muslim? Let the king's servitors go against Perekop through the tsar's lands, as if they were on their own territory. Let the tsar's servitors cross the king's lands both overland and over water as if on their own land so that between the rulers everything should be as one. The king also related to Antonio, that he, Stefan, a newcomer to the realm, is neither a Pole nor a Lithuanian, but by birth a Hungarian who came to his station in search of truth and love, to emancipate Christendom from the Muslims, and that under his governance there had been no Christian bloodletting at the hands of Perekop."

"We cannot at this time send our army against Perekop," replied Ivan, "because our servitors are worn out from warring against King Stefan. Moreover, our ambassadors have written from the Crimea that they have made a peace treaty with the khan. We do not yet know the conditions of the peace negotiated. If the king wishes to ally with us against the Muslims, he shall give orders in that regard to his ambassadors."

II

RELATIONS WITH OTHER FOREIGN POWERS

THE TSAR AND POSSEVINO DISCUSS MATTERS OF FAITH

After this exchange Possevino requested permission to speak with the tsar about the unification of the faiths. "We are prepared to speak with you," answered Ivan, "but not about union. How can we exclude our privy councillors at this time? Think about it. You, by order of His Holiness the Pope and by your service as an intermediary between us and King Stefan, concluded a peace agreement and now, thank God, Christianity is at peace. If we start to speak of faith, since each of us is zealous for his own belief each will glorify his religion, and there will be an argument, from which we fear enmity will rise."

Antonio persisted, saying that quarrels could not arise in a discussion of religion. "You are a great ruler. How can I, the least of your subjects, speak abusive words? Pope Gregory XIII, the holder of the throne of Peter and Paul, wishes to be united in belief with you, as a great sovereign, for the Roman and Greek belief is one. The Pope wishes that there be only one church in the entire world. We would attend the Greek church, and Slavs of the Greek faith would come to our churches. If the Greek books are not fully translated in your realm, we have the original Greek texts, written by the hand of St. John Chrysostom and other great holy men. You will be in amity with the Pope, the emperor and other rulers, and will be sovereign not only of your ancestral seat of Kiev, but also of Constaninople. The Pope, emperor and all other rulers will strive to that end."

"It is not for us to come together in faith," said Ivan. "Our religion is Christian, from time immemorial it has been its own, just as the Roman church. We were born into the Christian faith, and with God's blessing we have reached our present age. We are already fifty-one years of age, we have no reason to convert, nor do we have any desire for a bigger kingdom. We want to accept little in the future, and in this world we do not desire the goal of universality, because this is an occasion of sin. We have our true Christian faith, and have no need for any another. You say that your Roman faith is one with the Greek, but we hold the true faith,

Christian, not Greek. The Greek is known because the prophet David prophesied 'From Ethiopia will be foretold the hand of God.' Ethiopia is the same as Byzantium, which was famed for its Christianity. We follow the true Christian faith into which the Roman religion does not fit comfortably, but we do not wish to speak of this so as we can avoid inimical words. Moreover it would be impertinent for us even to consider such an important matter without the blessing of our father and priest, the metropolitan and all the consecrated assembly. You, Antonio wish to speak, but you are sent by the Pope and are yourself a priest, thus you can speak authoritatively."

Possevino continued to reassure the tsar that no quarrel would arise. Ivan again began to speak. "We do not wish to speak to you any longer," said he, "about such important matters lest you be annoyed. Here is a minor matter. You have a trimmed beard, but it is forbidden to trim or shave beards, not only for priests but also for laymen. You are a priest in the Roman religion, yet you cut your beard. You tell me, from whom did you adopt this behavior, from which teaching?"Possevino answered that he neither shaved nor trimmed his beard.

"Our young servant[1] who was sent to Rome," Ivan continued, "told us that they carry Pope Gregory to the throne, and that on the Pope's shoe there is a cross. Here is something that differs between our belief and the Roman. In our belief, the cross of Christ is a victory over our enemies, we honor it and we do not wear the cross lower than our belt."

"We must honor the Pope," replied the Jesuit, "for he is the head of Christianity, the teacher of all rulers, the inheritor of the throne of the apostle Peter, Christ's heir. You are a great ruler also, and your ancestor was Vladimir, the grand prince of Kiev. How can we not raise you and glorify you and not fall to our feet?" At this point Possevino bowed down to the tsar and fell at his feet, but this action did not create a good impression. "You praise Pope Gregory," Ivan answered, "saying that he is the inheritor of the throne of Christ and the apostle Peter. You say this philosophizing about yourself, not about your predominant beliefs. Yet you are not just an ordinary teacher, or the like. It is more fitting to honor us as imperial majesty. Moreover all prelates, as apostolic students, must display humility and not ascend higher than an emperor in pride. The Pope is not Christ. The throne on which he is carried is not a cloud. Those who carry him are not angels. Pope Gregory does not have to liken himself to Christ and to be the inheritor of his throne, neither is it fitting to equate the apostle Peter to Christ. The Pope, according to Christ's teachings, follows the path of previous Popes from Sylvester to Adrian. This Pope is the inheritor of these great Popes and apostles. The Pope who does not live according to Christ's teachings and does not follow the paths of the apostles will live as a wolf, not as a shepherd." "If the Pope is a wolf," Possevino replied, "I have nothing more to say," and fell silent.[2]

Having realized failure in his primary mission, the Jesuit wanted to reach what in his opinion were at least two attainable goals which would work towards the gradual union of the Russian and Western churches. He proposed that it would be beneficial for Catholics to have their own church in Moscow, and that the tsar permit several young Russian servitors to study Latin in Rome, but neither was he able to achieve even these ends. "Now on such short notice," the tsar replied, "we cannot find men suitable for such a matter. As soon as our servitors can gather such people we will send them to the Pope. As for what you said about the Venetians, they are free to travel to our realm with their own priests, as long as they do not try to spread their teachings among Russian people or build Roman Catholic churches. Let everyone stay within his own faith. In our country we have many different faiths, we do not try to change anyone's mind, everyone lives freely as he wishes, although as yet no churches of different religions have been built."

Possevino left Moscow with the tsar's courier. In his letter to the Pope, Ivan wrote "We received your letter with great joy and heard it with kindness. We received your emissary Antonio with great affection. We wish to be in brotherhood with you, with the emperor, and with the other Christian realms, that Christianity be liberated from the hands of the Muslims and be brought to peace. When you send word to the emperor and the other Christians rulers, and when your envoys come to us, we will instruct our boyars to enter into an appropriate agreement. You sent us with Antonio a book about the Council of Florence, and we ordered that the book be accepted from your envoy. As for what you wrote to us, and what your ambassador said to us aloud about religion, we spoke of it to Antonio."

The courier received these instructions. "Should the Pope or his councillors say 'Your master called the Pope a wolf and beast of prey,' answer that they must believe no such thing occurred."

ARMISTICE WITH SWEDEN

We have observed that Ivan decided at the boyar council to reconcile with Bathory to make it easier to attack the Swedes and deprive their king of the towns he had conquered, including Reval, then to add Estonia as compensation for the loss of Livonia. The Russian armies enjoyed some success against the Swedes in one instance, when the latter's two-pronged assault against Orsha was turned back. When in the beginning of 1583 De la Gardie once again prepared to attack Russian holdings the Novgorod governors proposed peace. The authorized negotiators met on the Plius river in May and concluded a truce of just two months, and then met again in August and signed another for three years on condition that each party retain possessions held at that time. As a consequence the Swedes retained the Russian cities of Yam, Ivangorod, and Koporie.

The instability of the truce with Poland and the dangerous uprising of the Lowland Cheremiss in the Kazan region help explain this hasty peace treaty with the Swedes. Even so, possibly the major reason was that Ivan had lost hope of achieving any gains in war against European nations until the Russians equaled them in military science. The successful defense of Orsha was not enough to renew the tsar's hope that it would be easy to seize Narva and Reval from the Swedes. Moreover he had promised Bathory not to fight for Estonia.

PROPOSED ENGLISH ALLIANCE

Ivan did not abandon the idea of controlling the Baltic even though convinced this could be achieved only through alliance with some European country which would supply Russia with the fundamentals of Western culture. This motivation is most clearly visible in the negotiations between Ivan and Elizabeth, the English queen.

As early as 1569 Ivan secretly sent Elizabeth a proposal through her agent Jenkinson. The tsar asked that the queen be a friend to his friends and enemy to his enemies, and conversely the tsar promised the same to the queen. England and Russia needed to be as one in all matters. The Polish king was an enemy to the tsar and the queen. His agent had been seized the previous summer with letters to English merchants in Russia in which the king wrote "I, Sigismund, king of Poland, ask you English merchants, servants of my trusted ones, to help the provider of this letter and to assist my Russian friends with moneys as well as with all other means."

At first the tsar was greatly insulted, then the agent confessed that the letters were sent especially to awaken the tsar's mistrust of Englishmen, to undermine the friendship between him and the queen as well as to arouse suspicion of treason by the tsar's advisers. Thus Ivan asked the queen to unite with him against the Poles and to bar her people from trading with the Polish king's subjects. The tsar requested that the queen permit experts in ship construction and navigation to come to him, and that she allow the export from England to Russia of all artillery and equipment necessary for war. Ivan also sincerely requested that there be a sacred promise between the queen and himself. Should either be forced into exile because of misfortune, each enjoyed the right of asylum with the other to save life, each would be received with honor and might live without worry or danger until fortune changed, or until God intervened. This obligation was to be held in the deepest secrecy.

For Elizabeth there was no purpose in entering into such a close alliance with the tsar and becoming involved in wars with his neighbors. She waited for a time, finally answering evasively and unspecifically that she would not permit any person or ruler to harm Ivan or his possessions insofar as her ability, justice, or good conscience could prevent this. She promised to act defensively and offensively against common enemies, and also promised to receive and maintain the tsar and his family in England with honor.

Ivan grew angry and wrote to Elizabeth a letter (in October 1570). "You have set this matter aside, and your boyars discussed only trade matters with our ambassadors. We supposed you were mistress over your land, wielding power over government and seeking honor for yourself as well as profit for your country. It was for this reason that we sought to enter relations with you. Now we perceive that other men rule, not only men without rank, but lowly traders seeking not the wealth and honor of our majesties but their own profit, while you remain in your maidenly state like a (common) old spinster. If this is the way things are, we also shall put these affairs aside. As for these boorish merchants who seek their own wealth while neglecting our wealth and honor, they will discover what trading is! When the Muscovite realm was without English commodities it lacked nothing. As to the letter which we sent to you in regard to trade affairs (the letter of privileges to the English merchants), if you do not send similar letters to us we are not bound by your initial letter to grant anything, and those privileges we granted formerly shall no longer be in force from this day forth."[3]

To please the "small trading men" Elizabeth sent her beloved Anthony Jenkinson[4] with a letter in which she wrote "Jenkinson will truthfully tell your majesty that no tradesmen direct our state for us and do our business, but that we ourselves oversee our business as is appropriate to a

mistress and queen appointed by God, and that our subjects give us obedience like no other ruler receives. In order to win your goodwill, our
subjects have brought with them to your country all kinds of things,
which we have not permitted to be exported to any other ruler on the
whole earth. We can assure you that many rulers have written to us asking us to end our friendship with you, but none of their letters could impel
us to fulfill their wishes."[5]

Ivan softened his position, restored most of their privileges to the English merchants, yet he never stopped reminding Elizabeth that she did
not wish an alliance with him. He also expressed his displeasure that
while the queen had promised to receive him in England, she did not
discuss receiving the same treatment for herself in Russia. In this the tsar
saw Elizabeth's pride and his own humiliation. "Should you want for
yourself our love and great friendship," the tsar wrote to her, "you would
have thought about it and committed yourself to such a matter as would
increase our love for you. If you were but to order your people to bring
us armor and weapons and copper and tin and lead, and hot sulphur for
sale you would succeed."[6]

Elizabeth fulfilled the last wish, sending people the tsar needed. Having sent him a physician, Robert Jacoby, pharmacists and barbers
[physcians], Elizabeth tried to show in her letter how important a sacri-
fice she had made for the tsar. She wrote that Jacoby was needed by her,
and that she had sent the pharmacists and barbers unwillingly, for there
were too few within her own realm. Ivan asked Jacoby if there were not
in England a bride for him, either a widow or a maiden. Jacoby answered
that there was, namely Mary Hastings,[7] the daughter of the earl of Hun-
tington, the queen's niece on her mother's side. His curiosity aroused,
Ivan instructed Bogdan Belsky[8] and Afanasy Nagoy, his wife's brother,
to question Jacoby about the maiden, as she was called in those times.

In August 1582 the noble Fedor Pisemsky was sent to England with
instructions to negotiate an alliance between Russia and England against
Poland, and to begin the business of the proposal. On Ivan's behest he
was to say to Elizabeth "Be our loving sister, Queen Elizabeth, and
present your niece to our ambassador Fedor, send us her portrait on a
board, and describe on a piece of paper her suitability to our exalted state,
then we will attend to the queen's business as seems appropriate."

Pisemsky was to take a portrait and the measurements of her height,
to review carefully whether the bride was portly, and whether she was pale
or dark in complexion. He was also to ascertain her age, her relationship to

the queen, her father's position, and whether she had brothers and sisters. If it was pointed out that Ivan was already married, Pisemsky was to answer "Our master sent to many lands to seek a bride, but was unable to do so, and he took the daughter of a noble from his own country, but not of equal rank. If the queen's niece is buxom, and appropriate for such a great position, he will put his current wife aside for the queen's niece."

Pisemsky was also to say that Mary must accept the Greek faith, as also the noblemen and women accompanying her who wished to live at court. Those not wishing to convert could not live at court. They would be free to live in the ruler's domains and enjoy his bounty, although it would be inappropriate for them to live at court, whatever their rank. The envoy also was to make it clear that the successor to the throne would be Tsarevich Fedor, and any children born to Mary would receive an appanage. This was necessary for otherwise the matter could not come to fruition.

On November 4 Pisemsky presented himself to the queen at Windsor. When he made his speech Elizabeth answered with a cheerful smile. "I hope," she said, "that God will give me the opportunity to see my brother, your master, with my own eyes and wish him brotherly love and goodwill." "Our master has communications with many emperors and kings," the ambassador responded, "but not with anyone else is there such affection. You are his beloved sister; he loves you not only in words but truly with his entire soul." "I am humble before my brother's love, happy to be with him in brotherly love and stand with him as one against all enemies until the end. Is there not some kind of disturbance (precariousness) among your people in your land of Russia, or Muscovy as it is known of old?" "Our land and the Muscovite realm," the ambassador replied, "were given by God, are as of old, but his people are under a hard hand. Among those who were disloyal, when they realized their fault they humbled themselves before the tsar, asking mercy. The tsar showed them his mercy, and now all the tsar's subjects serve him truly and the tsar rewards them." Then the queen asked the ambassador what impression England made upon him. "The English land," replied Pisemsky, "is very densely populated, very pleasing, and well provided with everything."

After his first reception, much time passed. The envoy began to experience boredom. When nobles in the queen's name proposed that he go deer hunting on the island game reserves, he replied "I am much gratified by the queen's favor, but it is not a good time to go wandering because we were sent by our master to the queen on important business. We came before the queen in our embassy, still no one has taken any initiative as yet on matters of state. Moreover, at the moment we are fasting and do not eat meat, so for whom would the venison be of any use?" "We eat meat," replied the English, "and if you do not ride with us on the hunt, the queen will be annoyed with you." The ambassador went to the islands.

In mid-December at Greenwich Pisemsky had his first meeting with the English ministers. He stated that the Polish king, the ally of the Pope and the emperor, was the tsar's enemy, that Ivan wished a close alliance with Elizabeth so as to have the same friends and enemies, to assist one another with men, and in instances where this was impossible, with funds enabling the queen to permit the passage to the tsar of firearms, armor, sulphur, oil, copper, tin and lead, and sundry master craftsmen, soldiers and artisans. In exchange the tsar would export many goods to England without tariff.

The English ministers agreed to the alliance on condition that prior to the declaration of war on the tsar's enemy the queen undertook to make peace between him and Ivan. In exchange for this mediation they demanded exclusive trading rights. "Let the queen's councillors themselves decide," Pisemsky responded. "Can England exist only with Russian trade, without trading with other countries and without permitting other merchants with any other goods? If England cannot exist only with Russian trade, how then can the Russian people exist only with English trade?" They decided that to settle the negotiations they would send an emissary from the queen to Moscow with Pisemsky. During the dinner following the negotiations the ministers said to Pisemsky "Is it true that the Pope is bragging that he made peace between the tsar and Bathory?" "The will of the Pope," the ambassador replied, "is simply wishful thinking. Would our master call the Lithuanian king his enemy, had he made peace with him?"

After negotiations with the ministers Pisemsky turned to the queen on the matter of the marriage proposal. "Out of love for my brother, your master," Elizabeth answered, "I would be pleased to be related to him. Still, I heard that your master likes pretty young women, and my niece is not pretty and your master is hardly likely to love her. I am flattered that your master, in love for me, wishes to be related, but I am ashamed to paint her portrait and send it to the tsar. She has been ill, suffering from smallpox, and her face is now red and scarred. As she is now, her portrait cannot be painted even for all the money in the world."

Pisemsky agreed to wait several months until Mary recuperated completely. In the interim they learned in England that Maria Nagaia had borne the tsar a son (Dmitry). Pisemsky sent word to the ministers that the queen should not believe such quarrelsome words. Evil people were spreading dissension because they did not wish to see good relations between the her and the tsar. Finally in May 1583 Pisemsky was shown the prospective bride in the garden so that the envoy could see her clearly in an open space. Mary Hastings, Pisemsky reported to the tsar, was tall, slim and pale in face. She had gray eyes, reddish hair, a straight nose and thin, long fingers. When she saw Pisemsky after his viewing Elizabeth once again said to him "I think that your master would not like my niece. Did she appeal to you or not?" "It seemed to me that your niece is pretty," the ambassador replied, "and that this matter is up to God's judgment."

Having completed his business, Pisemsky returned to Russia with letters from Elizabeth to the tsar. The queen expressed her desire to meet personally with Ivan, writing "Our wish and desire is that all our empire and provinces always be open to you that you will come to see your true friend and beloved sister." She sent the English ambassador Bowes[9] to accompany Pisemsky back to Moscow.

Bowes took upon himself the very difficult and unpleasant task of soliciting exclusive rights for duty-free trade for English merchants in Russia while simultaneously declining an alliance between Elizabeth and Ivan against his enemies, for such an alliance served no purpose for the English. He was also to decline the engagement of the tsar to Mary Hastings because, despite the desire of the aging maiden to change her status, the potential bride was frightened by the things she had heard about the bridegroom's character. It is easy to understand the awkwardness and nervousness Bowes experienced because of the difficulties of his situation.

In his discussions with the boyars Bowes declared that his queen could not begin war with the tsar's enemies without first seeking peace between them and the tsar. "How can we," the boyars responded, "write such a condition in a treaty? If we must treat with our enemy, he will prepare himself during this time. How can we defeat him if he is prepared?" "We do not conduct ourselves in this way," Bowes commented. "We do not send our armies against our enemies without first having tried to come to a peaceable settlement."

Then Bowes sought exclusive trade rights for the English. "What kind of love for our master is it from Queen Elizabeth," the boyars retorted, "that she wishes to expel all merchants from other countries' rulers from our land, and not permit one of them to see our master on his own land? Only the queen shall profit from this, but our master will suffer a loss." "Our mistress's merchants," Bowes replied, "found the way to the White Sea, let them alone use that route."

The nobles reported the negotiations to the tsar who instructed them to write into the treaty that Elizabeth must send to Bathory that he make peace with the tsar, that he return Polotsk and Livonia to him, and if he did not return them Elizabeth would send her armies against him. Bowes upon hearing of this said "This is a new matter and I cannot refer it to the queen, else she will call me a fool."

The tsar agreed that the English might enter the areas of Korolsk, Vorguz, Mezen, Pechenga and Shumsk, whereas Pudozhersk would be allocated to the Spanish merchant Ivan Beloboroda [John the White Beard],[10] and the Kola peninsula for the French merchants. The ambassador responded that according to the previous trade agreement the English had exclusive rights to all the northern ports. They answered him that previously the Muscovite state had a seaport at Narva, but the Swedes began to blockade that port. The Swedish captives taken on that occasion included some English mercenaries. Accordingly the first and second charters of privileges were annulled and a third, less advantageous, charter was granted.

"The French king," said the boyars, "has just sent a message through the Kola seaport asking for amity and brotherhood with our master. We heard that Queen Elizabeth has good relations with the French king, and with the Netherlands as well. How then can we not admit them, you tell us." "I cannot say anything else," Bowes answered, "because I have no instructions from the queen. Let the tsar send his emissaries to the queen."

The nobles persisted. "The tsar permitted the Spanish merchant from Antwerp, John Whitebeard, to enter Russia and granted him privileges on the mouth of the Pudozhersk. John Whitebeard brings to his majesty every kind of patterned fabric." Bowes said that the English merchants serve the tsar more than others. The nobles replied that the English merchants had conspired with the enemies of the realm, the Swedes and Danes, and dispatched letters home criticizing Muscovite people and the Muscovite realm. They suggested that Muscovites did not recognize quality, and recommended sending thin and rotten English merchandise. Imagine thinking that Muscovites cannot be good judges of quality! The cloth the English exported was ordinary. In comparison to the old it was much worse. "I am not a good judge of cloth," replied Bowes. "The previous chief merchant, Thomas, was indeed a thief. Englishmen also were caught together with the Swedes, though English mercenaries are free to take service anywhere."[11]

They went on to discuss other conditions. Because he had lost the Baltic provinces Ivan wanted foreign ambassadors to travel to him through England, the North Sea and the White Sea. Elizabeth agreed, although she requested that papal emissaries, ambassadors of Catholic countries, and those not recognizing her, not be allowed to travel to Russia by way of England. Ivan conceded in the case of the papal emissaries but did not wish to make similar concessions regarding the others. "Faith is no impediment to friendship," said the boyars. "Your mistress is not of the same faith as our master, but our master wishes to have amicable and brotherly relations with her as with all rulers."

Finally they came to the business of the marriage proposal. When asked whether Elizabeth agreed to give her niece's hand to Ivan, Bowes replied "The queen's niece Lady Mary unfortunately is ill. Moreover I believe that she will not deny her faith for there is only one faith—Christianity." "I see that you did not come to do," Ivan replied, "but rather to frustrate it. We will not speak any more of this business, which began as a result of Doctor Robert's eagerness." The ambassador was frightened by Ivan's displeasure, which could interfere with the Englishman's primary task, and therefore said "This niece of the queen is only distantly related to the queen, as well as unattractive, but there are at least ten other maidens closer to the queen." "Who are they?" asked the tsar. "I have no instructions on this matter," replied Bowes, "and without instructions I cannot reveal their names." "What instructions have you?" said the tsar. "We cannot conclude a treaty as Queen Elizabeth desires."

The ambassador was dismissed. Bowes ordered Jacoby to let the tsar know that he wished to speak to the tsar alone. Ivan commanded him to appear before him and asked what he wished to say. "I have with me," the ambassador answered, "no instructions in regard to the matters about which you ask, for the queen ordered me to listen and to report to her what was said."

"You are not aware of our court customs," said the tsar. "An ambassador speaks in this manner only to our boyars, who debate with ambassadors over who is to speak first, but you are not speaking with the nobles. We do not debate with you about who will speak first. Had your mistress come to visit us, she could speak in this manner. You say a great many things, but you say nothing about the matters at hand. You say on one hand that you have no instructions, but Dr. Robert told us yesterday that you wished to speak to us alone. Now say what you have to say!"

Bowes. I did not speak with the doctor. I have been on several previous embassies to sovereigns, to the king of France and other rulers, and spoke with them face to face on various matters.

Ivan. Tell me what our sister said regarding the marriage, and do not cite the example of the French realm. It is not our custom to speak with ambassadors in person.

Bowes. I have heard that our sovereign Queen Elizabeth wishes to hold you in affection above all other rulers, and I wish to serve you and actually to render you some service.

Ivan. Tell me exactly which of the queen's relatives are unmarried, and I will send my ambassador to look at them and take their portraits.

Bowes. In this I can be of service and I will look at their portraits myself, so that you can write to them directly.

Not having gained anything from the ambassador through personal conversation, Ivan ordered his boyars to continue their negotiations with him. When the nobles again asked him exactly which maidens were related to Elizabeth the ambassador, who had grown exceedingly tired of this question, answered "I said nothing of the maidens to the tsar." When the boyars expressed disbelief at his disavowal, he replied "I spoke of the maidens, but I have no instructions on this matter. I will be happy to serve the tsar, but my time of service has not as yet arrived."

The boyars were forced to end their discussions about the marriage proposal, then began to speak about another matter, that Elizabeth permit the tsar's messenger to King Henri of France to pass over English soil. "Half the French land," Bowes answered, "has seceded from its king and placed itself under the protection of our sovereign, who in turn gave it aid. I will escort the tsar's messenger, and I think that my sovereign will permit him to go through."

Afterwards, the tsar summoned Bowes and asked him to explain definitively what instructions he had received. Bowes answered that he had no instructions. Then Ivan said to him "You illiterate! How did you dare come to us and not conduct any ambassadorial business? Our major enemies are the Lithuanians and the Swedes, and you do not tell us for sure whether the queen will stand with us against these enemies. You say one thing, that she wants to first negotiate with them, but that means to give them news about us. Because of this it is impossible for us to make the queen our first friend. You spoke about the seaports, asking that English merchants use them exclusively. How can we place such a great burden on our own land? Giving tribute would not be so disadvantageous. Here is another reason that it is impossible to be in alliance with the queen. We cannot consider buying peace from her. When you spoke of the marriage proposal, you belittled one maiden and said nothing about any other. Who can propose to someone who is anonymous?"

Instead of answering the ambassador complained about Crown Secretary Shchelkalov, who had maintained him poorly. Rather than chicken and mutton, he was given ham, and was unaccustomed to such meals. The tsar gave orders to investigate the matter, and Crown Secretary Shchelkalov was barred from all relations with the ambassador, while those in charge of meals were thrown in jail. The tsar sent the boyar Bogdan Belsky to explain to Bowes why he had called him illiterate, in order to ameliorate the impression that the use of such a word had made on the envoy. Bowes in turn justified his actions by saying that he had done nothing to deserve the tsar's anger. He said merely what he was instructed to say. As to the maiden, he described what she really was like. As for the other maidens, he spoke as he was ordered by the queen. As to the conditions of the treaty, it would be as God and the sovereign willed. If the tsar wanted amity and blood ties with the queen, he must dispatch further ambassadors to England.

After this conversation the tsar again summoned Bowes, announcing that he could not agree to the queen's requests for exclusive trading rights, for while he would give the English certain seaports he could not permit them to enter the Pechora and the Ob. ["]These lands are distant and without seaports. Sable and gerfalcons breed there, and were such valuable goods to flow exclusively to England, how could our own realm survive without them?["] "If God and you, the sovereign, so will it," Bowes replied. "Yet, this will not be pleasing to the queen. As to what you say about sables, since there are none in our kingdom no one wears them." "My request," Ivan persisted, "is that the queen stand as one with me against the Lithuanians, Swedes and Danes. The Lithuanians and the Swedes are my chief foes but we can make peace with the Danes, for they are not my greatest enemies." "Should you grant the English merchants the former treaty," answered Bowes, "the queen will be as one with you against the Lithuanians and Swedes. Send it to her with your ambassadors, who also might view the maidens." "If the master of all the seaports," Ivan asked the ambassador, "yields them to the English, might he then write in the letter of agreement that the queen shall unite with the tsar against the Lithuanians and Swedes?" Bowes who declined to answer because he lacked instructions, instead said "The tsar wants the queen to ally with him against the Lithuanians in order to seize Livonia. Yet the queen is pious. She took neither the Netherlands nor France when they were offered to her. Is Livonia the hereditary property of the tsar from ancient times?" Ivan was insulted by this questioning of the justice of his demands and answered that he did not ask his sister Queen Elizabeth to act as judge between himself and the Lithuanian king. He wished her to unite with him against those who would make war upon his Livonian domains.

THE HOLY ROMAN EMPEROR AND DENMARK

On this note the negotiations with the English ambassador ended. Ivan was prepared to concede the rights for exclusive trade to England which "were more onerous than tribute" if only to create an active alliance with a European state against the enemies who had taken Livonia from him. Understandably he also sought alliance with the Austrian ruling house against Bathory, which efforts were unsuccessful. Maximilian II's son and successor Rudolph II[12] sent word to the tsar of his father's death, expressing the hope that Ivan would continue the same faithful, good, honest and familiar arrangements towards him and the Austrian court which he had accorded Maximilian. Yet he too requested that the tsar not permit war to hurt the unfortunate Livonians.

The tsar sent the messenger Kvashin to Rudolph with the announcement that he wished to be with him in amity and brotherhood much as he was with his father, standing united against enemies. "We hope that we will be in good relations with you," Rudolph replied, "and before the arrival of our ambassadors we would hope that you will not send sword and fire against the wretched Livonians."

When the war with Bathory took an unsatisfactory turn the tsar, in the spring of 1580, sent a messenger to Rudolph with a letter. "Your ambassadors, dearest and most gracious brother" he wrote, "for reasons unknown to us have not as yet arrived. Would you write to us and explain why your ambassadors have lingered, and send your envoys to us without delay, commanding them to sign a treaty with us to stand with us as one against our enemy." "Should they ask how the tsar gets on with the Lithuanian king," the courier was to "answer 'When I left my master the Lithuanian messenger had visited him and was given leave to return to

Lithuania, and a courier from our master to King Stefan had just left. I know nothing of significance for I am the tsar's most junior servant, and how can I possibly know of important business between rulers?' Should they ask about Polotsk, or how the Lithuanian king seized Polotsk from your master, answer 'Lithuanian emissaries arrived at the tsar's court and peace was made for three years. His error was that he did not keep more able servitors in Polotsk. If kissing the cross does not bind, what is there to believe in? The king attacked Polotsk unexpectedly, in violation of his sworn word, and he even seized the city. When someone violates truth and his own word, how can he be trusted?'"

In August of the same year when Bathory was approaching Velikie Luki the tsar dispatched another envoy to the Holy Roman emperor, writing "Your emissaries, our dearest and most gracious brother, have not as yet arrived although we do not know why. Stefan Bathory, the lord of Transylvania, now holds the Polish crown and the grand principality of Lithuania. He strengthened himself by corresponding with the Turkish sultan and in allying with him and other Muslim rulers, and is spilling Christian blood and plans to spill yet more. The Muslim rulers and the Turkish sultan's puppet, Stefan Bathory, stand against us because we had correspondence with your father and with you, desiring only the prosperity of all Christian rulers, wishing no one other than you to be the ruler of Poland and Lithuania. You, brother, must assist us against them and confirm our brotherly love. You must write to King Stefan about his intemperance, his spilling of Christian blood and his liaison with the Turkish sultan, that he will not do such things again.

"The burgomaster and aldermen [Ratmänner] from Lübeck have written to us that you did not permit shipment of various goods such as copper, tin and lead to our domains. Are those who wish to see us quarreling with one another spreading such rumors? I cannot think that you gave such an order."

Rudolph answered the first messenger. "Until now," he wrote, "we have considered diligently how we might send you emissaries for the impoverished Livonians, but one of the men named for this embassy died, while the others became ill. The Livonian land belongs to the Holy Roman empire. In your present letter not a word is said in that regard." The imperial courtiers comforted the Muscovite envoy, saying that soon Bathory would have nothing with which to pay his mercenary armies.

Through yet another messenger Rudolph replied further. "The ambassadors have not departed because there has been no meeting of the imperial princes in regard to Livonia, which is a part of the empire. The tsar would display his regard for the imperial princes were he not to attack the remaining Livonian towns. He, Rudolph, had not prohibited the import of tin, lead and copper by the Muscovite realm. The export of arms and everything related to military matters was banned by Emperor Charles V, and the ban again confirmed under Emperor Maximilian II. Your self-interest in this matter was considered, whereas I have been vindicated amicably and nobody was angry with me."

At the finish of the war with Bathory the tsar sent the emissary Yakov Molvianinov with Possevino to both the Pope and the emperor. In his letter to the Pope Ivan proclaimed his readiness to participate in an alliance of Christian rulers against the Muslims, in exchange for which all the allies were to send their ambassadors to Moscow. Because an alliance of all the Christian rulers was at stake, the emperor was to lift the prohibition against exporting arms to Muscovy.

In conversation with the English ambassador Ivan also referred to the Danish king Frederik[13] as his enemy. In 1578 Frederik sent Jakob Ulfeld[14] to Moscow to settle the matter of Estonia, a part of which was claimed by Denmark. The tsar refused to recognize these rights and Ulfeld was forced to accept a fifteen-year truce. The king recognized Ivan's rights to all Livonia and Courland, in exchange for which the tsar ceded Øsel Island to Denmark. The king undertook not to assist Poland and Sweden in their wars against Muscovy. He also promised not to delay German artisans traveling to Moscow through his lands. Frederik was unhappy with the agreement, grew angry at Ulfeld and expressed his enmity toward Moscow by demanding duties from English merchants on their way to the White Sea, announcing his claims on several places bordering Norway.

CHEREMISS DISTURBANCES

Muscovite forces were distracted during the war with Bathory by the ongoing danger of Crimean attacks. Even though the Muscovite ambassador displayed every courtesy to the khan, humbling himself before him and promising annual gifts, the khan refused to swear an oath without Astrakhan. If nothing was heard from the Crimea during the entire remainder of the war with Bathory, for this Moscow had to thank the war between the Turks and Persians, in which the khan was obliged to participate. Stymied by this war, the khan could only threaten Moscow by igniting disturbances among the Cheremiss. "Thirty-one years passed since the conquest of Kazan," wrote the chronicler, "yet the cursed Muslims did not wish to live under the tsar's hand, they raised an army and captured many cities. The tsar, having seen their ferocity, sent boyars and commanders to Kazan with orders to capture them. The pagans resisted the Muscovite armies like wild animals, killing the Muscovites both in their camps and on campaign, with the boyars and commanders unable to tame them."

III

THE STROGANOVS AND YERMAK

FIRST DEALINGS WITH SIBERIA

On the middle Volga and lower Kama the savage natives were making their last desperate efforts to avoid subjugation to the Russians. Meanwhile in the West, thanks to Bathory's personal qualities, by their combined efforts Poland and Sweden succeeded in shutting Muscovy off from the sea. Moscow was thus deprived of close and direct contact with Western Europe, and of benefitting from the fruits of enlightenment so necessary for the rapid and final triumph over Asia. At this time the movement of Russian population did not cease, on the contrary it grew even more intense, until finally Russians crossed the Ural mountains.

Following the conquest of Kazan[1] the Nogay princes personally invited the Muscovite tsar to take Astrakhan,[2] even as the petty Caucasian rulers turned to Moscow for assistance in settling their internecine disputes. They sought Muscovite clientage in hope of finding a strong protector and reliable aid. The ruler of the Tatar yurt in Siberia, situated in the center of the present-day Tobolsk government, came forward with such a request. Although the yurt was insignificant in and of itself, it was important because it was surrounded by empty land inhabited by scattered small tribes of various origins and modes of life.

According to the chronicle, in January 1555 the Siberian prince Yediger[3] sent congratulations to Ivan on his conquest of Kazan and Astrakhan. Yediger's emissaries petitioned the tsar to take them and the entire Siberian land under his protection, to defend them against their enemies, levy tribute upon them and send his official to collect it. Ivan granted the petition, placed the Siberian prince and his holdings under his wing and ordered tribute assessed. On behalf of their prince the ambassadors pledged their entire land to Ivan and promised a sable and a Siberian squirrel[4] for each of the common people who, according to their estimates, numbered some 30,700.

The tsar sent to Siberia his envoy and tax collector[5] Dmitry Kurov, who returned at the end of 1556 together with the Siberian ambassador Boianda. Yediger sent merely seven hundred sables as tribute. The ambassador explained the absence of the remainder by saying that there had been war with the Shibansk prince[6] who had taken many people prisoner, leaving no one from whom to collect the furs.

Contradicting the Siberian, Kurov said that it would have been possible to collect the entire tribute had they wished to do so. As a result of these accusations the tsar laid his disfavor upon Boianda and, placing him under guard, ordered the seizure of all his possessions. Ivan sent his service Tatars to Siberia with a letter instructing them to repair the situation.

In September 1557 the Tatar emissaries returned with new Siberian ambassadors who brought one thousand sables, and also one hundred and six sables in lieu of the arrears. They also brought with them a charter with the prince's seal in which Yediger promised to be the tsar's servant and to pay the whole tribute directly each year.

FRAGILITY OF DEPENDENCE ON MOSCOW

The Siberian yurt's ties to Moscow were tenuous. Yediger subjugated himself with the goal of getting help from the Russian tsar against his enemies, or at least to reinforce himself through their fear of his powerful protector. The distance of his domains from Muscovite lands made it difficult to receive assistance and tended to decrease his enemies' fears. They hoped to take possession of the Siberian settlements without penalty and then, should the need occur, to placate the Muscovite tsar with their promise to pay the same tribute as the previous prince. In Siberia the situation and the character of the relationship with Moscow were clearly understood. So it was that the Siberian prince spoke to one of the Russian servitors, saying "Now that I am collecting tribute, I will send emissaries to your ruler. But I am now at war with the Kozatsk tsar (Kirghiz-kaisatsky)[7] who, if he conquers me, will rule Siberia, then also will start to pay tribute to your master."

Indeed there were many changes in Siberia as princes were run off or destroyed each other, while Moscow, a non-participant in these events, demanded only one thing, its tribute. Whether the princes agreed to pay or declined, they hoped that there would be no penalty because of the great distance. For example Kuchum,[8] the last prince or tsar who established himself in Siberia, seemingly agreed to pay tribute to Ivan, but killed the Muscovite ambassador instead.[9] Complete subjugation of the land beyond the Urals to Moscow was accomplished only as a result of the movement of the Russian population to the Northeast, when Russian traders settled closer and closer to the "Stone Girdle"[10] and then decided to cross beyond it.

EARLIEST INFORMATION ABOUT STROGANOVS

The Stroganov family played an important role in the history of this movement to the Northeast and in the history of colonization of Northeastern Europe. According to a long-standing opinion, the entire vast area known as the Dvina lands was thought to have belonged to Novgorod the Great. We have seen that in addition to Novgorod domains, Rostov and then later Muscovite princely holdings were intermingled throughout the area. Legal records from the second half of the fifteenth century describe how when Ivan III had the opportunity of dividing the Dvina lands with Novgorod he removed those which previously belonged to him and to the Rostov princes. An extract from the judicial lists survives to this day concerning the Dvina lands. It specifies which lands taken from Novgorod belonged to the Rostov princes as well as to the Moscow grand prince, and enumerates those individuals who had claims against Novgorod for unfair seizure of their lands. Luka Stroganov is listed as claiming lands under the control of the Muscovite grand prince as well as several lands that belonged to Prince Konstantin Vladimirovich of Rostov. It is unclear from the court's decision whether Luka Stroganov claimed these lands because his quitrent holdings were located on them, or because he was authorized to do so by the Muscovite and Rostov princes in his capacity as a native of these areas possessing wealth and knowledge of native customs.

In addition to Stroganov, we see that the Rostov princes' lands were claimed by various individuals, among them Fedor Vasilisov, the elder of Vasilisk and Penza. Fedor claimed against three men of Novgorod, who answered in place of Archbishop Jonas. Consequently the Stroganovs and their friends could make claims as well as the Muscovite and Rostov princes. There exists a curious indication regarding the Stroganov's wealth during the reign of Vasily the Dark. In a letter dated 1610 Tsar Vasily Ivanovich Shuisky[11] tried to convince Stroganov to loan him a large sum of money. "Remember," he wrote, "when in previous times, you ransomed Grand Prince Vasily Vasilievich from captivity, of what great honors you were considered worthy."[12]

GRIGORY STROGANOV RECEIVES LANDS ALONG THE KAMA

We have discussed how the princes quickly ceded large pieces of land to those who promised to populate them, granting concessions including several years' emancipation from all taxes and from maintenance of passing officials as well as judicial control over local populations, except in cases of homicide or trials involving litigants from different jurisdictions, and so forth. The Stroganovs with their vast wealth became the primary colonizers of the empty lands of the Northeast. Under Grand Prince Vasily Ivanovich (Vasily III),[13] Luka Stroganov's grandsons received the right to populate an empty section of the Ustiug region in the Vondokursk district. During the reign of Ivan IV the Stroganovs turned their hunting-trading activities further to the East, to the Kama region. In 1558 Grigory Anikiev Stroganov petitioned the tsar noting "that eighty-eight versts downstream from Great Perm, on both sides of the Kama river to the Chusovaia river there lie empty lands, deep forests, small rivers and wild lakes, and empty islands and portages. The entire uninhabited area totals one hundred and forty-six versts. Hitherto there have been no plowed fields, no buildings nor taxes contributing to the tsar's treasury. As of now these lands have been given to no one, no one is assigned to them in either the cadastral books, or the merchant or debtors books."

Grigory Stroganov petitioned to build a town on this place, "a city supplied with muskets and arquebuses complete with musketeers, arquebusiers and gatekeepers gathered to defend against the Nogay people and other hordes." He offered "to clear the forest along the rivulets to the very headwaters and along lakes, cultivate the fields, establish households, invite untaxed and unregistered people to settle, search for brine, find salt, and build saltworks for its manufacture."

The tsar's treasurers inquired about these areas from the emissary Kodaula who arrived from Perm with tribute. Kodaula said that these areas were perpetually empty from ancient times, that there was no income from them and that they were of no use to Perm. The tsar then conferred these lands[14] upon Grigory Stroganov on condition that he not invite or accept any people registered or obligated to other cities, thieves, those in bondage to boyars, fugitives with property, robbers or brigands. If registered taxpayers from another city arrived with their wives and children, and the viceregent [namestnik], the rural district chief [volostitel][15], or the elected chiefs wanted them back, Grigory was obligated to return them to their previous residence. Merchants who arrived in Stroganov's town could trade there duty-free. The Stroganovs might build saltworks, manufacture salt, and fish in the rivers and lakes without payment of quitrent. When they found silver, copper or tin ore, they were to notify the tsar's treasurers, and not develop these resources without the tsar's knowledge.

Stroganov's tax exemptions, of twenty years' duration, covered all unregistered and untaxed people who came to live in his city, in the town quarter, near the town on cultivated land, in the countryside or in forest clearings. For these twenty years there would be no tribute, neither postal relay taxes nor excise on saltpeter, nor plowland tax, nor fortification work, nor any other kind of tax, nor quitrent from salt-making or fishing in these locations. When people passed through or near this town, either from Muscovy or from any other lands, with goods or without, no duties could be assessed, whether they traded there or not. When Stroganov transported or sent salt or fish through another town he was obligated to pay all taxes on the salt and fish, just as taxes were collected from all others.

The Perm viceregents and agents[16] were prohibited from bringing any people settling on Stroganov lands to trial for any crime. Neither might bailiff or constable enter his town for any purpose, nor could they accept his people in surety, nor could they dispatch them anywhere for any reason. Grigory Stroganov was to judge and have authority over his people in all matters. Should people from other towns have complaints against Stroganov they must obtain official warrants from Moscow. The plaintiff and the defendants then must appear without judicial officials before the tsar's treasury on Annunciation Day [March 25].[17]

At the expiration of the specified twenty years Grigory Stroganov was obliged to convey all taxes to the tsar's treasury in Moscow on Annunciation Day. When the tsar's envoys traveled from Moscow to Siberia and back again, or from Kazan to Perm and returned, by way of the new town, Stroganov and his inhabitants were not required to provide them with transportation services, guides or food during the twenty years of the grant. Bread, salt and all other supplies held by the traders in the town were to be sold to the envoys, messengers, passing people and travelers at the same price as the townsmen bought and sold to one another. Similarly, transitory people were permitted to bid freely to hire carts, sailing vessels, oarsmen or helmsmen.

During the the twenty years Stroganov was exempted from taxes or any obligations to the people of Perm. If it appeared that Grigory Stroganov lied when he petitioned the tsar, or did not comply with the charter, or acted contrary to law, the grant would be void.

The charter authorizing the settlement of the Kama wilderness was generally similar to those given to the settlers of all empty areas throughout Muscovy, although it differed from them in several respects. The Kama side was the borderland area attacked by wild Ural and trans-Ural tribes. Since the government could not defend them, the settlers had to defend themselves relying on their own resources. This meant building towns or watch points, fortifying them with artillery, and maintaining military forces there. Understandably, the only colonizers capable of this were those with extensive means, thus is it possible to understand the crucial importance of the Stroganovs. Only they possessed the wealth to populate the Kama lands, bringing Russian settlements into the Urals and enabling them to spread across the Urals. It was not only in pursuit of extensive monetary resources that they performed this feat on behalf of Russia and civilization. They needed rare courage, energy, and adroitness to colonize a wilderness where settlers were subjected to attacks by savages. They cultivated fields and prospected for brine with weapons in hand. To show them the principles of civilization they lured the savages by whetting their appetites with peaceful commerce.

Stroganov needed saltpeter for the artillery, muskets and arquebuses in his new town. The tsar granted his petition and permitted him to make saltpeter in the Vychegda commercial area and in the Usolie district, but no more than thirty puds. As he wrote to the elders in these locations, "Take good care that in making the saltpeter the peasants are not offended by Grigory Stroganov in any way, that in the settlements where the huts are all grouped together, that he not dig up litter and dirt, nor ruin them altogether. Also look well that he does not sell the saltpeter to anyone."

Stroganov built a town, which he called Kankor. Within five years it became apparent that one such town was insufficient for his purposes. In 1564 Stroganov petitioned the tsar for permission to build another town twenty versts from Kankor. Brine was found there and the Stroganovs wished to build a saltworks, although nobody dared live there unless there were a town. A rumor reached them through prisoners and the Voguls that the Siberian saltan and the Shibanids were bragging about launching an attack against Perm, and that earlier they had taken Solikamsk twice. The tsar fulfilled this request and a new town of Kergedan appeared, with walls thirty sazhens long, covered by rocks instead of clay from the assault side to the lowest point.

In 1566 Grigory's brother Yakov petitioned the tsar on behalf of his father Anika Fedorov to accept Kankor and Kergedan and all their production into the oprichnina [crown estates] and this request was fulfilled. In 1568 the same Yakov petitioned for land another twenty versts from the previous site. He also promised to build, at his own cost, fortresses equipped with quick-firing cannon. He received land under the same conditions as before, although settlers were excused from their tax obligations for only ten years.[18]

Prior to 1572 it was peaceful in the Kama region but that year the governor of Perm reported that forty rebels including Cheremiss, together with Ostiaks, Bashkirs and Buints attacked Kama, killing eighty-seven people, including local citizens, traders and cotton wagoneers. When he heard the news Ivan sent the Stroganovs a letter.[19] "You must live with great care," he instructed them, "and choose a good commander and gather as many volunteer cossacks as possible, armed with all kinds of weapons, handguns and bows. You should also assemble Ostiak and Vogul volunteers loyal to us and command their wives and children to live inside the fortress. Send these commanders with volunteers, cossacks, Ostiaks and Voguls, to fight the traitors, the Cheremiss, Ostiaks, Votiaks and Nogay who have betrayed us. As for the good Cheremiss or Ostiaks who would lead their friends to leave the outlaws and turn themselves over to us, do not kill such people, but protect them, and we will reward them. Those who were outlaws previously, but who now wish to turn themselves over to us and can prove this to you, to these you may speak our sworn word that we will not punish them, but make everything easy for them, if only they gather themselves and join the pursuing forces to fight our betrayers. Let them take for themselves the property, wives and children of those against whom they make war, and do not let anyone deprive them of these possessions or prisoners."

The Stroganovs fulfilled the order. Their commanders and volunteers fought against the traitors to the government, defeating several while the others were forced to swear their future loyalty to the ruler.

THE STROGANOVS SETTLE TRANS-URAL LANDS

Once established on one side of the Urals the Stroganovs naturally turned their attention to the areas beyond, promising even more profit than the lands of the Kama basin. Stroganov soon found a reason to request permission to found new settlements across the Urals. In turn Kuchum, the new Siberian saltan, demonstrated his enmity by capturing and killing the Ostiaks who paid tribute to Muscovy. In July 1573 the Siberian prince Mahmet-Kul[20] appeared with an army at the Chusovaia river to scout a path towards the Stroganov towns and approach Great Perm. During the expedition he killed many Ostiaks who were Muscovite tributaries, took their wives and children prisoner, and murdered the tsar's emissary to the Kirghiz-Kaisatsky horde. Yet when he came within five versts of the Stroganov towns Mahmet-Kul retreated, frightened by his captives' stories of the towns' large military garrisons.

The Stroganovs informed the tsar about the attacks by Kuchum and Mahmet-Kul, petitioning him for approval to send their mercenary cossacks against the Siberians.[21] They dared not dispatch them without the tsar's permission. Meanwhile the trans-Ural Ostiaks requested that the tsar defend them from the Siberian saltan, in exchange for which they would pay tribute to Moscow. To accommodate these requests Yakov and Grigory Stroganov asked the tsar for permission to build strong points at fortifiable places among the Takhchciam at the confluence of the Tobol and the rivers that flow into it, to employ watchmen, and maintain artillery at their own expense, to mine iron ore, cultivate land, and supervise everything in the area.

Ivan must have been pleased by the Stroganov proposal. By extending Russian control across the Urals Moscow acquired new tribute-payers while providing for their defense without hindrances and crown efforts. He gave the Stroganovs the right to settle on the other side of the Urals under the same conditions that pertained in the Kama and Chusovaia regions. They undertook to supervise the other traders who decided to settle along the Tobol and the other Siberian rivers. "Where the Stroganovs find iron ore," the tsar's grant stipulated, "they may work the site. They also may work copper, tin, and lead ores on trial. If someone else wishes to do the same, they will permit him to do so and make him pay quitrent on his business for the benefit of our treasury. Should someone take on this enterprise he must write to us how this business will be done, which ore, and how much[22] will be produced, who will pay the quitrent and how much. Everything must be written to us and we will prepare our decree.

"We will grant twenty-year exemptions for the Takchey lands, the arable lands, and the rivers and lakes to their headwaters. During these years the settlers will not pay taxes. Whichever Ostiaks, Voguls and

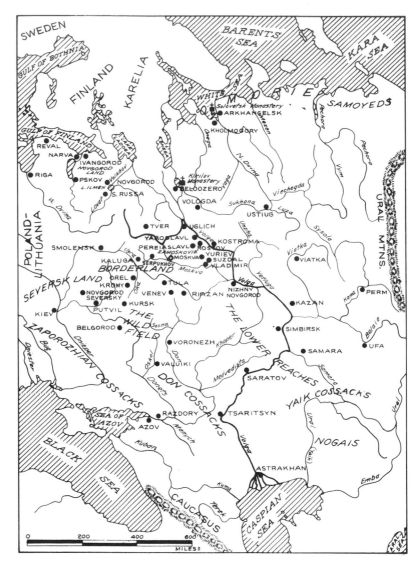

MUSCOVY AND THE URALS

Yugorians leave the Siberian saltan and pay us tribute, these people are to send their taxes directly to our treasury. Yakov and Grigory are required to protect the Ostiaks, Voguls and Yugorians along with their wives and children from attack by Siberian bands in their fortresses, Grigory and Yakov are to gather volunteers from among the Ostiaks, Voguls, Yugorians and Samoyeds to fight alongside the mercenary cossacks and artillery to capture the Siberians and to bring us tribute.

"Merchants from Bukhara, Kirghizia and other places who are not continuing on to Moscow will be coming to trade with Yakov and Grigory in these new settlements, bringing horses and many other goods with them. Trade with them freely and without duty in all goods. Similarly we grant Yakov and Grigory the same rights on the Irtysh, Ob and other rivers. Wherever appropriate they are to build fortresses, maintain guards with firearms for the reassurance and protection of the volunteers and to fish and hunt without quitrent for the duration of twenty years."

Thus the Stroganovs received the right to conduct business across the Urals along with the rights and obligation to build fortresses for the protection of their enterprises, and for the conduct of defensive wars. They also were expected to wage aggressive war, sending troops against the Siberian saltan, capturing Siberians, and collecting tribute for the tsar.

Declaring the land theirs and conducting business on it necessitated eliminating the Siberian saltan who considered these areas his property. Although the Stroganovs promised to conduct this war at their own expense using their own army, they had few resources for recruiting fighters. It was not a good idea to rely entirely on non-Russian volunteers such as Ostiaks, Voguls, Yugorians and Samoyeds. Peaceful traders needed an adventurous vanguard to seek new routes and new lands in areas utterly devoid of peace and civilization. They needed cossacks.

COSSACK SETTLEMENT ALONG THE DON

We have already noted that one of the dominant factors of Ancient Rus was its geographical situation consisting of open borders from every direction, contiguity with the steppe and empty wilderness areas. Consequently throngs of the discontented regularly distanced themselves from organized society by seeking the freedom of the steppe and thus became the vanguard of colonization. While nominally dependent on the government, in fact they paid little attention to its interests because it was against their fundamental character to do so. The wildness of the steppe and its lack of penalties occasioned both by the crown's weakness and their distance from the center, permitted colonizers to live in relative freedom.

As early as during the reign of Vasily [III] Ivanovich we have learned that the Riazan Cossacks were very familiar with places on the Don.[23] Under Vasily's son [Ivan IV] they settled there, taking their name Don Cossacks[24] from their location, and became even more of a threat than the Nogay,[25] Crimean Tatars,[26] and the people of Azov.[27]

In answer to the complaint of a Nogay murza that Russian cossacks were stealing from his people the Muscovite government replied "Don't you know that there are evil people everywhere? There are many kinds of cossacks in the steppes, from Kazan, Azov and the Crimea as well as other wayward cossacks entering from our borders who mix with them. These people are just as much thieves and vandals to us as they are thieves to you. No one teaches them evil, but after committing every sort of outrage they disperse to their own lands."

Those from the Riazan region were not the only ones to make up the mass of the Don Cossacks. Included among them were tribes like the Severians of the northern Ukraine who like those of Riazan recently had gained a reputation for their fearlessness. "Our people," wrote the Nogay prince Yusuf to Moscow in 1549, "traveled to Moscow with trading goods, and as they returned your cossacks and Severians who live on the Don killed them." Town cossacks who found themselves under close government supervision when doing something against its interests also fled to the Don. Thus the Putivl cossacks who were implicated in the robbery of the Crimean courier Levon But and his escort recounted that there were six of them out in the steppe, that they spent the spring on the Donets, and then they were to go on to Putivl. On the Murav road they encountered some ninety Cherkass (Little Russian) cossacks who forced them to join them and then robbed the Crimean courier. After the robbery Levon But himself and four of his retinue came to Putivl, while two of his companions left him and went on the Don. "We went along the Volga from Kazan to Astrakhan," the Russian[28] courier reported, "and as we neared the mouth of the Irgyz, Prince Vasily Meshchersky and the cossack Lichuga Khromoy from Putivl took from us a boat belonging to Tsar Yamgurchey. I asked them to give it back, but they did not return it to me, and I was disgraced."

Once again the tsar answered the Nogay Yusuf's complaints. "These thieves," he wrote, "live on the Don without our supervision and run away from us. We have more than once sent forces to capture them, but our men cannot catch them. We are again trying to get these thieves, and those whom we catch we will execute. If you could, personally, order them caught and having done so, send them to us. Your merchants must look out for themselves along the road because, as you yourself know well, there are always many people from different realms on the steppe. Who can know these people? He who steals will not give his name. It is impossible for us to protect our merchants in the steppe even though we safeguard and are gracious to them in our own possessions."

Yet Yusuf persisted in his complaints. "Your servants," he wrote to the tsar, "someone named Sary-Azman and his comrades, sailed on the Don and in some three or four towns assaulted our emissaries, and they shot and hurt people. What kind of friendship is this!? If you want our friendship and brotherhood, remove your servants from there!"

HOSTILITIES BETWEEN COSSACKS AND CROWN

The sultan often complained about the Don Cossacks, accusing them of activities such as attacks against Perekop,[29] and attempting to take Astrakhan.[30] No contemporary sources confirm his stories. There was consistent enmity between Turkish cossacks of Azov and the Don Cossacks of Russia. The Muscovite ambassador Nagoy wrote to the tsar that he could not send news to Moscow "because the Azov Cossacks are not at peace with your service cossacks."

The cossacks were necessary to the Muscovite government more than once to counter the rapacious Asiatics in these empty lands. Ivan sent his emissary Novosiltsev to Constantinople[31] by way of Rylsk and Azov with the Don ataman[32] Mishka Cherkashenin (whose nickname indicates that Mishka was a Little Russian cossack), accompanied by fifty of his contracted men,[33] atamans and men, to escort him as far as the Don winter quarters. Novosiltsev was to speak to the Don ataman and cossacks on Ivan's behalf, asking them to serve the tsar by deferring to his emissaries on crown business.

The tsar's letter was sent to all atamans and cossacks on the Northern Donets asking them, without exception, to obey Novosiltsev on all government matters, and to go wherever he sent them. "We would have you serve us in this way," the tsar wrote, "and we would like to reward you for your service."

The ambassadors' reports about their very difficult journey best illustrate the importance of the cossacks' assistance to Russian envoys in the steppe and the way of life to which they had to accustom themselves.

YERMAK'S CONQUEST OF SIBERIA
V.I. Surikov, 1895
Russian Armory, Moscow

Novosiltsev, for example, wrote from Rylsk on March 10. "There is a great deal of snow on the steppe and they have been enveloped in fog since Shrovetide. As a result we cannot push forward with horses since the fog is not lifting. We are thinking of taking sledges and we ourselves will forage our way[34] to the Northern Donets. Mishka's recruit, the service-tenured cossack Sila Nozrunov, refused government service, and returned from Rylsk to his own Rylsk patrimony." "We foraged our way to the Donets on foot," Novosiltsev later wrote, "but your majesty's treasury and its strong box we carried on sledges ourselves. When we came to the Donets on April 1, I ordered boats built on which we would go by water to Azov, and we lingered on the Donets for a week waiting for these boats. Mishka Cherkashenin, the atamans and cossacks did not all have used boats suitable for the Donets, and they made skiffs for themselves." On the return journey from Azov, Novosiltsev reported "As we left Azov I received news that the cossack ataman Senka Lozhnik and eighty men were following us from Azov into the steppe, where the Kazyev Tatars were gathering two Crimean atamans and three hundred followers to attack us from two sides on the Don or in the Ukraine. There were but a few atamans and cossacks with me for protection. Several atamans and their cossacks did not go with me, nor did they heed your letter." Interestingly, Senka Lozhnik was the Azov Cossack leader, whereas Sary Azman was the Russian Don Cossack commander.[35]

The following report from the Crimea to Moscow illustrates how Mishka Cherkashenin took revenge for his son who was taken prisoner and executed by the Crimeans. "The Turkish sultan sent a messenger to the Crimean ruler and wrote to him, saying 'Why did you execute the son of Mishka Cherkashenin? Now the Don Cossacks have taken Azov from me for Mishka's son and they have taken twenty leading citizens, including my brother-in-law Hussein, as well as people of the lower classes.'"

The Don Cossacks relied on the crown's inability to penalize them because of their distance from the realm, and chose either not to fulfill the tsar's or his ambassadors' orders, or fulfill them only partially. They attacked the Nogay, the people of Azov and Crimeans. As they sailed along the Volga they also stole from the tsar's boats, beat up people, robbing the Persian and Bukharan ambassadors as well as Russian traders. The tsar thus was forced to send his commanders with numerous soldiers against them. They caught and executed some cossacks while the others, in the words of the chroniclers, "scattered like wolves." Another band went up the Volga where they received an invitation from the

Stroganovs to enter their service, and they joyfully agreed. Although this overture occurred no earlier than the spring of 1579 it was not unexpected, for the Stroganovs had started recruiting volunteer cossacks as early as 1574 when they received the tsar's charter granting them rights to expand their enterprises to the other side of the Ural mountains. This slow pace of finding volunteers is best explained by events in the Stroganov family.

YERMAK JOINS THE STROGANOVS

Yakov and Grigory Anikiev died and only the third brother Semeon remained with two nephews, Maxim, Yakov's son, and Nikita, Grigory's son. Apparently Nikita did not live in great harmony with either his uncle Semeon or his cousin Maxim. The cossacks who came to the Stroganovs were some five hundred and forty in number under the command of Ataman Yermak Timofeev. The other atamans included Ivan Koltso (who according to the tsar's letter to the Nogay was sentenced to death), Yakov Mikhailov, Nikita Pan and Matvey Meshcheriak. They arrived in the Chusovaia hamlets at the end of June 1579 and remained there until September 1581. During that time, in the words of the chroniclers, they helped the Stroganovs defend their towns from attacks by barbarians. In July 1581 six hundred and eighty Voguls under the leadership of Murza Begbely-Agtakov attacked the Stroganov holdings unexpectedly, burning villages and taking people captive. The military stationed in the towns easily attacked them and took Murza Begbely prisoner. According to the tsar's letter of 1582 it seems that the Stroganovs were not content with the defense of their towns, for they had sent their forces to fight the Voguls, Votiaks and the natives of Pelym.

After Begbely's defeat the Stroganovs decided to dispatch the cossacks, Yermak and his comrades, across the Urals to accomplish the goal their fathers set in their letter to the tsar in 1574. According to the chronicle, on September 1, 1581 the Stroganovs, Semeon, Maxim and Nikita, sent Yermak Timofeev and his cossacks against the Siberian saltan,[36] supplementing Yermak with soldiers from their towns, Lithuanians, German prisoners, Tatars and Russians, three hundred in all, bringing the total army, including the cossacks, to eight hundred and forty. The Stroganovs also paid them, supplied them with various foods, clothing and weapons such as guns and arquebuses, and in addition sent escorts familiar with their Siberian route, as well as interpreters who knew Muslim languages.[37]

On the first of September, the very day that Yermak and his retinue departed to pacify the Siberian lands, hordes of natives gathered by the Pelym prince[38] attacked Perm locations along the Cherdyn, as well as the Stroganov holdings. Semeon and Maxim sent a letter to Moscow complaining that the Voguls set fire to their free settlements and villages, to their saltworks and copper mines, as well as to much grain and hay. Moreover, peasants with their wives and children were taken prisoner. In view of these events the Stroganovs petitioned the tsar to order soldiers with firearms to help them. Ivan ordered the Perm viceregent Prince Eletsky to gather two hundred armed soldiers from among the village elders and service men of the Perm and Solikamsk villages. Since the elders had only agricultural people, they permitted Perm and Usolie to gather their own soldiers to avoid penalities by the viceregent. Once formed in this manner, this militia was to help Semeon and Maxim in their fortifications. In exchange, if the Voguls attacked the Perm and Usolie settlements the Stroganovs must help these settlements. The tsar wrote to Nikita Stroganov ordering him to help his relatives.[39]

THE TSAR'S ANGER AGAINST THE STROGANOVS

The following year, when the Cherdyn governor Pelepelitsyn apparently failed to come to an agreement with the Stroganovs, he accused them of sending their cossacks to fight the Siberian saltan rather than protecting Perm against the Pelym prince's attack on the region. As a result of this report the tsar ordered this letter sent to the Stroganovs. "Vasily Pelepelitsyn has written to us from Perm that on September 1 you sent the Volga atamans and their cossacks, Yermak and his following, from your strongholds to fight against the Votiaks and the Voguls in the Pelym and Siberian settlements. On the very same day the Pelym prince, having assembled his Siberian forces with the Voguls, warred against our Perm settlements to the city of Cherdyn, attacking up to the fortification, killing our people and causing them many losses. This [attack] occurred because of your betrayal. You drove the Voguls, Votiaks and natives of Pelym from our service, fought with them, made war upon them, and in the same way embroiled us with the Siberian saltan. Then, having recruited the Volga Cossack leaders and their thieves, you placed them in your strongholds without our order. These atamans and their cossacks previously involved us in a quarrel with the Nogay Horde, having attacked the Nogay ambassadors on their transports on the Volga, assaulted and robbed the Horde merchants, and caused depredation and loss among our own people. They attempted to conceal their crimes by claiming to defend our Perm lands. They did this with you exactly as they [robbed and pillaged] along the Volga. On the very same day, September 1, that the Voguls came to Cherdyn, Yermak and his friends left your forts to fight the Voguls, and did not aid Perm in any way. All this was because of your criminality and treason. Had you been serving us, you would not have sent the cossacks to war at this particular time, you would have sent them as well as your troops from your strongholds to defend the Perm land.

"We have sent Voin Onichkov to Perm and have ordered him to take Yermak and his friends to Perm and Usolie on the Kama, where we have ordered them to remain, divide into smaller groups, and march in the winter with sledges together with the inhabitants of Perm and Viatka against the Pelym prince. After you have corresponded with Pelepelitsyn and Onichkov you are to send your own men to fight the Voguls and the Ostiaks. Immediately upon receipt of our letter send all your cossacks, as soon as they return to you from the war, to Cherdyn. Do not delay them. If you cannot hold your fort against enemy attack keep for yourself some troops, up to a hundred, with an ataman, and send the rest to Cherdyn immediately. If you do not send the Volga Cossacks under Ataman Yermak Timofeev with his friends from your strongholds to Perm, and keep them for yourself, and if you do not defend the Perm settlements, we will hold you in great disgrace for whatever occurs as a result of your treason. If there are further attacks by the Voguls, natives of Pelym or the Siberian saltan, the cossacks and their leaders who served you will be hanged."[40]

Clearly, the expression in the letter "you drove the Voguls, Votiaks and natives of Pelym from our service, fought with them and made war against them" cannot relate to Yermak's famous attack on Siberia of September 1, 1581. These words cannot even refer to it grammatically because of the use of the plural. Neither can they refer to this event because news of the call to Yermak was released later without any tie to former Stroganov attacks on the Voguls, Votiaks and natives of Pelym. Furthermore, in his last campaign Yermak could not have provoked the Pelym prince, who did not know of this campaign and who, when he found out, retreated. Consequently, prior to Yermak's expedition of September 1, 1581 the Stroganovs already had taken advantage of the tsar's [first] letter and attacked Siberian native populations.

What caused Ivan's annoyance was the Stroganovs' reason for enlisting the Volga Cossacks without his order. Still, Ivan, did not express strong displeasure, and he used similarly mild language in condemning their past dealings on the Volga. Words followed expressing the idea that the cossacks could have compensated for their guilt entirely had they defended the Perm land from the Siberian savages. This idea led to instructions on the employment of the cossacks for this defense, allowing the Stroganovs to retain some of them in their forts. The tsar's anger was not the result of the Stroganovs soliciting volunteers among the Volga Cossacks, nor a consequence of the cossack mission across the Urals, for they held that right according to his first letter. Rather, Ivan was angry because the Stroganovs preferred their own interests to the tsar's. The attacks angered the natives, and at the time of their assault on the Perm lands and the Stroganov properties the Stroganovs did not possess the resources to defend their lands and to assist the tsar's governors. The cossack army needed for defense already was sent to fight in Siberia. The tsar threatened the Stroganovs with great disgrace only in the event they continued this conduct and continued to pursue primarily their own advantage. He threatened to hang the cossacks only if they preferred service to private individuals over service to the tsar, to heed the Stroganovs and serve them, while betraying the tsar's land.

YERMAK'S SUCCESSES IN SIBERIA

The tsar's envoy Onichkov could not fulfill the tsar's orders. Yermak and his friends never returned to the Stroganovs from their campaign. Yermak traveled for four days up the Chusovaia to the mouth of the Serebrianaia river. They paddled on the Serebrianaia for two days until they came to the Siberian road, where they laid out an earthwork town, calling it Yermak's Kokuy town. From there they portaged as far as the Zharovl river, down which they sailed to Tura, where the Siberian lands began.

Sailing down on the Tura the cossacks attacked many Tatar towns and villages.[41] On the Tavda river they captured several Tatars one of whom, Tauzak, had lived under Kuchum and revealed to the cossacks numerous details about his saltan and those close to him. Yermak then returned this prisoner to Kuchum to frighten the khan with his stories about the cossacks.

Tauzak, according to the chronicle, said the following to Kuchum. "The Russians are strong warriors. When they shoot from their bows, they shoot fire, and smoke comes out and there is a terrible noise, the arrow is unseen and people appear with wounds and are brought to death's door. It is impossible to defend yourselves against them with any kind of shields. They can push a hole through anything."

These stories made the khan sad and pensive. He gathered his army, sent his relative Mahmet-Kul with them to meet the Russians, and fortified himself by the side of the Irtysh river, under the Chuvash mountains. Mahmet-Kul met Yermak on the shores of the Tobol, by the Babasan clearing, and was defeated. Guns triumphed over bows. Not far from Irtysh, one of the chiefs defended his village. The cossacks destroyed it, captured the mead and the ruler's treasure. The enemy overtook them on the Irtysh, a new battle erupted and again Kuchum's army fell defeated. The cossacks paid for their victory, losing several of their men while the rest were wounded in some way. Toward nightfall the cossacks seized the town of Atik-murza and settled in it. The next day their fate would be decided. Kuchum must be flushed out of his [Irtysh] refuge.

The cossacks gathered in their circle and debated whether to go forward or retreat. Those who wished to go on at all costs prevailed. "Brothers," they said, "Where do we have to run? It is already autumn, and ice is beginning to freeze in the river. We will not run, we do not accept disgrace, we will not reproach ourselves, we will have faith in God, who will help even the helpless. Let us remember the promise we made to the honorable people (the Stroganovs)! We cannot go back in shame. If God helps us, after death our memory will not fade in these lands, and our glory will endure forever."

At dawn on October 23 the cossacks left the town and assaulted the defenses. The besieged shot mulitudes of arrows at their attackers, breaking out of their refuge in three places to counterattack. After stiff hand-to-hand combat the cossacks triumphed. Prince Mahmet-Kul was wounded. Seeing his misfortune, the Ostiak princes abandoned Kuchum and dispersed to their own lands. Then the old khan himself abandoned his refuge, fled to his city of Sibir, where he gathered as many of his followers as he could and fled even further. The cossacks entered into an empty Sibir on October 26.[42] On the fourth day an Ostiak prince with his retinue came to Yermak and brought him many presents and supplies. Afterwards the Tatars and their wives and children began to arrive and resettle in their previous yurts.

The cossacks controlled Kuchum's capital, but Mahmet-Kul was not far away. Once, in December, several cossacks went fishing at Lake Abalak, where Mahmet-Kul crept up on them and killed them all. Hearing of this, Yermak went to revenge his comrades, caught up to the infidels at Abalak, and fought them until nightfall. They escaped during the night and Yermak returned to Sibir. During the spring flood a Tatar came to the city saying that Mahmet-Kul was camped on the Vagay river. Yermak detached a part of his cossacks who attacked the prince's camp that night. They killed many of the infidels, taking Mahmet-Kul himself a prisoner and bringing him to Yermak in Sibir.[43] The capture of the brave Mahmet-Kul was a terrible blow for Kuchum, who at that time was positioned on the Ishim river. Bad news followed one event after the other. The old khan soon learned that Prince Seidek, son of Prince Bekbulat who was killed by the khan earlier, was moving on him. Then the Tatar nobles and their followers left him. The old man Kuchum cried bitterly. "Those upon whom God does not have mercy, their honor is turned into dishonor, and they are abandoned by their beloved friends."

YERMAK INFORMS IVAN OF HIS ACHIEVEMENTS

In the summer of 1582 Yermak made use of the subjugation of the Tatar towns and villages on the Irtysh and Ob. He captured the Ostiak city of Nazym and its prince but in that attack he lost the ataman Nikita Pan and his retinue. Upon his return to Sibir, Yermak notified the Stroganovs of his accomplishments, that he had overcome Saltan Kuchum, seized his capital city and captured Prince Mahmet-Kul. The Stroganovs informed the tsar of these events and Ivan, in turn, as a reward for their service and zeal, granted Semeon the Volga towns of Great Salt and Little Salt.[44] To Maxim and Nikita he accorded the right to engage in trade without customs duties for themselves and all who arrived in their towns and strongholds.

The cossacks immediately sent several of their comrades directly to Moscow[45] to inform the tsar of the capture of the Siberian land.[46] Ivan granted these cossacks great favors in money, cloth, and damasks. To those remaining in Siberia, Ivan sent his full reward.[47]

ARRIVAL OF THE TSAR'S GOVERNORS

Ivan sent his governors Prince Semeon Bolkhovsky and Ivan Glukhov to occupy the conquered Siberian towns. The tsar's letter to the Stroganovs dated January 7, 1584 in regard to the dispatch of these governors to Siberia reads in part as follows. "According to our decree, Prince Semeon Bolkhovsky was ordered to take fifty men on horseback from your forts for our service in the Siberian winter campaign, but now a rumor has reached us that in Siberia it is impossible to travel in winter on horseback.

We have prohibited Prince Semeon from taking the winter route from Perm to Siberia until the spring thaw, and we have ordered him not to take soldiers from you. In the spring we have instructed him to take fifteen boats from you, complete with all necessary provisions for our army, for which we will provide, so that the boats each carry twenty men with supplies. We have ordered them not to take soldiers, carts, and escorts from you and not to offend your people and peasants. So, too, you are immediately to command the construction of boats for the spring and order the commanders of your fortresses not to interfere with these boats. If you delay in providing the boats, and as a result our enterprise comes to naught, you will be in great disgrace before us."[48] This was Ivan's last statement in regard to Siberia, for he did not live to receive news of Bolkhovsky's services, nor of Yermak's fate.[49]

IV

IVAN IV'S CHARACTER AND REIGN

PREMATURE AGING

In 1573, at the age of just forty-three, Ivan remarked to the Lithuanian ambassador Haraburda that he was already an old man. Truly the terrible life that Ivan lived and the awful illness he suffered combined to age him prematurely. The unfortunate war with Bathory, the loss of Livonia, and the humiliation endured by Ivan also must have had a destructive effect on his health. Finally even the strongest constitution when combined with his total lack of self-control could not withstand such abuse.

MARRIAGES

After the death of Anastasia[1] Ivan courted the sister of the Polish king, which effort was unsuccessful.[2] He then turned in the opposite direction, to the East, and in 1561 married the daughter of the Cherkess prince Temriuk, who was given the name Maria at the time of her conversion in Moscow.[3] Under the circumstances of the time the usefulness of a marriage to a non-Russian, and a Circassian beauty at that, must have been very appealing to Ivan. Moreover, it is easy to understand how he might benefit from a formal union with the barbarian princess.[4]

Maria died in 1569. In 1571 Ivan decided to enter into a third marriage and selected as his bride Martha Sobakina, daughter of a Novgorod merchant, but the young tsaritsa did not live even a month.[5]

Ivan disliked holding to conventions and in the beginning of 1572, despite the church's objection, he married for the fourth time, to Anna Koltovskaia. He called the church hierarchs, archimandrites and abbots to his tsarist council of clergy and prayed for pardon and their permission for a fourth marriage, daring to do so for the following reasons. His first marriage to Anastasia, the daughter of Roman Yurievich, which lasted for thirteen and a half years, ended when evil people, using hostile slander, sorcery and poison destroyed Tsaritsa Anastasia. As his second wife he had taken a young woman from the Piatigorsk Cherkess, and lived with her eight years, then she too was poisoned by the same hostile perfidy. Having waited some time, he wanted to enter into a third marriage for the sake of satisfying his physical needs and for the sake of his children, for they were still underage and therefore he could not enter a monastery. Ivan argued that to live in the world without marriage was to fall into temptation, thus he found himself a wife, Martha the daughter of Vasily Sobakin. The devil turned many courtiers against Tsaritsa Martha, and she was poisoned while still a maiden. The tsar placed his hopes in God's generosity and took Tsaritsa Martha for himself in the hope that she would heal. She was with him only two weeks and apparently was still a virgin. After her death the tsar grieved a great deal and thought of becoming a monk, then reconsidered. In light of the ruined and fragmented state of Christendom,[6] and because of his underage children, he dared to enter into a fourth marriage.[7]

When the assembled clergy, the archbishops and bishops beheld the tsar's humility and supplication they cried many tears and chose to be merciful. Gathered in the Dormition cathedral they stipulated that in compassion and because of his fervent prayers they would pardon and absolve the tsar by commanding him not to enter into a church before Easter. At Easter he might enter a church by the lesser door and receive a bite of the Easter cake, and then remain a year with the catachumens.[8] During the year he might walk to the smaller and great door, then was to stand for a year with the faithful, and when the year passed he might receive the eucharist and holy sacraments.[9] The following year, 1573, they permitted the tsar to partake of the Virgin bread,[10] the holy water and the miracle workers' mead[11] on prelate's holidays and the Feast of the

Virgin. The tsar might distribute as many alms as he wished.[12] If, for the sake of the holy church and for the Orthodox faith, the tsar was called upon to fight against the infidel, he would be allowed to do penance which the hierarchy and the entire consecrated assembly would take upon themselves. Nevertheless, others, from the tsar's council down to the common people, must not dare a fourth marriage. If someone in pride or thoughtlessness entered into one, he would be cursed.[13]

Ivan's fourth marriage lasted no more than three years, when Koltov-skaia was banished to a convent. The tsar's two concubines, Anna Vasil-chikova and Vasilisa Melentieva, could not rightly be called tsaritsas for he did not marry them and they never were referred to as tsaritsas in contemporary accounts.[14] For the fifth and final time Ivan in 1580 married Maria Fedorovna Nagaia, who bore him a son, Dmitry.[15] We have seen that he regarded the dissolution of this marriage as a minor matter, should he arrange to wed an Englishwoman. At the time of Possevino's arrival in Moscow Ivan admitted his marriage although he did not take communion, by reason of his marriage to a fifth wife.

SLAYING OF THE TSAREVICH

Ivan's habit of giving free vent to his anger as well as to his hands was not without fearful punishment. In November 1581, having become angry with his eldest son Ivan over some matter, the tsar struck him a mortal blow. We used the phrase *for some matter* because there exist various accounts of the causes of his anger. In the Pskov chronicle "*It is said* that the tsar struck his son Prince Ivan with a rod because he had spoken to him of the obligation to rescue Pskov (from Bathory)."[16] Some foreign writers repeated the same thing but Possevino, who was in Moscow only three months after the event, relates that the death took place as a result of a family quarrel during which the prince spoke out on behalf of his pregnant wife, whom his father had thrown to the ground. According to Possevino's version the killer was in despair, jumping out of bed at night and wailing.[17] He gathered the boyars, announced that he had killed his son, and that he no longer wished to rule. Since Prince Fedor, who was unsuited to rule the country, was next in line, it was up to them to decide which of the boyars was qualified to occupy the tsar's throne. Fearing that this proposal was made with guile, the boyars announced that they did not wish to see anyone on the throne other than the tsar's son, and requested that Ivan not abandon governance.[18]

ILLNESS AND DEATH

Ivan did not live for more than two years after his son's death. In the beginning of 1584 he developed a frightening illness, the outcomes of a terrible life, a decayed interior and an external tumor.

In March letters were sent to all the monasteries, "To the great and highly honored cloister, to the holy and reverend monks, churchmen, deacons, cathedral elders, servants, clergymen, prebendaries and to all the brothers in their cells. *Grand Prince* Ivan Vasilievich reverently kisses your feet and humbly asks that you pray and give your reverence, that you have mercy for my damnation, and that in your cathedrals and cells you pray to God and the Virgin for the sake of your holy prayers to grant me remission from my sins and my damnation, to free me from my present mortal illness and give me health. If we have offended you in any way, forgive us, have mercy on us, and that for which you are at fault before us, may God forgive you for everything."

They say that the ailing Ivan left instructions concerning the fate of his realm. He spoke to the boyars gently, admonishing his son Fedor to rule in a pious, loving and merciful manner, avoiding war with Christian states. He lowered taxes, and freed prisoners and captives. During his seizures he constantly called for his murdered son Ivan. It is also said that even at the end Ivan's self-indulgent nature never ceased manifesting itself... [.] The fatal seizure occurred on March 18 when, because he was feeling better, he insisted on playing checkers. As he lay on his deathbed he was tonsured as a monk and received the name Jonas.[19]

IVAN'S CHARACTER AND ACTIVITIES

For a long time Ivan the Terrible has been a mysterious figure in [Russian] history whose character and affairs have been the subject of contention. Immaturity of historical scholarship combined with historians' lack of attention to the connections between successions of events accounted for the perplexity and argument. Ivan IV was misunderstood because he was evaluated differently from his father, grandfather, and ancestors. Yet, even the appellation "Terrible," which we customarily associate with the name of Ivan IV, is enough to illustrate how this historical personality was connected to his predecessors, for his grandfather, Ivan III, was also called "Terrible."[20]

We complain that North Russian[21] sources prior to the second half of the sixteenth century are dry and lifeless, contending that historical personalities act silently, without revealing their convictions, sympathies or

IVAN IV THE TERRIBLE

Reconstruction by N.N. Gerasimov
Published January 1964 Following Exhumation on April 23,1963.

hostilities. During the second half of the sixteenth century, a period of conflict between the old and the new, the resultant dislocations no longer permitted participants to remain silent, and they began to speak out. Moreover in Moscow, from the second half of the fifteenth century on, growth in literacy facilitated outspokenness, causing this conflict to be waged through the written word. As a result of this process two major adversaries emerged, Ivan IV, grandson of Ivan III and Sophia Paleologus,[22] opposed by the scion of the appanage Yaroslav princes, the Muscovite boyar Prince Andrei Kurbsky.

To us, Kurbsky symbolizes the advent of boyar hostility to the processes of centralization and subjugation of all the Northern Russian principalities to Moscow. As a boyar and prince, in his writing Kurbsky casts Sophia Paleologus as the major culprit in causing the transformation, illustrating how, during the reign of Ivan III, relations between the Muscovite grand princes and their retinues began to change. Kurbsky is even more emphatic in setting himself against Ivan III and Sophia's son Vasily, viewing Ivan IV as the natural successor to his father's and grandfather's ambitions.

Kurbsky's writings give us a full explanation of how Ivan IV's aspirations were formed very early in life and recount the ways in which he constantly and consciously expressed them. Thus we can understand Ivan's hasty acceptance the title "tsar," his desire to protect it, his efforts to share his genealogy with Augustus Caesar and Tsar Vladimir Monomakh,[23] while at the same time separating and raising himself to heretofore unreached heights. This framework also makes it possible for us to understand Ivan's contempt both for the Swedish king to whom land was deeded, and for Stefan Bathory who was elected by a rebellious Sejm. Thus Ivan declares them unequal in stature to the Muscovite tsar.[24]

We have observed why even during childhood Ivan was conscious that he faced a conflict between these two contradictory principles, one he had to defend against its opposite. During his minority opposition to centralization was strengthened further by new conditions. His character was formed under the influence of this struggle in which each side revealed its methods and meaning, and carefully scrutinized earlier relationships in the history of Ancient Rus.[25]

To clarify the character of the relationships between the ancient princes we need only consult the chronicles to see how these princes referred to one another and how they referred to their subjects. Do we find the titles prince of Kiev, Chernigov, Pereiaslavl, Turov or Polotsk in the ancient chronicles? No, instead we discover that only princely names are used, which usually create difficulties for novices in the study of early Russian history.[26]

We need not pursue issues in ancient society about which the ancient sources say nothing. The princes did not use titles corresponding to the names of their holdings; consequently their domains were not of great importance to them, and they actually changed them. They called one another brothers, and considering that they argued over seniority according to family genealogies, the dominant relationships between them were familial, not determined according to holdings.

We now turn to the princely retinues and to the boyars with the same questions. Let us ask how they were titled. The names of the great magnates of Western Europe often were prefixed with *von* or *de* denoting the titles of their castles or landed holdings. If all the information about the ancestry of the Western European higher estates disappeared we could conclude from their family names that these men were landowners, and that ownership of land was the basis of social standing. In turning to the names of our own Russian boyars, what do we discover? We find "Daniel Romanovich Yurievich Zakharin" or "Ivan Petrovich Fedorovich." Just as among the ancient princes, so too among the boyars there was no sign of a relationship to landed property. One development explains the other. If the princes did not have permanent territories and changed them according to family ranks, so too their retinues exchanged their territories along with them, never settling and driving deep roots into these localities to acquire landownership and independent landed status. Instead the retinue depended upon and received its means of support and status from the prince or from the entire princely family, for members of the retinue moved from one prince to another.

A Russian boyar's primary concerns were expressed in his name. To the name he received at birth or christening he added the name of his father, grandfather, and great-grandfather. Thus he carried with him his genealogy and vehemently opposed any attempt to lower or compromise his standing. These were the origins of the phenomenon of precedence[27] in which family or clan interest predominated.

In a time when there were many princes the advantageous position of member of the retinue was guaranteed entirely by the possibility of moving from one prince to another. Upon the establishment of autocracy this possibility disappeared, and the member of the retinue was forced to accept whatever situation the autocrat accorded him. Distinctions between estates and the privileges of each were never worked out or formulated into law. We have seen that when in the field, or when a judicial clash developed between junior boyars on the one side, and peasants on the other, the junior boyars, heeding the demands of their estate, declined to fight with peasants. In these situations the judges prosecuted them, for the law was silent on differences between estates.

In Northern Russia a change in princely relationships occurred, destroying the family tie. Territories were isolated from one another, so that by the time all were brought under Moscow the princes' names were based on their domains. When princes removed from their original domains, according to the then current expression "were driven into" the old boyar families, they could not retain their privileged positions for long. Soon nothing differentiated them from the rest of the members of the serving class other than their titles. Many even forgot their territorial titles and kept only their personal names and their ancestors' nicknames. All this explains why in Ivan IV's minority the struggle for primacy took place only among certain well-known families, as well as why the service classes held onto the custom of ranking by precedence for so long and so strongly. The family principle took root in popular culture, and as it disappeared from one sphere it appeared with great strength and resiliency in another.

The family principle waged a strong persistent struggle against a sovereign entity that already had entered into its seventh century and begun to unify. Thus the old and the new began to come to a final reckoning by raising many important issues and creating pressing demands. One of the primary characteristics of the second half of the sixteenth century, the reign of Ivan IV, was the advancement of these critical questions pertaining to governance. Even had these principles been raised before, what mattered was the manner in which these questions were discussed, for in history nothing occurs all of a sudden. Thus it becomes possible to interpret the oprichnina [crown estates] as a response to hostilities between the tsar and his old boyars. Yet the oprichnina also illustrates how old families jealously guarded their family honor and exclusivity by citing precedence against the more numerous service estate. The expanding realm demanded more service nobility, especially as untrammeled attacks on Muscovy grew more widespread and frequent. Consequently, a whole array of people were able to take advantage of the hostile relationship between the tsar and his senior retinue.

In his testament to his sons Ivan regarded the oprichnina as much a problem as an opportunity. It was only in a later period that the important question of the relationship between the junior retinue and the senior was resolved.

The government centralized, the new settled accounts with the old. Following a period of strident questioning of how to change administration, deal with inadequate resources and remedy the abuses arising from them, efforts were made to settle these issues. These activities resulted in the creation of criminal statutes, enhancement of the status of crown secretaries in relation to governors, and the like. Understandably, at this moment the critical problem arose of acquiring the resources essential to the crown's prosperity to compete with those available to other European peoples. It was in this context that the first attempts on Livonia occurred. During this difficult time when so many crucial issues arose the head of government was an individual whose rash temperament demanded their immediate resolution.

It would not be necessary to add anything to what already has been said about Ivan's character were the historical literature not replete with contradictory opinions. While some who admired him tried to exonerate Ivan from responsibility for some very unflattering deeds, justly attributed to him, others wanted to remove him from any participation in the events which lent his reign any significance. These two contradictory orientations resulted from a general undertaking to find consistency in the character of historical personalities.

The human mind deplores too much diversity in life, for it makes it difficult to perceive and explain unity. Moreover, the human heart cannot abide discovering imperfection in those who have become objects of adulation since doing so can lead to total disillusionment. Biographers of famous "good" people are reluctant to criticize their subjects for fear of blemishing their records. If the sources describe a specific event or action they make every effort to vindicate their hero. On the other hand, rarely are historians willing to acknowledge the virtues of an individual who has left behind an evil reputation.

Thus it was with Ivan IV. According to one school of thought all important achievements during Ivan's reign were the product of the tsar's wise counsellors Sylvester and Adashev,[28] in whose hands Ivan was merely a blind, unconscious tool. To prove their point, advocates of this view use sections of the Kurbsky correspondence where Ivan apparently personally acknowledged that under Sylvester's aegis he had no power whatsoever. Yet in reading this famous correspondence it is imperative to recall that both Ivan and Kurbsky wrote with intensity, tending towards exaggeration and often falling into contradiction.

If Kurbsky's fundamental point was the principle that the tsar must listen to his counsellors, Ivan's basic notion was that subjects must defer to the tsar rather than try to bend the tsar's will to their own. In Ivan's view, Kurbsky's aspirations were the greatest of all crimes and he sought to blame Sylvester and his adherents for harboring similar motives. This is why he accused Kurbsky of the most criminal abuse of his trust, independence of action, and arbitrariness, why he wrote that Sylvester and Adashev ruled in his stead and that he personally vested in them their unlimited power through his trust.

These are the excerpts in question. "Were you corrupt or was I? Was it that I wanted to rule over you or that you no longer wanted to live under my power? Was it because of this that I became angry? As you grew more corrupt not only did you cease to be dutiful and obedient, you ruled for me and took all my power from me. I was ruler only in name, but in reality I had power over nothing."[29]

Elsewhere Ivan, in flaunting his wit, his deftness and his contentiousness, flattered Kurbsky with this subterfuge, not realizing that afterwards its advocacy could be used against him. "You say that because of military absences you rarely saw your mother, rarely lived with your wife, abandoned your patrimony, always took up arms in cities against enemies, endured natural diseases, were covered with wounds at barbarian hands and that your body is entirely covered by wounds. But all this happened to you when you wielded power with the priest and Alexis. If this was not in your best interests, then why did you do it? If you did this for the sake of enhancing your power, then do not blame us!"[30]

These advocates cite yet a third section of the correspondence to prove that Ivan did not undertake the campaign against Kazan voluntarily, rather that Sylvester's adherents forced the tsar to go under duress. "When we moved on the godless people of Kazan carrying the cross, the banner of all-Orthodox Christianity, we achieved victory through the ineffable mercy of God. Yet on the return home what kind of well-wishing did those you call martyrs show us? Like a prisoner on a ship they conveyed me through a godless and faithless land, escorted by a paltry detachment."[31]

Yet, there is not the least indication of an involuntary campaign. Ivan states directly "When we moved." He also clearly writes that there was little concern about his security, and he was carried like a prisoner only on the return journey after the taking of Kazan.

Kurbsky accuses Ivan of lacking courage at the time of the Kazan campaign because of his desire to return to Moscow quickly. Ivan responds to these accusations and describes his conduct and that of the boyars in the Kazan wars in the following manner. "When we sent our commander Prince Semeon Ivanovich Mikulinsky and his comrades to the Kazan land, what did you say? You claimed that we sent them not for our campaign but in disgrace, desiring to punish them! Is it possible that bravery in service puts people into disgrace? This is how we force the proudest in our realm to submit! Afterwards, on how many campaigns against the Kazan land did you go freely without being forced? Even when God subjugated this barbarian people to Christianity you did not wish to fight, and because of your reluctance there were more than fifteen thousand not with us at that time. During the siege you always offered bad advice. When supplies were getting short you wanted to return home after having been there three days! You never wanted to wait for a favorable time. You and your men never felt regret nor were you much concerned about victory. You could win or accept defeat, only to get home the sooner. To speed your return you left the battle causing a great spilling of Christian blood. On the attack, had I not held you back, you would have been the undoing of an Orthodox army by not having begun the action on time."[32]

How can the words "I sent, had I not held you back" and the words "You ruled and I did not have power over anything" be reconciled? These inconsistencies clearly illustrate the sort of sources available to us, and how we must use them.

All the sources make it indisputably clear that Ivan placed his full trust in Sylvester and Adashev. At the same time it is also clear that Ivan was never a blind tool in the hands of the people closest to him. He undertook the Livonian war despite their advice, they having suggested subjugating the Crimea. After taking Kazan, says Kurbsky, all the wise and thoughtful (in other words Sylvester's side) advised the tsar to remain in Kazan for some time to complete the subjugation of the country in its entirety. Yet the tsar "did not listen to the advice of his wise commanders and heeded the counsel of his brothers-in-law." Therefore Ivan was free to follow anyone's advice and was not under the exclusive influence of one specific side.

In 1555 the tsar was setting out on campaign against the Crimean khan when news reached him that a Russian army already was destroyed by

the Tatars. Many advised him to turn back whereas, according to
Kurbsky, the brave ones insisted that they must meet the Tatars. The tsar
listened to their advice, in this case heeding the counsel of Sylvester's
adherents, because when Kurbsky gives praise, he praises his friends.
Thus we see how on one occasion Ivan acted after the advice of certain
people, and on another on that of others. Moreover, in several instances,
having endured their debates, and irrespective of his own ideas, he followed his counsellors' advice.

All sources speak unanimously of Sylvester's enormous influence. We
must not overestimate this influence, rather establish reliable measures for
it, for a curious memoir has come down to us clearly revealing the relationship between Sylvester both to the metropolitan and to the tsar. In it
Sylvester wrote to Metropolitan Makary on the subject of Bashkin's
heresy.[33] "Sylvester the priest of the Annunciation cathedral humbly
makes his petition to the master, his holiness Makary, metropolitan of all
Russia and to all the consecrated assembly. Ivan Viskovaty wrote to you,
master, that Bashkin with Artemy[34] and Semeon are in council together,
that the priest Semeon is Bashkin's holy father and that he praises their
activities. He also wrote that I, Sylvester of the Annunciation cathedral,
threw out the old ways and introduced my own new philosophy.

"My master, holy metropolitan! The priest Semeon told me about Matiusha[35] at Matins during the St. Peter's [May 31-June 29] fast. An unusual
son of a priest came to me and asked me many perplexing questions. And
as soon as the tsar arrived from the St. Cyril monastery Semeon and I told
our lord the tsar everything that I had heard about Bashkin. Archpriest
Andrei and Alexis Adashev heard it all. Semeon also said that Matiusha
asked about the interpretation of many details in the Acts of the Apostles,
and not only did he give his own interpretations on their essence, but did
so in a corrupt manner. We told all this to our sovereign. The tsar commanded Semeon to order Matiusha to write down all his discourses regarding the Acts of the Apostles. Soon thereafter the tsar and ruler went
away to Kolomna and the matter lay dormant.

"As for Artemy, the former abbot of the Trinity monastery, Ivan [Vis-
kovaty] says that he and I must have a meeting. Prior to his becoming
abbot of the Trinity monastery I had not known [Artemy] at all. They
elected him as the Trinity monastery's abbot in the following manner.
Artemy was brought from the wilderness, the sovereign ordered him to
stay in the Miracles monastery and ordered me to visit him and report
regarding his disposition and spiritual dedication. Simultaneously his

student Porfiry came to the priest Semeon at the Annunciation cathedral and engaged in many discussions with him over different matters. Semeon told me everything that Porfiry discussed with him. I grew cautious and summoned Porfiry, conversing with him sufficiently about spiritual matters two or three times, and related everything to the tsar. Then the tsar, using his God-given intelligence and sense of judgment, began to notice the mistaken teachings of Porfiry and his teacher Artemy."

On one hand this document indicates the high level of trust which Sylvester enjoyed. The tsar sent him to Artemy to assess his fitness to occupy the position of abbot of the Trinity monastery. On the other hand it is also evident that Sylvester had to report on everything to Ivan, who decided for himself how to rule, and his own intelligence alerted him to things that Sylvester overlooked. When Ivan departed Moscow matters came to a halt. After such testimony it is difficult to accept literally Ivan's word that Sylvester managed the government, leaving him as tsar in name only. It is even stranger to propose that someone with Ivan's character could have been held at a distance from matters of state!

Finally we must discuss Ivan's conduct with respect to the Crimean khan after the burning of Moscow by Devlet-Girey,[36] then towards the Swedish king and especially in regard to Bathory. Although we may be unpleasantly startled by such a rapid transition from heroism to humiliation we are prepared, even on our own terms to see hesitation here. Nevertheless, we must not forget the great differences in understanding between contemporary culture and that of our predecessors in the sixteenth century. In the present era an upbringing within a set of clear-cut rules and values gives us strength yet prevents us from seeing radical transformations even as they occur within ourselves. People of preceding centuries did not have these developed characteristics and constraints. Thus they were not embarrassed by sharp transitions from one sentiment to its opposite. Even today less educated people who are closer to the values of their ancestors behave in a similar manner. Moreover we must not forget that Ivan IV was the grandson of Ivan III, the descendant of Vsevelod III.[37] If some historians found it necessary to present him as a hero in the beginning, the subjugator of kingdoms, then later as one shamefully fainthearted, they are not entirely at fault.

Ivan undertook the campaign for Kazan because he was convinced it was necessary, further strengthening his will to succeed through the religious conviction that the campaign would emancipate Christians from pagans. Yet, he never conducted himself as Achilles. In its direct and

detailed recounting of the scene in church at dawn when the army attacked the chronicle presents the most truthful picture of Ivan, who appears here not at all as a hero. Ivan personally undertook to attack Kazan,
then Polotsk and Livonia, because he was convinced that these actions
were necessary and might have beneficial outcomes. The same Ivan hastened to shorten the war with Bathory as quickly as possible because he
saw he had too few resources to achieve success. Just as his grandfather
Ivan III personally accompanied his armies to Novgorod and Tver, expecting them to succeed, Ivan III also tried to avoid Akhmat because the
chance of victory was decidedly unsure.[38] All Muscovite and North Russian princes, the gatherers of the land, behaved similarly.

The motivations of historians are mixed and at times peculiar when it
comes to evaluating the role of Ivan IV in Russian history. Some tried to
deprive him of any importance as a significant and independent actor.
Others, strangely, made Ivan a hero at the beginning of his career, then
accused him of shameful cowardice at the end. Strangest of all was the
desire of some to vindicate Ivan by mingling historical explanations of
events with their own moral justification.

Ivan's character and methods of action were explained as a struggle
between the new and the old. Could the events of the tsar's youth, during his illness and after, be morally justified by this struggle? Can someone of moral deficiency, unable to withstand temptation or govern the
depraved inclinations of his nature, receive exoneration? Indisputably in
Ivan there nested a terrible illness, but why did he have to permit it to
develop? We may display a deep sympathy and admiration for those
fallen in struggle, but only when they have fallen after using every means
available to them to defend themselves. In Ivan there is no visible inner
struggle with his passions at all, although there is a consciousness of his
fall. "I know that I am evil, " he said. Still, this awareness is an accusation, not a vindication. It is impossible for us not to concede his great
achievements and, for his time, great erudition. Achievements and erudition were not so much a vindication as an indictment.

Some wish to justify his cruelty by citing the brutal customs and
manners of the time. The moral conditions of society in Ivan IV's time
truly may appear to us as completely unattractive. We have seen how the
struggle between the old and new was in progress for some time, developing a character incapable of promoting gentle manners, or inspiring
prudent behavior and personal honor. The brutality of the customs of that
time was expressed even in contemporaneous written memoirs, whose

demands for restoring order and ending abuse suggested that brutal methods were singularly effective in banishing evil. In Ivan Peresvetov's[39] well known work, *About the Turk Tsar Mahmet who Wished to Burn the Greek Books,* the sultan's strong judgment and cruel punishments were glorified as qualities worthy of imitation. "Sultan Mahmet used to say, 'If you do not threaten a great people with such terror, you cannot introduce law into the land.'"

Being able to explain the society of the time does not exonerate a historical personality. Moreover, we dare not blame Ivan the Terrible's actions on sixteenth-century Russian society for the following reasons. It was based on different principles from that society [a conquered Byzantium] ruled by Sultan Mahmet. Indeed, Muscovy was capable of advancing an individual who instructed Ivan in the demands of moral principle. Russian society produced a St. Philip[40] who articulated these fundamental principles as part of his pastoral duties, proclaiming disapproval of Ivan the Terrible's methods of action. In demonstrating that Russian society possessed laws and prophets, it is cleansed and justified before history. Therefore Ivan, who refused to accept the exhortations of Philip's supporters, cannot be absolved.

Ivan clearly was conscious of the loftiness of his place and he zealously guarded his rights. Yet, he did not acknowledge one of his greatest prerogatives, that of supreme mentor and educator of his people. Just as in private and public education, so too in the education of the nation the example of the mentor, the figure of highest standing, the spirit of his words and deeds, exerts the most powerful influence. The people's customs were brutal, accustomed as they were to cruel and bloody measures. It was obvious that they must be educated away from them, yet what did Ivan do? He was a man of flesh and blood like all others yet he did not acknowledge the moral and spiritual agencies for establishing law and order. Even worse, although fully aware of their importance, he neglected them. Instead of healing it he aggravated the illness by acclimating the Russian people to torture, death by burning and the executioner's block. He planted terrible seeds which yielded a terrible harvest, the slaying of his son by his own hand, the murder of his youngest at Uglich,[41] the pretenders to the throne[42] and the horrors of the Time of Troubles![43]

No historian can say a single word to exonerate such a man. He can use only words of sympathy if, after having carefully observed the terrible face, he notes beneath the tormentor's gloomy features the doleful characteristics of victimization. For here, as everywhere, the historian is obligated to explain the connections between phenomena. Through their corruption and contempt for public good, disdain for the life and honor of those closest to them, Shuisky and his friends[44] sowed the seeds out of which Ivan the Terrible grew.

Like Ivan III, his grandson Ivan IV was of unusual height, well built with high shoulders and a broad chest. According to foreign accounts he was stout, whereas Russian descriptions have him lean. He had small and lively eyes, a bent nose and a long mustache.[45] The habits he acquired in the second half of his life lent his face a mournful, unhappy expression even when he laughed. He had an extensive memory, displayed great energy, personally reviewed all requests, and anyone might to turn to him personally with complaints about officials. Like his father he loved the monastic life, yet because of his lively nature he was not content merely to stay at a monastery to contemplate the way of life there. In Alexandrov Village he followed the monastic customs, he himself the abbot and the oprichniks the brethren.

In Russian and foreign accounts, during the first part of his life Ivan spent little of his time hunting, rather he devoted himself to administrative matters. When at the conclusion of the war Bathory requested red gerfalcons Ivan answered that he expressly sent to the Dvina and the seacoast for them. He once had good gerfalcons, which for sometime now were fewer and, because so many sorrows had befallen him he went hunting rarely. Bathory in thanking him for the gerfalcons asked what things especially pleased him that he might present to him. Ivan replied that he admired argamak horses,[46] good stallions, good iron helmets with brims and hand pistols of good quality, made entirely of metal, and light in weight.

APPENDIX I

A NOTE IN REGARD TO THE CONQUEST OF SIBERIA

We cannot leave our story of Yermak's conquest of Siberia without certain clarifications because a number of historically controversial and contradictory sources exist for the tale. Karamzin,[1] the most truthful of those writing about the subjugation of Siberia, cites the chronicle published by Spassky (1821) and suggests that it was actually composed about 1600. "The author," (writes Karamzin), "had in his hands Ivan's letters to the Stroganovs, and writes thoroughly, simply. I will call this the actual historical chronicle the *Stroganov Chronicle*."[2]

P.I. Nebolsin in his 1849 essay *The Subjugation of Siberia*[3] wrote to counter the information in the *Stroganov Chronicle* (we will refer to it in this manner following Karamzin's example) and tried to give priority to another chronicle, the Yesipov, named for its compiler. "The Yesipov Chronicle," Nebolsin wrote, "without even taking into account its rhetoric and phraseology, is shorter. It describes events simply, succinctly, without scholarly pretensions, without particularly exaggerating anyone's personal motives. It explains the circumstances of its creation, names the authors, indicates the time of composition, and makes no effort to conceal the chronicler's expansion upon the original which served as the model for his version.

"Apparently Yesipov, whether for good or ill, did his work critically, describing events by developing them in chronological order and in accordance with local conditions. He made no special mention of the Stroganovs, the Perm merchants, and accentuated the role of 'that great and wise rhetorician, Yermak' and his men. In his manuscript's first draft Yesipov even rejected references to another chronicle. 'Other chroniclers tell the story a different way, as if they (Yermak and his comrades) were summoned from the Volga by the Stroganovs who gave them properties,' and so on. Yesipov understood that here every word... [implied] some impossible event, so he simply wrote that Yermak and his comrades departed to Siberia from the Volga of their own volition.

"Another anonymous chronicle[4] repeats much of what Yesipov contains but even more than the Yesipov document it rounds off the time periods and exaggerates the volume of activities. Moreover, it is replete with eloquently colorful phrases and turns of language, suggesting that it was compiled much later than the Yesipov chronicle. Despite the chronicle compiler's great efforts to imitate Old Church Slavonic grammar, the work is full of major errors. It is impossible therefore, to treat this document with the same credibility as the Yesipov Chronicle, and because certain details increase this mistrust, it must be subjected to strong criticism.

"From its very beginning" [Nebolsin continues,] "the anonymous chronicle makes every effort to acquaint the reader with the importance of the revered Perm salt-workers in the crown's way of life, long before the appearance of Yermak on the scene. The anonymous chronicle deletes all expressions from the tsar's letters which could lead to the truth, and concentrates its efforts on depicting Yermak's cossacks as indispensable, totally different from others of their ilk. Yermak's cossacks are not thieves (in the meaning of the term at that time), but saccharine heroes, always prepared to weep emotionally. They are not the usual mortals whom an enemy might on occasion destroy in battle by overcoming their strength. Rather, they are almost everywhere victorious heroes. The author also goes to great pains to dismiss accusations of any kind of indelicacy on the part of the conqueror and to each deed he gives the appearance of the greatest propriety, even though in order to do so he must alter the significance of events. A similar predilection brings yet another kind of error with it. The author deduces events unsupported by any official document, adding wherever possible anything that could give luster to the Stroganov name.

"Karamzin characterizes both chronicles as very old and trustworthy in Note 670, concerning the Yesipov and Stroganov chronicles, in the ninth volume of his *History*. In Note 664 to the same ninth volume he explains that he unconditionally followed the Stroganov Chronicle but does not deem it necessary to reveal exactly why this was the case. In Note 644 to the same ninth volume, concerning the Stroganov manuscript, he calls it the most trustworthy of all the various accounts and dates its composition to approximately 1600. Since at its very outset the Stroganov manuscript refers to the Siberian archdiocese, which was not established until at least 1621, Karamzin's opinion is itself untrustworthy. In its conclusion the Stroganov Chronicle speaks of building cities and churches, the purification of the 'entire Siberian land,' of the propagation of the Gospels in every part of Siberia and of the spread of Christianity among the alien nations, pushing the composition of this manuscript to at least to the second half of the seventeenth century, or perhaps even later."

Anyone who has compared the Yesipov and Stroganov manuscripts will agree with us that a review of the manner in which events are presented in both which, incidentally, we find in Nebolsin, could be nothing other than the result of the author accidentally mixing the two manuscripts, and incorporating one part instead of another. Otherwise it would be impossible to explain how, for example, Nebolsin permitted himself to say that the Yesipov manuscript sets forth events in a simple, concise manner without pretensions of erudition. It takes only a glance at Chapters III, VI and VIII of the Yesipov Chronicle to discover that the author [Nebolsin] confused the two manuscripts. Did he make any real pretensions to scholarship by telling of Siberia, citing Italy, speaking of Kuchum, and filling an entire chapter with citations to Moses? Is it possible to find anything comparable in the Stroganov manuscript?

Before us are two manuscripts, one of whose compilers had an evident penchant for his hero, Yermak, minimizing the importance of his summons from the

Stroganovs. The compiler of the second described events by fully utilizing indisputable sources, namely official documents.

Which of the two is preferable? Should we denounce the latter [chronicle] for tending to favor the Stroganovs, only because it recalls their participation in the Yermak affair, and because it is based on official documents which refer directly to this participation? Therefore the Stroganov manuscript must be preferred to all other known Siberian chronicles because its story uses and conforms to undeniably trustworthy sources.

Even if we did not know the importance of the sources for the Stroganov manuscript we would still have to prefer it over the Yesipov for it explains the problem in a fully satisfactory manner by depicting an incremental pace of events and the connections between them. Settlement occurred in the areas neighboring Siberia, and colonizers by custom received greater special rights. Because of unique conditions in newly populated areas wealthy colonizers had to undertake responsibility for defending their settlements with their own resources, building forts and supporting mercenaries. In its charters the government specifies they were to obtain mercenaries from among the free cossacks. The cossacks became especially necessary to them when in order to transfer their enterprises across the Urals they obtained the tsar's charter granting them the Siberian saltan's domains. Thus they invited the free cossack band from the Volga and sent them off to Siberia. What could be more satisfying to the historian than such a narrative?

Nevertheless, an effort is being made to convince us that it is much more accurate and satisfactory to repudiate evidence of the Stroganovs' participation in the subjugation of Siberia as recorded in the tsar's treaties. Rather we are to acknowledge that the cossack band left the Volga on its own to cross the Urals and conquer Siberia!

Perhaps the compiler of the Stroganov manuscript, basing his work on trustworthy sources, the tsar's documents, really overindulged. Yet, did he form such great preference for the Stroganovs that he would make the researcher suspect his story? Indeed Nebolsin reproaches the compiler of the Stroganov manuscript for omitting all expressions in official documents which might reveal any vestiges of truth. Nebolsin, however, did not deem it necessary to demonstrate the justice of his reproach, nor did he document any such omissions because clearly there are none! Nebolsin also criticizes our chronicler for distorting the character of Yermak's cossacks as supposedly emotional knights prepared to shed tears when confronted with refined sentiments. Yet in the entire manuscript there is only one instance in which Yermak tearfully, at a decisive moment when many cossacks were frightened, urged them to pray to God. Even had the chronicler forced his cossacks to cry several times, how does Nebolsin know whether our strong ancestors wept more often than we, their weak descendants? According to this outlook, was Monomakh also an emotional knight if he often cried?

Most importantly, why attribute something to the chronicler which he did not intend? Why fault the chronicler for seeming to make the cossacks appear everywhere as conquering heroes? In fact, the chronicler relates how the cossacks were frightened when they saw Kuchum's defensive earth and tree barrier defended by many warriors and recounts the instances in which the cossack detachments were annihilated. The very subject under discussion implies that the cossacks had to win more often than be defeated for they conquered Siberia. Did Nebolsin find additional information about cossack defeats in other chronicles? Is there more information in his own account? Finally, Nebolsin criticizes the compiler of the Stroganov manuscript for his pleas to dismiss charges of violence against the cossacks. Is there information in other manuscripts that meets Nebolsin's claims of what he calls "indelicacy?" Only then is it possible to reproach the chronicler for bias if he hid something found in other sources. The Stroganov manuscript purposely contains nothing praising Yermak's morality or that of his friends, nor is there any information that the cossacks took vows of chastity. Nebolsin postulates the cossacks' conduct in an entirely different manner and introduces good Tatars into the scene. Nebolsin's version was compiled to counter several chronicles, but not the Stroganov. Why then does Nebolsin set himself against the Stroganov version?

Nebolsin criticizes Karamzin for dating the compilation of the Stroganov manuscript to the beginning of the seventeenth century. In Nebolsin's opinion, it must be dated at least to the second half of the seventeenth century, since its beginning mentions the Siberian archbishopric and its conclusion speaks of the propagation of the gospels in all parts of Siberia. The archbishopric is not mentioned in the beginning of the chronicle. It is found in the chapter headings, which clearly were written by a later transcriber, not by its compiler. At the conclusion of the same manuscript, where references to the archbishopric might have been expected, there are none. "Here is the story of the establishment of cities and fortresses in the Siberian land," the conclusion reads, "of the release of the atamans and cossacks of Yermak Timofeev and his comrades and their campaign in the Siberian lands, of the victory over Tsar Kuchum, the capture of his son Prince Mametkul, and the seizure of the Siberian land by Russian crown servitors. These words come at the end of the story. Everyone who reads it will think of it and not forget such things. These writings are written to be remembered. Indeed, these things will be forgotten only with difficulty."

This is the actual title of the memoir, written by the same compiler and unchanged by a later transcription. Its contents regarding the propagation of the gospels throughout Siberia could have been written as easily at the beginning of the seventeenth century. Moreover, what was understood as the Siberian land was not today's Siberia, the area from the Urals to the Pacific Ocean, but Siberia in the more succinct sense, the realm of Kuchum.

The compiler of the Stroganov manuscript bases his information on official charters granted the Stroganovs. To promote his idea that the Stroganovs did not participate in the Yermak adventure, Nebolsin had to review these documents. He criticizes earlier scholars of Siberia and the Stroganovs for having misunderstood the documents. Curiously he contends that the Stroganov lands were not given as hereditary property but as service tenures, as leases, as rentals! Consequently we must inquire in which document Nebolsin found the fixed terms for the use of chartered lands that would have necessitated granting them as service tenures, leases and rentals.

An even more important error in Nebolsin's work is based on an incorrect understanding of ancient relationships. Empty expanses of land granted for cultivation and colonization had no value in the eyes of the crown. These lands did not lend themselves to time limits specifying when labor and investments would make them valuable and capable of bringing the government income at the conclusion of the exempted years. When the Muscovite ambassadors were speaking of the election of Tsar Fedor Ivanovich to the Polish throne they mentioned that among the advantages Poland would gain from this election was that the tsar had land on the Don and Donets for the poor gentry. "In such empty lands," responded the nobles, "what gain will there be? Beyond Kiev we have many lands of our own such as these. How can you dirty yourselves by including such lands in your articles? Would the tsar grant our people lands in the Muscovite realm, in Smolensk, or in the cities of Severia?"[5]

It would have been the same sort of trash to write in a charter for empty lands that they were granted temporarily. "Why over the course of time they (the Stroganovs) were made the hereditary lords of the Chusovaia lands—that is another question," writes Nebolsin. No, it is not another question, it is the same one, and it is impossible so blithely to escape important, insuperable objections. Had the Stroganovs not received the land in perpetual ownership from Ivan IV, if the silence of the charters on the term of the grants does not point to this perpetuity, when, it must be asked, did they receive the right to perpetual ownership?

In a petition of 1574 the Stroganovs requested a charter to settle and trade on the Siberian rivers. Then we see that the Stroganovs summoned the cossacks, sent them across the Urals to pacify those places to which the charter referred. This matter is clear to everyone. Nevertheless Nebolsin sought to prove that the Stroganovs had no role in the Yermak campaign. In keeping with his goal he concluded that many years passed between the time the Stroganovs received the charters for Siberia and the time of Yermak's campaign. Consequently they did not have their sights on Siberia, and furthermore they could not have done so because of their lack of funds. For what purpose, then, did they accept the charter for Siberia if they did not have their sights on that country and could not have because of lack of funds? It would seem that Nebolsin fails to answer that question.

Afterwards Nebolsin attempts to deny the possibility of the summoning of the cossacks by the Stroganovs. "How could the honest, God-fearing Stroganovs," he writes, "the faithful servants of the tsar, send a kindly letter to doomed brigands sentenced by the tsar's courts to death? How could the idea enter the heads of clever traders like the Stroganovs of inviting this whole crowd, this army of thieves who in the far-off backwoods could rob them with impunity? Just how great was the Stroganovs need to win general admiration? For this did they need to act against the will of their ruler and benefactor?"

All this was written from a nineteenth-century perspective, without taking into the least consideration sixteenth-century ideas. That the Stroganovs were able to hire the Volga Cossacks better explains the tsar's angry letter to them, sent after the receipt of Pelepelitsyn's report. At least here is a rebuke to the cossacks for their previous conduct on the Volga. They are accepted nevertheless into the tsar's service and ordered to the defense of the Perm region, and the Stroganovs were permitted to keep some of them in their own service.

The tsar threatened the cossacks with punishment only if they continued serving the Stroganovs exclusively without heeding the tsar's interests. We must also remember how at that time, as in later years, with what ease cossacks were pardoned who *"gave up brigandage." Once Yermak* and his friends agreed no longer to earn their living along the Volga they had retired from brigandage to serve the Stroganovs. Finally, it must be noted that of all Yermak's ataman friends only Koltso was condemned to death for previous crimes.

"It is said," Nebolsin continues, "based on the Stroganov manuscript, that the Stroganovs sent to Yermak and all the cossacks an inviting, warm letter, signed on April 6, 1579, and that Yermak with five hundred cossacks appeared at the Stroganovs' on June 21 of the same year. He took shelter with them for two years and prepared for war with Kuchum, and on September 1, 1581 went to make war in Siberia." Let us see if there is some kind of logic in this information. Is there the least shadow of truth?

"The messenger carrying the Stroganov letter" [wrote Nebolsin] "could leave Perm for the Volga no earlier than the thawing of the waters. He must reach the Volga, then secretly discover Yermak's whereabouts. While keeping his mission secret from local authorities he must find and persuade him, the other atamans and their entire horde of thieves to accept the Stroganovs' invitation, and allow them time to assemble for their council.

"Yermak was supposed to think about the proposition the Stroganovs apparently had offered him, consulting with his and the other atamans' men. Convinced there was advantage in this invitation, and decided on a campaign, they had to stock enough provisions, load the boats, and voyage along two great rivers. Traveling against the current for more than a thousand versts, they constantly had to evade detection in more heavily populated areas. It was physically impossible to start, organize and complete all this in seventy-five days, even if we assume that the rivers were indeed open on April 6!"

Indeed, it would have been physically impossible to accomplish this goal given the nonexistent difficulties Nebolsin devised. The Stroganov messenger, once arrived on the Volga, did not have to discover "by sleight of hand" the location of Yermak's camp. The Stroganovs must have learned beforehand the location of the cossack winter camp from their stewards and representatives. Neither did the messenger have to conceal himself from local authorities to find Yermak. Obviously, when describing sixteenth-century events, Nebolsin envisioned the banks of the Volga and Kama as having the same character as now, in the mid-nineteenth century. On this premise he created local authorities from whom it would be necessary to hide. Yet, based on descriptions of the Volga's course in the second half of the sixteenth century, we know the wilderness began from the river's Kazan estuary.

Further, Nebolsin presumes that Yermak had to think for a long time about the Stroganov proposition, but it is unclear on what he based this assumption. The manuscript says that the cossacks had no reason to think for long, that they were delighted with the proposal and came quickly. Thus, we have no reason to doubt the accuracy of this information. We do not know how long Nebolsin thinks it took the cossacks to load the boats with provisions which according to his own words (p. 72) consisted of small quantities of oat flour, groats, and salt. Nebolsin assumes that Yermak's voyage took him along two big rivers. This is quite uncertain, for it is not known where Yermak wintered nor where Stroganov's messenger found him.

"Yermak," Nebolsin states further, "with his group and the other atamans could not have lived for two years with the Stroganovs. Feeding five hundred useless non-farmers who were actually dangerous to the people living on Stroganov lands would have been impossible and incompatible with sound reasoning. To support such a cohort of warriors for two years without at the very least informing the Perm authorities or concealing their presence so the crown did not find out, also was impossible."

Once again this is based on nineteenth-century assumptions and suggests very minimal attention to the sources. Since they were entirely independent of the Perm authorities, why were the Stroganovs obliged to inform them about their cossacks? Moreover, they were permitted to gather a variety of servicemen including free cossacks, and use them for offense as well as defense. Nebolsin thinks it impossible for wealthiest family in the realm to feed five hundred men for two years. Can he possibly have been unaware of how many men were supported at the time by the great boyars and lords-in-waiting in Moscow, who had many fewer resources at their disposal than the Stroganovs? It is even stranger that men who were a necessity to the Stroganovs as much for defensive as offensive war could be termed "useless and dangerous!"

"The cossacks," states Nebolsin, "including Koltso, could not have come on the Chusovaia to the Stroganovs in 1579 for in the official documents of 1581 under the listing of Volga fugitives for 1580 we find the name of the name of Yermak's inseparable and trusted friend Ivan Koltso." The listing of Ivan Koltso in 1581 indicates only that he had not been captured. Evidently the reason he was not caught is because he was hiding with the Stroganovs.

"From the very beginning of 1581 the Volga-Ostiak tribes pushed into the Stroganov lands and menaced Perm" [Nebolsin writes]. "[H]ad Yermak been on the Chusovaia and was really the Stroganovs' employee and boarder in the spring and summer of that year, the direct result would have been that either the Stroganovs, or the local authorities, would have forced him to defend the Russian borders. In 1581 the Stroganovs could not have sent Yermak to God-knows-where at such a time. Calamity hung over their heads and every local force was needed to save the entire region from further destruction. The Stroganovs themselves could not have known of Yermak's campaign. Otherwise, we must conclude that (in the beginning of 1581) although they asked for soldiers to defend their communities and complained to Ivan about Nikita Stroganov's failure to assist them, they dared conceal from the tsar the presence of Yermak's band. By lying in this manner, they caused the tsar, in his letter of November 6, 1581, to order both Nikita and the Perm authorities to their aid."

It is incomprehensible how Nebolsin allows himself to use these "must have beens" about Yermak's actions with the Stroganovs. The chronicle directly tells us that this activity consisted of battles against the godless sons of Hagar, Murza Begbel. The Stroganovs were able to send Yermak to Siberia only in September 1581, for prior to this time they turned back Begbel's attack, and the murza himself was captured and imprisoned. They did not expect yet another attack and used the remaining time before the onset of winter for the Siberian campaign. Further, it is also incomprehensible how Nebolsin writes as though the Stroganovs asked the tsar for aid in the beginning of 1581, when in their letter the Stroganovs specifically discuss the attack by the Pelym prince of September 1 of that year, "in our time, in the ninetieth year of Semeon's days." At this time they said nothing about Yermak, for they already had dispatched him to Siberia.

Here we must stop, for Nebolsin's further statements and explanations in regard to Yermak's campaign to Siberia itself are inappropriate to our discussion. Our goal was to disprove the objections he directed against the sources which we used for our story.

APPENDIX II

ON THE PEACE WITH BATHORY

Possevino was greeted with suspicion and unfriendliness in the Polish camp. The Poles laughed at Possevino's pretensions, assuming he supported the tsar's side in the hope of turning him toward Catholicism. Thus, we find frequent attacks against the Jesuit in Zamoyski's correspondence with various individuals. In Zamoyski's letter to Zbarazski we read "I should think that by the end of the peace talks Moscow will have such faith in Possevino that his portrait will stand alongside St. Nicholas or the Immaculate Virgin of the Caves. Yet, they do not wish to write his name on the peace negotiations list."

In a letter to the king Zamoyski wrote "There are those who call all Jesuits rogues. This, naturally, is unfair. Unfortunately, whoever calls this particular one by that name does not err." Zamoyski accuses Possevino of favoring the Muscovite tsar in his general comments, and by his silence during negotiations on various localities relinquished by both sides.

Were Possevino really the tsar's friend he would have informed Moscow about the miserable state of the Polish army at Pskov. On January 15 Zamoyski wrote to the commissioners conducting the peace negotiations that they must conclude the matter as quickly as possible. The army at Pskov could hold out no longer than another eight days, nor could it advance further into enemy territory. Otherwise the Poles must retreat in shame with great losses because the Hungarians had destroyed all the crops, and the armies would die of starvation on their return. Zamoyski strongly feared war with the Swedes, and even advised the king in the event to make an alliance with Moscow, ceding to it the sea shore and estuaries of the Neva.[6]

NOTES

Additional information on personalities and topics found in the text and notes is available in Joseph L. Wieczynski, et al., eds., *The Modern Encyclopedia of Russian, Soviet and Eurasian History* (MERSH, formerly *The Modern Encyclopedia of Russian and Soviet History*); Harry B. Weber, et al., eds., *The Modern Encyclopedia of East Slavic, Baltic and Eurasian Literatures* (MESBEL, formerly *The Modern Encyclopedia of Russian and Soviet Literatures, Including Non-Russian and Émigré Literatures*); Paul D. Steeves, ed., *The Modern Encyclopedia of Religions in Russia and Eurasia* (MERRE, formerly *The Modern Encyclopedia of Religions in Russia and the Soviet Union*); and David R. Jones, ed., *The Military Encyclopedia of Russia and Eurasia* (MERE, formerly *The Military-Naval Encyclopedia of Russia and the Soviet Union*) all published by Academic International Press.

INTRODUCTION

1. Sergei M. Soloviev, *The Age of Vasily III* (History of Russia, Vol. 9). Edited, translated and with an introduction by Hugh F. Graham. (Academic International Press, 1976), p. 16.

2. The relevant collections, or *fondy*, in the Central State Archive of Ancient Acts are those pertaining to England (35), Denmark (53), the Crimea (123), the Nogay Tatars (127), Poland (79), the papacy (78), Sweden (96) and Turkey (89).

3. *Akty istoricheskie, sobrannye i izdannye Arkheograficheskoiu Kommissieiu* (Historical Acts Collected and Edited by the Archeographical Commission) (St. Petersburg, 1841); *Akty otnosiashchiesia k istorii Zapadnoi Rossii* (Acts Pertaining to the History of Western Russia) (St. Petersburg, 1848); *Dopolneniia k aktam istoricheskim, otnosiashchimsia k Rossii, sobrannye v inostrannykh arkhivakh i bibliotekakh, i izdannye Arkheograficheskoiu Kommissieiu* (Supplements to the Historical Acts Pertaining to Russia Collected in Foreign Archives and Libraries and Edited by the Archeographical Commission) (St. Petersburg, 1848). Polish sources include *Zbior pamiatników historycznych o dawnej Polszcze* (Collection of Memorials Concerning Ancient Poland) (Lipsk, 1838); Andrzej Fricz Modrzewski, *Commentariorum de Republica emendenda libri quinque* (Five Books of Commentaries on the Reform of the Commonwealth) (Basle, 1554, reprinted Warsaw 1953).

4. *Russkaia letopis' po Nikonovu spisku* (The Russian Chronicle in the Nikonian Transcription) (St. Petersburg, 1792). A more recent edition of the Nikonian Chronicle is contained in *Polnoe sobranie russkikh letopisei* (Complete Collection of Russian Chronicles), Vols IX-XIII (reprinted Moscow 1965). The *Tsarstvennaia kniga* (Book of Tsars) is contained in the same collection, Vol. XIII, Part 2 (St. Petersburg, 1906, reprinted Moscow, 1965).

5. Antonio Possevino, *Moscovia* (Wilno, 1583). For a modern English translation, see Note 14, below.

6. *Hakluyt's Collection of the Early Voyages, Travels and Discoveries of the English Nation* (London, 1809).

7. *Letopis' sibirskaia izdana iz rukopisi XVII veka G.I. Spasskim* (The Siberian Chronicle Edited by G.I. Spassky from a Seventeenth-Century Manuscript) (St. Petersburg, 1821).

8. N.M. Karamzin, *Istoriia gosudarstva rossiiskogo* (History of the Russian State) (St. Petersburg, 1842).

9. G.F. Müller, *Opisanie sibirskogo tsarstva* (Description of the Siberian Tsardom) (St. Petersburg, 1850).

10. Since Poland's history is so complicated readers seeking more information on Poland are advised to consult Norman Davies, *God's Playground. A History of Poland,* Vol. I (Oxford, 1981).

11. For histories of Sweden consult Franklin D. Scott, *Sweden. The Nation's History* (Minneapolis, 1977). For a more detailed treatment of this particular period, see Michael Roberts, *The Early Vasas. A History of Sweden, 1523-1611* (Cambridge, 1968).

12. Soloviev's view is far from the prevailing interpretation. German historians maintain that Ivan claimed Livonia as his patrimony, and Robert Crummey also downplays the search for technology. See Robert O. Crummey, *The Formation of Muscovy, 1304-1613* (London, 1987), pp. 158-159, 173-175; Norbert Angermann, *Studien zur Livlandpolitik Ivan Groznyjs* (Studies on the Livonian Policy of Ivan the Terrible) (Marburg, 1972); Knud Rasmussen, *Die livländische Krise, 1554-1561* (The Livonian Crisis 1554-1561) (Copenhagen, 1973). A Soviet historian expressing similar views was V.D. Koroliuk, *Livonskaia voina. Iz istorii vneshnei politiki russkogo tsentralizovannogo gosudarstva vo vtoroi polovine XVI v.* (The Livonian War. From the History of the External Policy of the Russian Centralized State during the Second Half of the Sixteenth Century) (Moscow, 1954).

13. For more information on this theory see Paul Bushkovitch, "The Formation of a National Consciousness in Early Modern Russia," *Harvard Ukrainian Studies*,10 (1986), pp. 355-376.

14. For a full translation of Possevino see *The Moscovia of Antonio Possevino.* Translated and edited by Hugh F. Graham (Pittsburgh, 1977).

15. See Volume 10, Chapter I of this series.

16. The foremost historian of the Time of Troubles was S.F. Platonov, whose *The Time of Troubles. A Historical Study of the Internal Crisis and Social Struggle in Sixteenth and Seventeenth Century Muscovy.* (Translated by John. T. Alexander, Lawrence, Kan., 1985) is one of the best works available in English. See also Crummey, *Formation,* as well as Volumes 14-15 of this series. More recent and authoritative is the notable modern Russian historian Ruslan G. Skrynnikov's *The Time of Troubles. Russia in Crisis, 1604-1618.* Translated and edited by Hugh F. Graham. (Academic International Press, 1988) as is his *Ivan*

the Terrible (Academic International Press, 1981). *The Tsardom of Muscovy* by the outstanding historian Alexander E. Presniakov (Academic International Press, 1986) is one of the best brief summaries of this era, while his *The Formation of the Great Russian State* (Academic International Press, 1993) is a classic full-length account.

17. Kliuchevsky's views are contained in his *Sochineniia* (Works), Vol. II (Moscow, 1957), pp. 157-199, as part of his lectures, A *Course in Russian History* of which there is still no really good English translation. Fortunately Platonov's *Ivan the Terrible*. Translated by Joseph L. Wieczynski (Academic International Press, 1974) is a good English translation, and has other essays of interest on that subject.

18. Crummey, "Ivan the Terrible" in Samuel Baron and Nancy Heer, eds., *Windows on the Russian Past. Essays on Soviet Historiography since Stalin* (Columbus, 1977), p. 58. This is one of the best discussions of the development of Russian and Soviet historiography on Ivan's reign and explains how each succeeding generation of historians has moved the content and source base of the discussion of Ivan's reign into exciting and ever more sophisticated levels.

19. Some of the books to which Crummey refers include A.A. Zimin, *Oprichnina Ivana Groznogo* (The Oprichnina of Ivan the Terrible) (Moscow, 1964), Zimin, *Reformy Ivan Groznogo* (The Reforms of Ivan the Terrible) (Moscow, 1960), Zimin, *Rossiia na poroge novogo vremeni* (Russia on the Threshold of Modern Times) (Moscow, 1972), N.E. Nosov, *Stanovlenie soslovno-predstavitel'nykh uchrezhdenii v Rossii* (Establishment of Estates-Representative Institutions in Russia) (Leningrad, 1969), R.G. Skrynnikov, *Nachalo oprichniny* (Beginning of the Oprichnina) (Leningrad, 1966), Skrynnikov, *Oprichnyi terror* (The Oprichnina Terror) (Leningrad, 1969), Skrynnikov, *Ivan the Terrible*. Translated and edited by Hugh F. Graham (Academic International Press, 1982).

20. Edward L. Keenan, *The Kurbskii-Groznyi Apocrypha. The Seventeenth Century Genesis of the "Correspondence" Attributed to Prince A.M. Kurbskii and the Tsar Ivan IV* (Harvard, 1971). For a good summation of the debate over Keenan's controversial views, see Charles J. Halperin, "Keenan's Heresy Revisited," *Jahrbücher für Geschichte Osteuropas,* NF 28 (1980), pp. 484-489.

21. George Vernadsky, *Russia at the Dawn of the Modern Age* (Yale, 1959) and *The Tsardom of Muscovy* (Yale, 1969).

22. W. Bruce Lincoln, *The Conquest of a Continent. Siberia and the Russians* (New York, 1994), especially Chapters 5 and 6. Lincoln's account is a narrative synthesizing original documents, chronicles and important secondary works such as G.F. Müller's *Istoriia Sibiri,* 2 vols. (Moscow-Leningrad, 1937). In addition to Lincoln, there are several other sources to consult for information on Yermak, the Stroganovs, and the chronicles in question. See Terence Armstrong, ed., *Yermak's Campaign in Siberia. A Selection of Documents.* Translated by Tatiana Minorsky and David Wileman (London, The Hakluyt Society, 1975), which in addition to a detailed and scholarly introduction includes English versions of the Stroganov, Yesipov, Remezov and New chronicles as well as the Royal charters

and letters relating to the crossing of the Urals. Another collection of documents about Siberia, *Russia's Conquest of Siberia. Three Centuries of Russian Eastward Expansion.* Translated and edited by Basil Dmytryshyn, E.A.P. Crownhart-Vaughan, and Thomas Vaughan (Portland, Oregon, 1985), contains the charters and letters as well as brief excerpts from the Stroganov Chronicle. It also includes a very useful glossary of Russian terms used in the various documents.

23. Skrynnikov, *Sibirskaia ekspeditsiia Ermaka* (The Siberian Expedition of Yermak), 2nd and expanded edition (Novosibirsk, 1986).

CHAPTER I

1. The term voevoda (pl. voevody) is an old Slavic term for military commander. During the Muscovite period the voevoda was either a military commander, or especially during the seventeenth century the governor of a province, an official holding both civil and military power. The Muscovite army in the field was divided into five units called polki (pl.), and at the head of each unit stood a voevoda, sometimes alone or with colleagues. See Sergei G. Pushkarev, compiler and George Vernadsky and Ralph T. Fisher, Jr., eds., *Dictionary of Russian Historical Terms from the Eleventh Century to 1917* (Yale, 1970), p. 176.

2. Soloviev is referring to the defeat of the Crimean Tatars under Devlet-Girey at the hands of a force commanded by Prince Mikhail Ivanovich Vorotynsky in the summer of 1572. Devlet-Girey advanced towards Moscow along the Oka and was met by Muscovite forces who overtook his Tatars some fifty versts from Moscow near Molodi on the banks of the Lopasnia. During late July and early August it became the site of a series of bloody engagements between the Tatars and the Russians, all of which ended as defeats for the khan. Devlet-Girey was forced to flee after his forces suffered heavy losses. See Volume 10 of this series, p. 190.

3. The Jagiellonian dynasty ruled Poland-Lithuania from 1386 to 1574. In 1386 Jagailo, grand prince of Lithuania, married Jadwiga, queen of Poland and last of the Piast dynasty. The marriage which was marked by Jagailo's conversion to Catholicism also brought Lithuania and Poland into a confederation in which the king of Poland also held the Lithuanian lands as its grand prince. Jagailo appointed his cousin Vytautas as *de facto* governor of Lithuania in 1392, thereby preserving its autonomous character. Thus, by the mid-sixteenth century Lithuanian identity remained quite distinct from that of Poland, and the Lithuanian and Polish nobility never assimilated with one another.

4. Here Soloviev is referring to Casimir IV, son of Jagailo (1447-1492).

5. Princess Bona Sforza of Milan married Sigismund I in 1518 at Cracow. Considered a brilliant and innovative consort and then ruler, she was responsible for bringing Renaissance art and culture with her from Italy. Her marriage marks the beginning of the period known as the Golden Age of Polish art and literature. See *Cambridge History of Poland to 1696* (Cambridge, 1950), Volume I. From the Origins to Sobieski (to 1696), passim.

6. The Polish nobility was divided between the great and powerful nobles and the rank-and-file gentry. Collectively the Polish-Lithuanian nobility was called the szlachta. The wealthiest group in the nobility were the magnates, beneath whom there were several classes of nobility who fell into categories defined by the size of their landed properties and number of serfs. The propertied nobility was composed of four classes: magnates, nobles with means (nobles born owners of both land and serfs), noble owners of fragmented properties, tenant nobles and leaseholders. The petty nobility, "without sufficient means," lacking either land or serfs or both was the other major category. This group included noble owners of fragmented properties, tenant nobles and leaseholders, noble small-holders, nobles "behind the wall," the rabble (landless and serfless), and town nobles. According to Davies (p. 206, see also diagram, p. 220), while it is not correct to refer to the entire noble estate as the szlachta, the term is "much used and much abused." "Even among those historians who weigh their words with discrimination, usages and translations differ considerably in accordance with varying criteria. Many modern historians insist on the antithesis of szlachta:magnateria whereby the szlachta becomes the 'mass of the nobility,' as opposed to a 'magnatial oligarchy' distinguished by disproportionate power and wealth. Anglo-Saxon historians beguiled perhaps by the English distinction between 'gentleman' and 'peer,' have tended to concur in this fashion, and szlachta is habitually translated as 'gentry.' However, it is important to stress that the Polish Nobility was not divided into separate legal sub-categories as in England or Germany, and that the term szlachta referred to the whole of the Noble Estate, not just part of it. While the magnates were not entitled to any special privileges, in fact they wielded a huge amount of power, disproportionate to their numbers and even to the amount of land under their control."

7. The Polish gentry or petty nobility were supposed to be largely service nobles holding landed estates obligated to perform military service if needed. In the sixteenth century they had achieved a highly complex structure with far greater distinctions than those of the Russian noble classes. According to Davies (pp. 211-212, 218-221, 228-229), although in practice not all landowners were noble and not all nobles were necessarily landowners, it would be fair to say that the nobility was the landowning class. In 1569 noble land accounted for sixty percent of all the land in Poland, another twenty-five percent belonged to the church and the remaining fifteen percent to the crown. Because increasing amounts of crown land were leased to noblemen, and bishops were also members of the nobility, in effect the percentage of land under noble control was actually even greater. The distribution of land between the great and petty nobility varied from province to province as well as within provinces. The great magnates held the largest amount of land and wielded power greater than their actual numbers. "The average nobleman was fortunate if he possessed two or three properties. Yet if his land was his own, and he had the serfs to work it, he owed his living to no one..." and some historians classify such a noble as a member of the middle nobility accounting for between one-third and two-fifths of the noble estate

as a whole. The most numerous element of all was the "seething mass of petty nobility without means." Some lived on fragments of larger estates which had been broken up for sale or tenancy, sharing the serfs and material resources of the original estates with their neighbors. Another group, noble smallholders, possessed land but no serfs, working their plot themselves. "Economically they were indistinguishable from the peasantry. Some of these... nobles behind the wall... lived in exclusive noble villages, whose perimeter wall protected them from the ignoble world around. But the group which with time became the far most numerous, the... 'rabble,' possessed neither land nor serfs. They worked as tenant farmers, as labourers, as domestics, as soldiers; or else, as... street nobility..., were reduced to eking out a penurious living in the towns." Several provinces were famous for their petty nobility. In Mazowsze more than half the land was owned by the so-called szlachta zagrodowa or noble smallholders, according to a 1571 estimate totalling 32,000 households working 51.5 percent of the arable land of the duchy. Each household made do with a little over sixteen acres on average. "In the Republic as a whole, well over half of the nobility did not possess land." Whereas in other countries the numbers of such landless petty nobility declined, in Poland they continued to multiply. Ultimately, writes Davies, "Numerically speaking, the petty nobility dominated the noble estate, providing both its distinctive colour and the material with which its political and social customs operated... From the sixteenth century onwards, the petty nobleman, incapable of equipping himself, none the less perpetuated the military tradition of his caste by serving either in the professional regiments of the royal army or in the retinues of the magnates." Davies notes that despite the huge economic differences the szlachta was united in protecting its status. The mechanism for this protection was the bicameral Sejm consisting of a Chamber of Envoys and the Senate. From the late fifteenth century onwards the Sejm passed a series of measures establishing that no new laws be introduced without the consent of both chambers, and after 1505 the slogan *Nic o nas bez nas* ("Nothing concerning us without us") remained the basic concept of this "Noble Democracy."

8. The Piast dynasty immediately preceded the Jagiellonians. The last Piast ruler was technically Jadwiga, granddaughter of Casimir III (died 1374). She was actually crowned "king" of Poland in 1386 along with her husband Jagailo.

9. Riurik (died 879) was the Varangian warrior who became the eponymous ancestor of the Rus princely dynasty.

10. Gediminas (reigned 1316-1341) was the ancestor of the Lithuanian grandprincely line.

11. The term used is pospolite ruszenie, a levy in mass similar to the *fyrd* in Anglo-Saxon England or the arrière-ban in medieval France.

12. The term used here is rokosz, denoting a sedition or rebellion.

13. Sigismund Augustus (Zygmunt August) actually ascended the throne twice. In 1529 he was formally elected to the Polish throne at his father's request. He began to rule as grand prince of Lithuania with his father's guidance. At this point Sigismund I was referred to as Sigismund "the Elder" and Sigismund Augustus

was known as "the Young Augustus" in Wilno. In 1548 he became king of Poland at his father's death. Davies (p. 145) describes Sigismund Augustus very differently from Soloviev. "Despite his regal manner and cosmopolitan education, Sigismund II entirely lacked the assertiveness of the typical Renaissance prince. His temper was mild, and in his later years distinctly melancholy. He was nobody's 'wise fool,' but he administered the realm with a grace and ease that bordered on the nonchalant. He was interested in all the progressive movements of the age, from Protestant theology to 'Executionist' politics, and naturally took the part of the lesser men who were battling against the privileges of bishops and magnates. Yet he would have nothing of violence and bias; and refused categorically to be drawn into the religious quarrels of the age."

14. Davies (pp. 145-146) blames many of Sigismund Augustus's problems on the interference of his mother Bona Sforza, whom he characterizes as "resorting to the tactics of a Renaissance harpy." According to Davies's scenario she ruined her son's first marriage in 1545, and actually "poisoned" the unlucky first wife. In 1547 she was offended at his secret marriage to Barbara Radziwiłł, daughter of Mikolaj Radziwiłł "the Red," the Lithuanian hetman. Bona was suspected of poisoning her as well. Sigismund never forgave the Sejm's intrusion into his marriage with Barbara. He actually submitted a detailed matrimonial interrogation to the Sejm, whereupon the Senate told him to arrange a divorce. In his statement to the Senate, Sigismund asserted he could not break his marriage vows without offence to his conscience, and that there were no grounds for divorce. One of the members of the Sejm is quoted as saying "It diminishes us, your majesty, that you should have taken as your wife a woman from such a family, and from a nation [Lithuania] which received its nobility and its Christian faith from us Poles one and a half centuries ago..." The Sejm penalized the king by withholding a year's taxes, then finally relented, and Barbara was crowned. According to Davies, when she died shortly afterwards Sigismund was inconsolable, and his third marriage to Catherine of Austria, a purely political affair, was disastrous. For the last years of his life Sigismund Augustus lived alone and dressed in black.

15. Davies's comments (p. 155) on Sigismund Augustus's death echo those of Soloviev but also contradict some of the details. The king "died on 7 July 1572, surrounded by a motley company of quacks, astrologers, and witches, in a room hung in black in memory of Barbara Radziwiłł.... The last of the Jagiellons, like the last of the Piasts 202 years before, was buried on Wawel hill. The king's private person was dead. His public person rode in effigy to the burial. The royal standard was broken asunder and, with the royal jewels, cast into the grave. The late King had ruled as the hereditary monarch of two separate principalities. He was leaving them united in one elective Republic."

16. Gian Francesco Commendone, bishop of Zacynthos, one of the most skillful papal diplomats of the era, was sent to Poland as the new apostolic nuncio. Commendone was instrumental in acceptance of the decrees of Trent by the king of Poland. *Cambridge History of Poland,* p. 402.

17. Prince Andrei Mikhailovich Kurbsky (1528-1583), one of Ivan IV's prominent boyars and generals, fled to Lithuania in 1564. The lengthy and sometimes acrimonious correspondence between Ivan and Kurbsky constitutes one of the most important sources on the development of the Muscovite monarchy during the mid-sixteenth century. Kurbsky was also the author of a *History of Muscovy*. His writings constitute a major primary source on which Soloviev based his information.

18. See Volume 5 of this series.

19. This refers to the election of Sigismund Augustus as grand prince of Lithuania. See Note 13, above.

20. Nicholas Radziwiłł, known as the "Black," was the most powerful lord in Lithuania during the reign of Sigismund Augustus. Although an eager defender of Lithuanian identity Radziwiłł, a prince of the Holy Roman empire, cooperated with the Poles and his court was an important center of humanistic studies. Radziwiłł was also the most prominent Protestant in Lithuania. In 1565 he published the "Brest Bible" which Davies claims (p. 184) "marked an important milestone in the progress of the Polish vernacular." During the reign of Sigismund Augustus Radziwiłł was chancellor, marshal and commander (wojewode) of Wilno. The king cared little about the religious beliefs of his nobles, and his toleration clearly extended to the Radziwiłł family, whose members enjoyed a very close relationship with the Polish king during this era.

The Radziwiłłs were one of several prominent families who became Calvinists. Davies maintains (pp. 182-183) that in Poland Calvinism attracted support from the "middling sort of nobleman, who was trying to preserve his independence from the patronage of the great families and who resented the wealth and influence of the Bishops. In the Grand Duchy, it attracted the greatest magnates themselves, as a means of bypassing the influence of Catholic and Orthodox clergy." In 1558 the Calvinists challenged the right of the bishops to participate in the Senate. During the following two decades they "constituted one of the most powerful groupings in political life" numbering an estimated twenty percent of the nobility and controlling an absolute majority of the Senate.

21. The term Rus refers to the Orthodox population residing in the Ukraine and Belorussia, areas often called Ruthenia. In the actual text Soloviev uses the word "russki" meaning Russian. During the nineteenth and early twentieth centuries Russian nationalists sought to underline the "Russian" character of these western provinces to justify their demands to limit the powers of the dominant Polish noble landowning class. Thus they referred to these Ruthenian populations as Russian. While it is unclear whether Soloviev used "russki " with such purposes in mind, we have chosen the more accurate form, Rus, when referring to Ruthenian peasants and to the Ruthenian lands.

22. The Union of Lublin of 1569 created a union between Poland and Lithuania that no longer depended on unity by both having one monarch. It meant that the king was elected jointly by the Lithuanian and Polish aristocracy and that the coronation of the king signified the consecration of both his royal title and of

his grand-ducal powers. The Diet henceforward was held jointly combining the Sejm of Poland with that of Lithuania. Warsaw was chosen as the seat of the Diet since it was in Poland, but close to the Lithuanian border. It should be noted that law and administration remained separate in Poland and Lithuania, and even after the Union of Lublin Lithuania preserved its own law code, the Lithuanian Statute of 1566, which remained in effect until the beginning of the nineteenth century. Lithuania also continued to maintain its own administration, separate chancellors, hetmans, and treasurers as well as its own army. The unified state now had a unified foreign policy and acted as one entity in external affairs. See *Cambridge History of Poland,* Volume I, p. 365.

23. Soloviev is referring to the absorption by Muscovy in 1654 of the East Bank Ukraine during the reign of Alexis Mikhailovich.

24. The pro-Protestant attitude of Queen Bona Sforza played a major role in the spread of the new beliefs into Poland and Lithuania. Lutheranism flourished in Danzig and other cities with German populations. In Danzig the crown protected the Lutherans, who received royal promises of toleration first from Sigismund Augustus then from Stephan Bathory. The Gymnazium in Danzig was an important Lutheran intellectual center patronized by Queen Bona. She also encouraged other Protestant sects. For example "[a] number of 'anti-trinitarians' came together in Cracow around 1550 in Protestant discussion groups organized by Queen Bona's Corsican Confessor, Francesco Lismanino. They included Adam Pastor, a Dutchman; George Blandrata, Queen Bona's Piedmontese physician; and Lelio Sozzini, a refugee from Venice and Zurich." See Davies, pp. 179, 185.

25. Mikolaj Radziwiłł "the Red" (1512-1584) was the brother of Sigismund Augustus's second wife Barbara. Serving as grand hetman of the Lithuanian army, he distinguished himself in the wars against Muscovy and in 1566, not 1569 as Soloviev would have it, succeeded his recently deceased cousin Mikolaj "the Black" as the chief Calvinist in Poland-Lithuania. Davies (pp. 216-218) writes that as a Calvinist Mikolaj "the Red" stood aloof from the Catholic establishment and actively opposed the Union of Lublin until the last minute. Davies's book also includes a description of his lavish court as noted by the English ambassador Sir Jerome Horsey, who passed through Lithuania on his way to Moscow.

26. Arianism and Socinianism were heretical Christian movements. Arianism maintained that Christ had only one nature, divine. Socinians, ancestors of present-day Unitarians, denied the Trinity. While these two heretical Christian movements were much older than Protestantism, they along with Anabaptism tended towards less centralized organization, and undermined efforts to organize the Protestants, who were primarily Calvinists, into a unified opposition. While not as popular as Calvinism, there were numbers of Polish-Lithuanian nobles who were attracted to Arianism and Socinianism. According to Davies (pp. 184-185), by 1569-1570 the sectarians whose ranks also included Anti-trinitarians, Unitarians, Polish Brethren, Racovians, Pinchovians, Samosatenians, Farnovians, Sabellians, Budneans, Theists, Ditheists, and Tritheists in addition to the Arians

and Socinians, had seceded from mainstream Calvinism. In 1569-1570 they refused to participate in the Compromise of Sandomierz and in the united Protestant front against the Counter-Reformation. Soloviev is probably referring to these splits in the Protestant community.

27. According to the *Cambridge History of Poland* (p. 342) Uchanski, as primate of Poland, was a strong advocate of a national church and willing to negotiate with Protestants to achieve this end. Such willingness ran counter to the spirit of Catholic reform.

28. Stanislaw Hozjusz (1504-1579), bishop of Warmia, as Cardinal Hosius later was president of the Council of Trent. Throughout his long and distinguished career Hosius served Polish interests as clergyman and diplomat, apparently a common activity for high-ranking Polish clerics. Hosius was one of the first Polish clerics to spread the ideas of the Council of Trent even while bishop of Warmia in 1551. Later, after being named cardinal, he presided over the Council and became closely associated with what came to be called the "Tridentine spirit."

29. According to Davies (p. 167) the Catholic Reformation in Poland was rarely violent. Following the advice of Hosius, the Society of Jesus began its activities in Poland in 1565, opening their first college in Braunsberg, followed by colleges at Pultusk (1566), Wilno (1569) and Poznan in 1573. In the East they opened colleges at Polotsk, Dorpat, Orsha, Kiev, Pereiaslav and Vitebsk.

30. In contrast to Soloviev's version of a very strong Catholic effort in Poland, Davies (p. 166) asserts that the Catholic counter-reform in the last decades of the sixteenth century was cautious, and even moderate in character. He points out that the Roman church never enjoyed a monopoly in Poland-Lithuania and, in addition to lingering remnants of pagan belief in parts of Poland and even more so in Lithuania, Judaism had a longer history in Poland than Christianity. The eastern lands were strongly inhabited by Orthodox populations and during the Reformation important congregations of Calvinists, Lutherans and other Protestant sects abounded. "In the united Republic between 1569 and the First Partition of 1772, the Roman Catholics formed the largest single religious group, but accounted for barely half of the total population."

31. Sierotka in Polish.

32. One of them, Jerzy Radziwiłł, became the bishop of Cracow and a cardinal.

33. Davies (p. 177) comments that in Lithuania, among some of the strongest magnate families, the adoption of Protestantism was an intermediary step in the movement from Orthodoxy to Catholicism. This became increasingly the case in seventeenth-century Ruthenia, but during the sixteenth century important signals in this process were evident, and probably played a role in the phenomenon Soloviev recounts here. According to Davies, the fragmentation of the Orthodox church was reflected in the lives of the leading families in Lithuania, many of whom ceased to hold any fixed religious loyalty. He cites the example of Prince Konstanty Ostrogski, who himself was married to a Catholic. His heir Prince

Janusz was a Catholic, two of whose three sons were also Catholic and one Orthodox. One of Prince Janusz's daughters married Krzystof "Thunderbolt" Radziwiłł, the Calvinist hetman of Lithuania, and the other married Jan Kiszka, the richest Arian in the grand principality. "The senior lines of the Radziwiłł, Chodkiewicz, Sapieha, Pac and Wisniowiecki all turned Protestant. The Sanguszko, Czartoryski, Czetwerynski and Oginski passed from Orthodoxy to Catholicism. In the history of many Orthodox families, the adoption of Calvinism in the sixteenth century acted as a stepping stone to their Catholic conversion in the seventeenth."

34. Maximilian II, Holy Roman emperor, 1564-1576.

35. Jagailo (1351-1434) became grand prince of Lithuania in 1377. According to Davies (pp. 116-117) he had no special love for his neighboring Poles "who to his pagan mind were servants of the 'German God.'" Yet because he was surrounded by two Catholic powers, the Poles on one side and on the other the Teutonic Order, chartered by the Pope to convert forcibly whomever it conquered, Jagailo knew that Christianity was inevitable. "Thus he was driven towards Poland by the coldest and most calculated reasons of state.... A conjugal and political union was proposed. It was a decisive moment in the history of two nations." The Poles viewed the Lithuanian connection as superior to their choices of Habsburg or Angevin rule. The Poles received some important concessions from Jagailo. "In return for the hand of Jadwiga, the Lithuanian prince was ready to accept Christian baptism, to convert all his pagan subjects to Roman Catholicism, to release all Polish prisoners and slaves in his possession, to coordinate operations against the Teutonic Knights, and to associate the Grand Duchy of Lithuania with the Kingdom of Poland in a permanent union. On this basis, in February 1386 a great assembly of Polish barons and nobility at Lublin elected Jogailo, whom they knew as 'Jagiello,' as their king."

36. Davies claims (p. 154) that Ivan's punishment of Novgorod in 1570 was linked to his knowledge of the Union of Lublin of 1569. "In Muscovy, Ivan IV was angered by news of the Union of Lublin and hastened to the crime which more than anything else earned him the name of 'Terrible.' Forged letters were produced to show that the Archbishop and Governor of Novgorod were guilty of treasonable contacts with the Polish King. The Tsar arrived to administer the punishment in person. The inhabitants of Novgorod were systematically seized and tortured, and killed in batches of five hundred and a thousand every day. In five weeks, Russia's most civilized city was depopulated, and reduced to a smouldering heap. Ivan returned to Moscow to prepare the cauldrons of boiling oil and meat hooks which were to chastise some hundreds of Muscovites suspected of treasonable contacts with Novgorod. What future for the 'Republic of goodwill' with such a neighbour?" Soloviev attributes Ivan's vicious attack on Novgorod to the discovery of a document hidden in the Holy Wisdom cathedral in Novgorod offering to surrender the city to the Polish king. The signatures of Archbishop Pimen and other leading citizens appeared genuine, but others maintained it was the forgery of a disgruntled vagrant named Peter of Volhynia who had been

punished in Novgorod. Soloviev also places it in the context of Ivan's execution of his rival, his cousin Prince Vladimir Andreevich of Staritsa in 1569. In January 1570 Ivan's armies arrived in Novgorod. Soloviev describes the events there in great detail, explaining the mechanisms by which the population was massacred during the six-week occupation of the city. Ivan then ordered his men to ransack Pskov. Upon returning to Moscow Ivan began an investigation of the events in Novgorod and Pskov, accusing his prisoners of desiring to turn the cities over to the "Lithuanian king" and placing Prince Vladimir Andreevich on the throne. The details have not survived, but several important boyars were executed, including some of Ivan's leading favorites. Archbishop Pimen was banished. See Volume 10, pp. 129-133.

37. Maliuta Skuratov was one of Ivan's closest associates in the oprichnina or crown estates (see Note 41, below) and among the most hated. In Russian folklore he personifies the excesses of Ivan's reign. Grigory Lukianovich Maliuta Skuratov Belsky apparently was a member of the lesser provincial aristocracy who joined the oprichnina when Ivan first created it. As one of Ivan's closest henchmen he was associated with the most dastardly deeds of the oprichnina, including the murder of Metropolitan Philip. (See Chapter IV, Note 40) Maliuta Skuratov not only married into Ivan's family, a sign of his high standing, one of his daughters became the wife of Boris Godunov. Maliuta was killed in 1573 during the Livonian War, storming the fortress of Weissenstein. In Russian folklore Maliuta Skuratov is remembered as the epitome of evildoers of the oprichnina. See Volume 10, pp. 128, 216.

38. Ivan is referring to Devlet-Girey's raid on Moscow in 1571. See Volume 10, pp. 186-187.

39. Here Ivan is referring to the untimely death of his beloved first wife, Anastasia Yurievna-Zakharina, later known as Romanovna, in August 1560, who he claimed was poisoned through a conspiracy of boyars, among whom he included Kurbsky. See Volume 10, pp. 100-105 for Ivan's accusations against Kurbsky.

40. The Lithuanian clerk Michal Haraburda was an envoy on prior occasions. In 1563 he accompanied the border official Jerzy Chodkiewicz to negotiate with Ivan. Chodkiewicz asked that Haraburda speak for him in his negotiations with Ivan because Haraburda's Russian was so much better than his. See Volume 10, p. 153.

41. "Crown estates" is the translation of oprichnina, a possession or property set apart. Derived from the term oprich', meaning to set apart, it referred to Ivan's claiming certain lands throughout Muscovy for his own private appanage, or crown estates. The remaining lands were termed zemshchina, land held by other landowners. Though technically a reference to specific landholdings, oprichnina came to mean not the just crown domains but the whole system of terror associated with the reign of Ivan. During the Livonian War, soon after the departure of Andrei Kurbsky in 1564, fearing the boyars' treason and having decided to exterminate every vestige of treason and traitors, Ivan established early in 1565 a special crown institution called the oprichnina. After establishing a special corps

of enforcers called oprichniki he introduced administrative reform, creating a state within a state, which he governed directly as his own appanage. The main seat of the oprichnina was Alexandrov village some sixty miles northeast of Moscow. Ivan confiscated the allodial estates of the nobles who lived in the areas under his direct control and granted estates to service gentry. Those boyars who survived the terror of the oprichnina received lands in other parts of Muscovy. The oprichnina abated after 1572 when Ivan disbanded the oprichniki and some boyar families actually had their confiscated lands returned to them. During this period perished many thousands of people, nobles, clerics, as well as commoners, city dwellers and peasants alike. See Pushkarev, p. 76. For Soloviev's discussion of the oprichnina, See Volume 10, Chapter III.

42. Here Ivan uses the word gospodar, the word that the Lithuanians used in referring to their grand prince.

43. Curiously Ivan uses here the word korolevstvo (kingdom) rather than tsarstvo (tsardom) when referring to Muscovy, perhaps out of courtesy.

44. These are Soloviev's parentheses as are all the parentheses in this volume. Here he is referring to the actual members of Ivan's oprichnina entourage, often called oprichniki in Russian.

45. During the sixteenth century France and the Ottoman empire shared a common enemy, the Holy Roman empire. Throughout the period and into the seventeenth century much of France's foreign policy was designed to avoid encirclement by the Habsburgs. During the seventeenth century French intervention in the Thirty Years War was predicated on this very principle. Since France sought to remain independent of the papacy it virtually ignored the Council of Trent, and regarded the Habsburgs as its natural enemies. It saw no problem in concluding alliances with the Ottoman Turks, to whom the Habsburgs presented an ongoing threat. From 1521 to 1559 France fought four major wars against the Habsburgs over disputed territories in Italy. At the same time the Turks actually overran Hungary and continued to threaten other parts of Habsburg-controlled Eastern Europe. Historians argue that Charles V's preoccupation with his Ottoman and Valois enemies greatly assisted the growth of Protestantism in Germany. He could neither afford to alienate the German princes, nor deal effectively with the growth of Lutheranism and then Calvinism.

46. The term okol'nichie (pl.) is translated here as "lord-in-waiting." According to Pushkarev (p. 74) the term refers to a court rank from the beginning of the fourteenth century. At first the term signified the men "around" the tsar, courtiers in his immediate entourage. In the sixteenth and seventeenth centuries the okol'nichie formed a high rank of the Muscovite serving aristocracy immediately below the boyars. They were members of the boyar council and served as military commanders, ambassadors, judges and administrators.

47. The term "crown secretary" is the translation of d'iak. These men were the mainspring of the Moscow bureaucratic apparatus in the fifteenth to seventeenth centuries. They were assistants or associates to the boyar council and other central government departments, and sometimes themselves were department heads.

They played a very important role in the Muscovite administrative, judicial and financial institutions. See Pushkarev, p. 12.

48. Here Ivan's men are using gospodar', the Lithuanian term for supreme ruler.

49. Archduke Ernst of Austria (died 1595) was one of Holy Roman Emperor Maximilian II's five sons. Although many Poles regarded the Habsburgs as potential enemies, there was still a substantial group supporting a Habsburg candidacy for the throne. Eventually Ernst served briefly and unsuccessfully as governor-general of the Netherlands during the revolt against the Habsburgs by the Dutch house of Orange. He ruled in Vienna as duke of Upper and Lower Austria until his death.

50. Jean de Montluc, bishop of Valence, was the French ambassador who proclaimed Henri's virtues.

51. The Polish name of Henri of Anjou was Henryk Walezy. In actuality he was Henri Valois, duc d'Anjou, who later became King Henri III of France. Soloviev used his ducal title as a name, whereas the Poles tended to refer to him by his family name.

52. Davies (pp. 151-152) describes Jan Zamoyski (1542-1605) as a Renaissance giant. Although Zamoyski concerned himself primarily with politics, serving as Poland's chancellor and hetman, he was a major intellectual figure at the court of King Sigismund Augustus. A graduate of the universities of Cracow and Padua, where he later served as rector, Zamoyski reconstructed his native Zamosc as a model city of the age. The intellectual center of the city was concentrated round its "academy" the famous *Hippeum*, which briefly constituted one of the most important seats of learning in Eastern Europe. "In his private microcosm, Zamoyski successfully organized the Renaissance life-style and encouraged the virtues in which the world at large were beyond his grasp."

53. Davies (p. 414) notes that the actual election was carried out in May 1573 in speed and harmony with forty thousand noble electors participating! The election was held on the Wola field outside of Cracow to accommodate the huge number of nobles eligible to participate. Despite the huge numbers, there was no major disturbance.

54. According to the *Cambridge History of Poland* (pp. 372-373), Grand Marshal Firlej refused to proclaim Henri king until Montluc officially signed the Confederation of Warsaw, the Henrician Articles, and the Pacta Conventa which safeguarded the Polish constitution and limited the powers of the "foreign king." The Henrician Articles then became obligatory for all elected kings of Poland. They were for the most part a written summary and re-affirmation of all privileges and rights acquired by the lesser nobility (the szlachta) since the Pact of Kassa of 1374. They provided for calling a Sejm every two years, prevented the king from naming his successor or marrying without consent, restricted his authority over the levée en masse, limited his power over legislation, and bound him to accept a permanent council of sixteen senators who, in relays of four every six months, resided at court and advised the king. To safeguard the principle of toleration the Confederation of Warsaw of 1573 was included in the Henrician Articles, together

with the general rule of 1501 known as the de non praestanda oboedientia, which released the king's subjects from their oath of obedience should he fail to carry out any part of the contractual agreement. Besides the Henrician Articles the lesser nobility also formulated the Pacta Conventa, special conditions just for Henri. He was required to conclude a political alliance with France and to supplement it with a liberal trade agreement. At his own expense he was to build a fleet in the Baltic, close navigation to Russia through the port of Narva, and ensure dominion of the Baltic Sea. In addition he was to pay the debts of Sigismund Augustus, replenish the treasury, provide for the education of a hundred noblemen in France, and subsidize foreign scholars in Poland. According to Davies (p. 335) the term pacta conventa also could refer to special articles drawn up in 1576 at the time of the election of Stefan Bathory. Since these particular articles were employed only one time, it became common to refer to the Henrician Articles of 1573 as the pacta conventa, and the two terms became virtually synonymous.

55. In August of 1572 Catherine de Medici conspired with Catholic forces to entice the rival Huguenots to Paris to celebrate the marriage between her daughter Marguerite and Henri of Navarre. On the eve of St. Bartholomew's Day thousands of Calvinists were slaughtered throughout France, although Henri of Navarre escaped to rally Huguenot forces against Catherine and her sons, extending the civil wars for at least another two decades. The massacre became the most notorious event in the French religious wars of the sixteenth century, and associated the Valois dynasty directly with pro-Catholic, anti-Huguenot sentiment in a highly partisan manner with which it had not been associated in the struggle heretofore. Because it involved the murder of members of the French nobility, the notoriety of this episode frightened aristocrats throughout Europe regardless of their religious beliefs.

56. For a description of the Paris festivities, see Davies, p. 413.

57. Davies (pp. 414-415) describes the events dramatically. At Henri's coronation on February 21 the king had taken communion and sworn the oath when Firlej came forward with his hat firmly on his head. The Protestant leader was dissatisfied with the wording of the oath and insisted that Henri swear specifically to the terms of the Confederation of Warsaw voted by the Sejm in January 1573. This stipulated complete freedom of conscience and religious toleration as a cardinal principle of public life. He said "You shall swear or you shall not reign." Firlej had no intention of allowing a Polish St. Bartholomew's. Henri replied "I shall take care to uphold it." The bishop of Kujawy, Adam Konarski, then proclaimed "Our laws are saved," to which Henri rejoined "Your laws are saved."

58. The Zborowski family were the most important supporters of the French party. There were five brothers of whom Andrzej and Jan, castellan of Gniezno, were Catholics. Piotr, Krzystof and Samuel were Calvinists. According to Davies (p. 415) the Zborowskis were "flushed with success" at Henri's coronation, and at the tourney held in the king's honor their arrogance provoked a murder that shadowed the king's reign. The youngest Zborowski brother, Samuel, had thrown down the gauntlet seeking a challenge from someone of substance. No one accepted other

than a common soldier in the service of the Teczynski family. Zborowski was mortally insulted and in front of the Castle Gate at Wawel, in full view of the king, attempted to assault Teczynski. When he struck with his mace he missed his target, hitting a courtier who tried to keep them apart, killing the man. The penalty for murder committed during a session of the Sejm was death. Although the slain courtier's widow and his family demanded the full penalty, the Zborowskis pleaded for leniency. Henri compromised and sentenced Zborowski to perpetual banishment, a sentence too harsh for the Zborowskis and too lenient for the nobility as a whole. For more details see Davies, pp. 416-420.

59. The description Davies (pp. 416-417) gives of Henri's kingship differs somewhat from Soloviev's in that it appears that Henri knew more Latin than Soloviev would have his readers believe. Davies reports that the Sejm could not be ruled, that its sessions were quarrelsome to say the least. Henri threatened a hunger strike unless agreement was reached, while the opposition continued to press for more explicit guarantees under the Confederation of Warsaw. Moreover there were promises that Henri would marry Anna Jagiellonka, the last of the dynasty, a spinster twenty-six years Henri's senior. He had no intention of marrying her inasmuch as the prospect of a childless marriage was totally inappropriate for the twenty-two-year-old king. According to Zamoyski, Henri also was disappointed at the poverty of the Polish countryside. He disliked the Italian furnishings of the royal castle, and was bored by the constant Senate debates which he could not follow either in Polish or Latin. He was affronted by the argumentative behavior of the senators and deputies, and disliked the Poles' drinking habits as well. Davies adds that he missed his beloved Marie de Cleves. To escape he took to pills and potions, and diplomatic absences from the Senate and court by spending time at the royal hunting lodge at Niepolomice. Finally he was extremely worried by the ill health of his brother King Charles IX of France.

60. For a dramatic description of Henri's secret departure, see Davies, pp. 417-418. Davies tells us that Henri acted as if he was unsure of what to do after receiving word of his brother's death. In reality he was preparing for a surreptitious departure fearing that if he tried to leave for France openly the Poles would delay him. Late on a Saturday night after the Wawel Castle was locked and bolted, with the help of his trusted French advisors, Henri escaped on foot through Cracow's Jewish Quarter dressed in "nondescript riding clothes" and walking across the Vistula bridge where horses were waiting. Unfortunately Henri was recognized and once his absence was confirmed two hundred horsemen and a troop of Tatar archers followed him towards the frontier in what must have been an hectic chase. Because of delays and disorganization Henri was able to keep ahead of his pursuers and crossed the frontier bridge at Harmeze near Oswiecim (Auschwitz). "As he crossed the old dilapidated bridge, his last glimpse of his Polish kingdom was of the loyal Starosta of Oswiecim manfully swimming towards him in the middle of the Vistula and shouting at the top of his voice: 'Serenissima Maiestas, *cur fugis*?' (Serene Majesty, why do you flee?)" (p. 418).

61. According to Davies (p. 420) the Valois candidacy was flawed from the beginning because it was next to impossible for a young man whose sole experience

with ruling was at an absolutist court consumed with sectarian warfare to assume control over a country with a new constitution. Moreover since there was no expectation that Charles IX would die so soon, Henri was expected to remain in Poland for the rest of his life and establish a new Valois line. Actually Henri never relinquished his claim to the title of king of Poland. It remained part of his title to the end of his life although he never renewed the Polish alliance and never returned to Poland. His reign as king of France was clouded by ongoing sectarian and civil war. He met his death at the end of a knife, wielded by the Dominican monk Jacques Coeur in August 1589, after a reign during which he murdered his principal Catholic rivals including Duke Henri and Henri Cardinal de Guise.

62. See Note 31, above.

63. The text uses the Russian expression "cherez pen' koladu valit" which literally means to cut a log through its stump. In other words, doing something in your peculiar way even if it is harder.

64. Maximilian II, the Habsburg Holy Roman emperor (1564-1576), had a reputation for tolerance of Protestants and sought good relations with Protestant nobles in Habsburg lands. It is likely that his reputation was an important factor in influencing at least some of the magnates in Maximilian's favor. See Robert A. Kann, *A History of the Habsburg Empire, 1526-1918* (Berkeley, 1974), pp. 40-41.

65. Archduke Ferdinand, born 1529, ruler of the Tyrol in 1564-1595, was brother of Emperor Maximilian II. He was a strong advocate of the Counter-Reformation and was regarded as one of the most experienced Habsburg rulers, especially when compared to his ineffectual nephew Rudolph, who succeeded Maximilian in 1576 and ruled as Rudolph II until 1612.

66. King John III Vasa (born 1537, reigned 1568-1592) married Katarzyna, sister of Sigismund Augustus. John was the son of Gustav Vasa, king of Sweden, who separated Sweden from Denmark in 1530. As one of four sons of the Swedish king he was originally duke of Finland, as well as a scholar and theologian. In 1568 he succeeded to the Swedish throne after his brother Erik XIV, a "homicidal maniac," was deposed. John's queen Katarzyna Jagiellonka was a fervent Catholic. At her instigation John introduced a new ecumenical liturgy, commonly known as the "Red Book," blending elements from Tridentine Catholic and Swedish Lutheran models, into nominally Protestant Sweden in 1576. He was received secretly into the Roman faith by Antonio Possevino in 1578. It was to his advantage to exploit his Polish contacts, and while he was unsuccessful in two Polish elections, in 1573 and 1575, in 1587 he engineered the election of his son and heir Sigismund to the Polish throne. Although the Vasa dynasty failed to hold the Swedish crown, they remained kings of Poland until 1668. See Davies, pp. 434-435.

67. Bathory, king of Poland 1576-1586, was elected prince of Transylvania (Sedmigrad) in 1571 by the anti-Habsburg national party and he became a national hero. Even his enemies acknowledged his administrative ability and his unusual diplomatic skills which avoided the absorption of the Transylvanian buffer state by either Austria or Turkey. Bathory was born in 1534, the youngest son of the palatine of Transylvania. He received a fine education, studying in Padua, touring

Western Europe and serving at the imperial court in Vienna. While he was a most fervent Catholic, he made his career resisting the Holy Roman empire. In 1575, with Turkish support, Bathory decisively crushed his rival the imperial candidate Gaspar Bekes. Bathory made himself a thorn in Austria's side because he did not limit himself to the administration of Transylvania. He attempted to extend his activities to Hungary in an effort to seize the Hungarian crown from the Holy Roman emperor. Bathory's possession of the Polish crown could only increase his chances of success against the Austrians. See *Cambridge History of Poland*, p. 377, and Davies, p. 422.

68. The sponsor of Alfonso d'Este, duke of Ferrara, was no less than a Jewish physician, Dr. Solomon Askenazi of Constantinople. Davies (p. 421) cites this curious event as an example of how far-flung were the various candidates for the Polish throne.

69. In Latin, pro posse.

70. Ivan III, grand prince of Moscow, 1462-1505.

71. Vasily III, grand prince of Moscow, 1505-1533.

72. Henri of Navarre, leader of the Huguenots, became King Henri IV of France in 1588, ruling until 1610 as founder of the Bourbon dynasty which lasted until the French Revolution. In order to claim his throne Henri became a Catholic. Nevertheless he did not forget the Huguenot cause, and in 1598 he issued the Edict of Nantes, which granted limited toleration to Protestants in France.

73. This must be one of the more ironic statements in this entire book. How peculiar that a monarch who had just killed thousands in Novgorod and Pskov expressed grief over a massacre perpetrated in much the same character by a ruler who sought to protect the throne from competing forces. Such are the niceties of diplomacy.

74. The word used in the text is efimki, the Russian word for Joachimsthalers, large silver coins minted in Joachimsthal (Jachymov) in Bohemia and frequently used in other European countries. According to Pushkarev (p. 18) "Joachimsthalers were used in 16th and 17th century Muscovy in the absence of Russian silver coins of large denomination. In the 17th century, efimki were worth approximately 50 kopeks."

75. Hans Kobenzl (dates unknown) is also known in historical sources as Johann or Jan, and the surname is sometimes spelled "Kobentzl." This envoy of the Holy Roman empire was the author of an *Epistle Concerning his Embassy to the Muscovites* in January 1575. By March Kobenzl was back in Vienna, where he at once set about composing the *Epistle*, which he completed in May of that year. Couched in general terms, the work from the diplomatic point of view contains little more than reaffirmation of Ivan's wish to remain on good terms with Emperor Maximilian II. The secret negotiations with respect to the Polish crown are not mentioned. The textual history of the *Epistle* remains obscure. Since Kobenzl served as vice-chancellor to Archduke Karl in Styria it has been thought that he knew Slovenian or Croatian and wrote the *Epistle* in one of those languages. On his own showing, Kobenzl was not familiar with Slavic languages and thus, since he was a diplomat, he probably wrote in Latin. The *Epistle* is clearly

a controversial work since it tends to magnify the power and size of the Muscovite armies. Hugh Graham suggests that it may or may not have been edited in the Holy Roman empire's chancellery to magnify the Muscovite forces for diplomatic purposes. See MERSH, Volume 17, pp. 83-86.

76. Daniel Prinz of Buchow (1546-1608) was ambassador of the Holy Roman empire to Moscow in 1576. He also conducted negotiations concerning the throne of Poland, Livonia and the war with Turkey. His account of Muscovy is called *Moscoviae ortus et prograssus* (The Rise and Development of Muscovy) (Neisse [Silesia], 1668), in the third chapter of which he describes his 1575 mission to Moscow. His book was translated into Russian by I.A. Tikhomirov and appeared as "Nachalo i vozvyshenie Moskvy," *Chteniia v Imperatorskom Obshchestve Istorii i Drevnostei Rossiiskikh pri Moskovskom Universitete* (Readings at the Imperial Society for Russian History and Antiquities at Moscow University) III, No. 4 (1876), pp, i-iii, 1-46, and IV, No. 4 (1876), pp. 47-74. See MERSH, Volume 8, p. 171.

77. Soloviev uses the Russian term udel'nyi kniaz', meaning "appanage prince" here. Pushkarev (p. 167) defines an udel as the portion of an ancestor's property inherited by one person as a result of the division of property among the ancestor's various heirs. The term was applied to princely holdings in the thirteenth to sixteenth centuries. Over the centuries, division of princely possessions turned some of the udely (pl.) into small districts where the prince was really more of a landlord than a political ruler. By the sixteenth century the process of centralization under Muscovite rule virtually eliminated the appanage regime and the princely title tended to connote a relatively minor position within Muscovy. In contrast the Holy Roman empire used the term "territorial princes" to distinguish them from "ecclesiastical princes" when defining the origin of the rulers of the various domains under nominal control of the Holy Roman emperor. As specified by the Golden Bull of 1356 there were seven "electors" whose task it was to choose the Holy Roman emperor. Three ecclesiastical princes, the archbishops of Mainz, Cologne and Trier, and four laymen, territorial princes, the count palatine of the Rhine, the duke of Saxony, the margrave of Brandenburg and the king of Bohemia constituted the original seven. In the course of the seventeenth century Bavaria and Hanover became electorates as well. Thus in the Habsburg context a territorial prince was an autonomous ruler nominally subject to the Holy Roman empire who could be an individual of substantial political and economic power, as opposed to the appanage princes of Russia, whose powers and positions had diminished greatly by the end of the sixteenth century.

78. Ivan is referring to the fate of Ladislas of Hungary who was also King Wladyslaw III of Poland (Wladyslaw Warnenczyk) who was slain at the battle of Varna in 1444 in the course of a crusade for which much of the help promised from the West failed to materialize. A similar fate befell Louis II of Hungary at the battle of Mohacs in 1526, which enabled the Habsburg Ferdinand I, then king of the Romans, to claim Hungary and Bohemia in the right of his wife who was the heiress of the slain king.

79. Concerning Magnus as Ivan's vassal "king" of Livonia, see Volume 10, pp. 165-167, 171-172.

80. The pejorative term Liakhi is used here.

81. Erik XIV, king of Sweden, was the eldest of Gustav Vasa's sons. According to some versions he was a homicidal maniac, and was deposed in favor of his brother John III Vasa in 1568. See Scott, pp. 142-143. When commenting on this event there are historians who point out that Ivan naturally would have had great sympathy for Erik's plight whatever his character. Some attribute Ivan's violent repression of Novgorod in 1570 as related to his fear of a noble revolt against his rule similar to Sweden's. Erik as king was interested in expanding Swedish control over the Baltic trade routes into Russia. According to Michael Roberts, Erik wanted to secure the monopoly of trade between Muscovy and the West. Noting that Russian timber and hemp built the fleet that defeated the Armada and Polish and Lithuanian grain supplemented grain deficiencies in Western Europe, Roberts claims the Swedish aim was to supplant the Hanseatic League. Erik was willing to make concessions to Ivan to achieve this aim. Roberts, *The Swedish Imperial Experience, 1560-1718* (Cambridge, 1979), pp. 27-29.

82. Erik became king in 1560 at the death of his father Gustav Vasa. At first Erik's relations with John, the eldest of his three brothers, were good. Erik, subsequently, feared that his brother might have designs on his throne and viewed John's marriage in 1562 to Katarzyna Jagiellonka as an unwarranted assertion of independence. John also made a loan to Sigismund Augustus, receiving a small principality in Livonia in exchange. Erik therefore threw them both into prison, where they languished for almost seven years. An aggressive imperialist seeking to control the Swedish side of the Gulf of Finland, Erik roused the antagonism of his neighbors by his restrictive trade policies, and in 1563 he found himself at war with Denmark, Poland and Lübeck. To avoid war with Russia as well Erik bowed to Russian demands, including what Scott calls the "barbaric demand" that John's wife, the Polish princess Katarzyna, be turned over to Ivan. The Swedes procrastinated in complying with this demand, finally using the excuse of Erik's insanity to avoid handing her over to Ivan. Scott, p. 150.

83. In 1558 King Gustav Vasa of Sweden sued for peace with Ivan IV after the fruitless siege of Oreshek. At the same time Moscow suspended its equally futile siege of Narva. The subsequent truce between the two rulers ended their warfare temporarily. Despite the truce the Swedes continued to be suspicious of Russian activities in Livonia, Gustav Vasa raising Swedish concerns about Russian power to new heights. See Volume 10, p. 56.

84. Gustav I Eriksson Vasa, born 1496, king of Sweden, 1523-1560, came to the Swedish throne after the expulsion of the Danes and restoration of an independent Sweden. Considered a reforming monarch, Gustav Vasa broke with Rome and formally established the Swedish Lutheran church and hierarchy, which helps explain the pro-Catholic peasant rebellions that rocked Sweden in the sixteenth century.

85. A knotty point in Russo-Swedish relations was that Moscow insisted on communications being channelled through the Novgorod authorities, declining to enter into direct relations with the Swedish kingdom.

86. Yaroslav "the Wise," in baptism "Georgii," son of Vladimir I who converted Rus to Orthodox Christianity, ruled Kiev from 1036 until his death in 1054. Yaroslav succeeded to the grand princely throne after two decades of civil war during which according to Simon Franklin and Jonathan Shepard "Vladimir's numerous children, aided by recruits from neighbouring and distant lands, set at each other's throats. Iaroslav re-established a semblance of his father's authority only after all of his eleven known brothers had either died, or been murdered, or been incarcerated." (p. 183) Heavily influenced by Byzantine culture, Yaroslav was responsible for extensive construction in Kiev including St. Sophia church. At his death Yaroslav divided his realm among his five surviving sons and one grandson, his eldest son Iziaslav inheriting Kiev. Florinsky tells us that Soloviev took the view that the testament of Yaroslav was the starting point for the mode of succession among the princes "to be determined by their lineage and their respective positions among Yaroslav's descendants. The rotations of the members of the dynasty, who in turn occupied the various princely seats, embodied, according to this theory, the idea of the indivisible right of Yaroslav's descendants to rule Russia." (p. 25) See Simon Franklin and Jonathan Shepard, *The Emergence of Rus, 750-1200* (New York, 1996) and Michael T. Florinsky, *Russia. A History and Interpretation*, Vol. I (New York, 1966), pp. 24-25.

87. The word used here is nemtsy, literally "Germans" but frequently applied to foreigners in general, especially those of Northern European origin.

88. The phrase the Soloviev presents in italics is "bil chelom" which we translate as petitioned. It literally means to bow so low from one's knees as to touch one's head to the ground, which was the manner in which the tsar's subjects bowed before him. Such a bow could be described as groveling.

89. Magnus originally was betrothed to Yefvimia, daughter of Prince Vladimir Andreevich of Staritsa, but she died and Magnus married her sister Maria instead, in 1571. See Volume 10, p. 172.

90. On Taube and Kruse, see Volume 10, Chapter IV, Note 17.

91. See Note 46, above.

92. Danzig backed the Habsburg candidate as part of a larger effort to assert its independence of Poland. In September 1576 Bathory put Danzig under a ban and commercial blockade. It continued to resist, and the Danzigers attacked and burned the abbey of Oliwa. In April 1577 Bathory's armies attacked Danzig with force, defeating its army in the field. Failing actually to take the city, Bathory signed the Treaty of Malbork with Danzig, withdrawing the hated terms Poland imposed on it in 1570, in exchange for a large indemnity and agreement to pursue further negotiations in regard to the city's status. See Davies, p. 425.

93. Rogvolod Borisovich was prince of Polotsk from 1144. After he assumed the throne there were severe struggles and he was exiled in 1151 to Minsk. In 1158 he returned to Polotsk with the help of the prince of Slutsk. Finally, in 1161 he was defeated by Vsevolod Glebovich and ended up in Drutsk. There are no other chronicle mentions of Rogvolod after 1161. See Volume 2 of this series.

94. This passage as well as others about Bathory and the Vasa dynasty of Sweden indicate the degree to which Ivan was concerned about the lineage of his fellow monarchs. Clearly, Bathory's worthiness to rule was based on his lineage

not his capabilities as a general. Ivan seeks to insult the Poles by suggesting that they elected an inappropriate king for reasons of generalship rather than family background.

95. According to Davies (p. 423) the Crimean Tatars attacked Ruthenia in October 1575 with a horde of over one hundred thousand men. They returned with their numbers doubled as a result of their capture of tens of thousands of prisoners, including 35,340 noblemen who were carried off to the Crimea.

96. In 1568 the Poles under Hetman Jan Chodkiewicz besieged the Muscovite fortress of Ulla for three weeks, finally lifting the siege because of strong Muscovite resistance. See Volume 10, p. 161.

97. The Muscovite armies of Ivan IV were defeated by the Poles led by Hetman Mikolaj Radziwill "the Red" in 1564, a year after their great victory at Polotsk. The battle is often called the "second Orsha." It was at the battle of Ulla that the commander Prince Peter Shuisky was killed, and it was shortly thereafter that Kurbsky defected to Lithuania. See Volume 10, pp. 154-156.

98. The battle at Orsha in 1514 stopped the Muscovite armies of Vasily III in their attempt to conquer Lithuania. Soloviev contends that the Muscovite losses were the consequence of lack of technological parity between Moscow and its western neighbors. Just prior to the defeat at Orsha the Muscovites succeeded in capturing Smolensk, albeit on the third try.

99. The term stol'nik here translated as "table attendant" originally referred to a court office where the stol'nik served the sovereign and his guests at table (stol means "table" in Russian). In Muscovy the court service of these officials was incidental to their main occupation. The stol'niki (pl.) were a rather high-ranking and numerous group of the tsar's servicemen, ranking immediately after the members of the boyar council. Some estimates claim that they numbered about five hundred, and served in the military, civil and diplomatic services as heads of office, provincial governors or commanded military units. See Pushkarev, p. 149.

100. In 1575 Ivan suddenly left Moscow, announcing that he was retiring from his rulership and becoming a plain boyar, giving his crown to the Orthodox Tatar prince Semeon Bekbulatovich. Born Sain-Bulat, he was Shah Ali's successor to the throne of the Kasimov Tatars, then took the name Semeon Bekbulatovich at the time of his baptism in 1573, when he also relinquished his Islamic throne. See Volume 10, p. 138.

101. Prince Ivan Fedorovich Mstislavsky was one of Ivan's chief commanders. He was an important figure in the campaigns against Kazan and Astrakhan, and a leading personage at Ivan's court. During the time of Ivan's illness in 1560 Mstislavsky was one of the few boyars who pledged his loyalty to Ivan's infant son Dmitry. Subsequently Mstislavsky was appointed one of the boyar administrators of the zemshchina, the non-crown lands. In 1571 after the successful Tatar attack on Moscow Mstislavsky admitted to receiving overtures from the Crimean khan, but apparently escaped major punishment. See Volume 10, passim.

102. This passage is somewhat puzzling. It would appear that the impudent or rude treatment was not necessarily physical abuse, but that Filon Kmita claimed

to be the military governor of Smolensk. In response the envoys then compare Filon to another more famous Philon. Philon (4th century B.C.) was one of Alexander the Great of Macedonia's "companions," the official term for the childhood friends who comprised Alexander's closest entourage. It is unclear whether these young men were his advisers as well as his companions in drinking, fighting and love-making, but Philon represents the closest advisers of a ruler. This section concludes with the observation that many a Filon (a false Philon) has been "displayed" on the walls at the fortress gates. Dead bodies were hung or displayed at the gates to a town but, according to Eve Levin, rarely impaled upon them at this time.

103. The Russian words are zatinnikh pishchalei (pl.) which I take to mean having something to do with defense since Pushkarev defines the word zatinshchik as a Muscovite stockade guard and *pishchal* means musket or arquebus.

104. Pontus de la Gardie was born in present-day Belgium but began his career as a soldier in France, where he fought on the Protestant side in the wars of religion. He then fought in Danish service, was captured by the Swedes and changed sides, founding one of the most prominent of Swedish families. In 1581 he commanded a mercenary force composed of English, Scots, Germans and Swedes which captured Narva. See Scott, p. 151.

105. Ostafy Mikhailovich Pushkin (died 1602) was a diplomat and member of the boyar council who during the reign of Boris Godunov became governor of Tobolsk. During Ivan's reign he was sent to negotiate with Antonio Possevino as well.

106. Fedor Andreevich Pisemsky (died 1592) was Ivan's ambassador on a number of occasions similar to that described here. Not only did he represent Ivan's interests in Poland, he also was sent to England in 1582-1583.

107. When Stefan accepted the Polish throne his brother Christopher remained in charge of Transylvania until his death in 1581. C.A. Macartney, *Hungary. A Short History* (Edinburgh, 1962), p. 79.

108. The actual words in Russian have a rhythm to them that cannot be duplicated in translation: Chto eto za mir: kaznu u nas vziavshi, obogateivshis' nas izubytchivshi, na nashu zhe kaznu liudei naniavshi, zemliu nashu Liflianskuiu vziavshi, napolnitivshi eio svoimi liud'mi, da nemnogo pogodia, sobravshis' eshche sil'nee prezhengo, nas zhe voevat', i ostal'noe otniat'.

109. Vasily Fedorovich Skopin-Shuisky (died 1595) was a prominent commander and administrator during the reign of Ivan IV. He was made a boyar in 1577 and commander of the area around Pskov and then Vladimir. His son Mikhail Vasilievich became an important military leader during the Time of Troubles. He relieved the siege of Moscow in March 1610, became very popular but died suddenly in April of the same year, most probably by foul play on the part of his jealous relatives.

110. Prince Ivan Petrovich Shuisky (died 1588) was one of the great heroes of the Livonian war. He helped storm Polotsk in 1563. He continued active in the area, participated in the Assembly of the Land of 1566 that approved the continuation of the Livonian war, fought the Tatars in 1571-1572 and became a boyar

in 1574 before returning to Livonia. Long the governor of Pskov, he was best known for his heroic defense of the city. In 1584 he was named by Tsar Ivan to a regency council to guide Fedor Ivanovich, and in 1585 he was granted revenues for his personal use, an honor no commander ever had received before. During the regency of Boris Godunov Shuisky was one of the leaders opposing Godunov's ambitions. Godunov retaliated, secured Ivan Petrovich's condemnation and had the prince tonsured and immured in a remote monastery, where he was put to death in 1588.

111. The Shuisky boyar family was one of the most important princely clans. One of the Shuiskys was among the boyars from the council who ruled during Ivan's minority, still others such as Mikhail Ivanovich Skopin-Shuisky were prominent Russian governors. During the Time of Troubles (1598-1613) Prince Vasily Shuisky occupied the Muscovite throne from 1606 to 1610, having been elected through a boyar coup.

112. Soloviev quotes the original Latin phrase, Patavium virum me fecit. Zamoyski studied at the University of Padua.

113. Possevino was a Jesuit diplomat whose account of his meetings with Ivan provides an important source of information about Ivan's Muscovy. For a thoughtful translation and discussion of his activities see *The Moscovia of Antonio Possevino*. Translated and edited by Hugh F. Graham (Pittsburgh, 1977).

114. Hans Schlitte was a German from Saxony in the employ of Ivan, who sent him on missions to Central Europe with the express purpose of recruiting scholars, doctors and artisans. See Volume 10, p. 58 for Soloviev's discussion of Schlitte's activities.

115. Julius III (Giovanni Maria del Monte), Pope, 1550-1555. See Sir Nicholas Cheetham, *Keepers of the Keys* (New York, 1982), pp. 207-208.

116. Pius IV (Gian Angelo de' Medici), Pope, 1559-1565, presided over the conclusion of the Council of Trent and is associated with the publication of the Tridentine Creed. See Cheetham, pp. 210-211.

117. Gregory XIII (Ugo Boncompagni), Pope, 1572-1585, is best known for commissioning a revision of the calendar, named in his honor, adopted in the West only gradually because the Protestant states initially declined to accept it when it was issued in 1582. See Cheetham, pp. 212-214.

118. According to Hugh Graham (*Moscovia,* p. ix) that courier was Istoma Shevrigin, who was sent to Rome in February 1581. When the Pope received Ivan's letter he and his chief advisors hoped that "their intervention might lead to the establishment of regular diplomatic relations between Rome and Moscow, the adherence of Muscovy to a 'League of Christian Princes' to attack the Turks ... and, above all the creation of channels of communication which would open the way to uniting the Muscovite church with Rome on the Pope's terms."

119. Literally the "sponsor" or "best man" at a wedding. This is a sarcastic reference to Bathory's position as prince of Transylvania. Since 1526 the western portion of the Hungarian lands, known as "Royal Hungary," were under Habsburg rule. The remainder, including Transylvania, was governed by native rulers under Ottoman suzerainty.

120. Doubtless meaning that the patriarch of Constantinople had to attain his position by bribing the Ottoman authorities.

121. Here Possevino means the Ukraine.

CHAPTER II

1. Once again this refers to Istoma Shevrigin. See Chapter I, Note 118.

2. Although Soloviev certainly had access to Possevino's *Moscovia,* he apparently is not basing his text on Possevino. For Possevino's version of the conversation, see Graham, *Moscovia,* pp. 67-75. In his introductory remarks Hugh Graham notes that Possevino presumed that the Russian church had accepted the Union of Florence of 1438, and many of his appeals to Ivan were based on this erroneous assumption. This particular conversation also reflects the very different minds of the disputants and the churches they represented. While Possevino thought that Ivan's questions about the Pope's appearance and conduct (riding around on a chair) were irrelevant and trivial, they clearly were central to Ivan and his courtiers. According the Graham (pp. xix-xxi) they were genuinely astonished when Possevino confirmed that the Pope indeed did wear a cross on his shoe, ride in a litter and was permitted to shave his beard. Possevino attributes Ivan's questions to the influence of Protestant heretics, Englishmen and a Dutch doctor who were present in Moscow. "[He] he kept on asking the same four questions, which these heretics had been drumming into him....'Why is the Pope carried in a chair?' 'Why does he wear a cross on his feet?' Why does he shave his beard?' 'Why does he pretend to be God?'" (pp.72-73).

3. The entire letter appears in George Tolstoy, ed., *The First Forty Years of Intercourse between England and Russia, 1553-1593* (St. Petersburg, 1875, reprinted New York, 1964), pp. 106-115.

4. Although the Soloviev text reads "Ivan Jenkinson" this is Soloviev's error, and he is actually referring to Anthony Jenkinson (1530-1611). It is difficult to understand Soloviev's confusing the name in view of the fact that in the same letter Ivan specifically refers to Elizabeth's representative as "Anthony Jenkinson." In 1557 Jenkinson was appointed captain-general of a fleet sailing for Russia, commissioned by the Muscovy Company, and he served as the Company's agent in Moscow for three years. Travelling to Russia on three subsequent occasions, Jenkinson continued to serve the Company and Elizabeth until 1572. In their introduction to Jenkinson's account of his first voyage, Berry and Crummey note that it is a valuable source of information about Muscovy during the reign of Ivan, particularly because of Jenkinson's description of court ceremonies. Similarly his description of Moscow "is an invaluable record of the city's appearance before the Tatar invaders destroyed much of it in 1571." Jenkinson also established trade with Turkey prior to his first involvement with the Muscovy Company in 1553. Lloyd E. Berry and Robert O. Crummey, *Rude and Barbarous Kingdom. Russia in the Accounts of Sixteenth-Century Voyagers* (Madison, 1968), pp. 43-58. Also MERSH, Volume 15, pp. 125-128.

5. For the complete letter as well as its Elizabethan translation, see Tolstoy, pp. 106-115. Apparently Tolstoy used a translation of Ivan's original letter in the Public Records Office.

6. This letter (Tolstoy, pp. 148-158) is dated August 20, 1574. This time the translation provided is in modern rather than Elizabethan English.

7. "Now was the Emperor [Ivan IV] more earnest to send into England about this long conceited match than ever; addressed one Fedor Pisemskii, a noble, grave, wise, and trusty gentleman, to confer and desire of the queen the Lady Mary Hastings, daughter to that noble Henry, Lord Hastings, earl of Huntingdon, whom he heard was her kinswoman and of the blood royal, as he termed it; and that it would please her majesty to send some noble ambassador to treat with him about it. His ambassador went forward; took shipping at St. Nicholas; arrived in England magnificently received; had audience of the queen; delivered his letters commendatory. Her majesty caused that the lady be attended on with divers great ladies and maids of honor and young noblemen, the number of each appointed to be seen by the said ambassador in York House garden. She put on a stately countenance accordingly. The ambassador, attended with divers other noblemen and others, was brought before her ladyship; cast down his countenance; fell prostrate to her feet, rose, ran back from her, his face still towards her, she and the rest admiring his manner. Said by an interpreter it did suffice him to behold the angel he hoped should be his master's spouse; commended her angelical countenance, state, and admirable beauty. She after was called by her familiar friends in court the empress of Muscovy." Sir Jerome Horsey, *Travels*, Berry and Crummey, pp. 300-301.

8. Bogdan Belsky (died 1611) was a powerful figure exerting considerable but not decisive influence upon affairs during the latter part of Ivan's reign. His family owed its rise to Maliuta Skuratov who was the commander of the tsar's personal bodyguard. Bogdan was Maliuta's nephew and began his career in the tsar's entourage in 1570. Ivan appointed him to the office of armorer in 1578, and in 1581 Belsky was named governor of Rzhev, and in 1582-1583 handled delicate negotiations with representatives of the English government. During Fedor's reign he continued to be identified with the family of Ivan. After Fedor's death in 1598 Belsky's fortunes fell dramatically and Godunov moved against him in 1600-1601. See MERSH, Volume 4, pp. 1-2.

9. Sir Jerome Bowes (died 1616) was Elizabeth's ambassador to Moscow, sent in 1583-1584 to negotiate on two questions raised by Ivan the year before, an alliance between England and Russia, and a marriage between Ivan and Lady Mary Hastings, Elizabeth's cousin. Bowes also was instructed to secure for the English a monopoly on the White Sea trade as well as to deal with specific grievances of the Muscovy Company merchants and those of other Englishmen in Russia. Bowes's negotiations were not successful since the English would accept the alliance proposed by Ivan only if the Russians agreed to attempt mediation of disputes with third parties before declaring war. Ivan would not accept such a stipulation, neither would he agree to the trading monopoly, which the English

made a condition of the alliance. Bowes was also to forestall the marriage proposal by every means possible. The negotiations at an impasse, Ivan decided to send his own embassy to England. Bowes was still in Moscow at the time of Ivan's death in March 1584, making the marriage question moot, while the discussion of an alliance was abandoned. It was decided not to dispatch a Russian ambassador to England at that time, Bowes returning home having accomplished very little except for the release of three English subjects held by the Russians. For a discussion of Bowes's embassy as well as the various descriptions of it, see Robert M. Croskey, "Hakluyt's Accounts of Sir Jerome Bowes' Embassy to Ivan IV," *Slavonic and East European Review,* 61, No. 4 (October 1983), pp. 546-564. Croskey concludes that the version of the embassy included in Hakluyt, a practically contemporaneous source apparently used by Soloviev, must be used with caution because of bias for political reasons.

10. John the Whitebeard was probably the Flemish merchant Jan de Waal. Since Antwerp was under the suzerainty of Philip II in the late sixteenth century, the term "Spanish" would apply.

11. This is probably a reference to one Thomas Glover whom Ivan charged with violating trading provisions by not trading on England's behalf and bringing trade from other countries, including France and Germany. The other reference is to an accusation that Englishmen, probably mercenaries, joined the Swedes in fighting against Ivan in the Novgorod territories, and that Ivan's governors informed the English interpreter Daniel Sylvester in that regard. See Tolstoy, p. 153, for English translation.

12. Rudolph II, Holy Roman emperor, 1576-1612, is recognized as an important patron of the arts, but otherwise is considered an ineffectual ruler. As emperor, Rudolph's foreign policy was to make no concessions to the Ottoman empire.

13. Frederik II, king of Denmark, 1559-1588. Until the accession of Christian IV (1588-1648) to the throne Danish domestic policy was in disarray after the loss of Sweden in 1523. Danish kings were forced to struggle against a nobility seeking to gain power at the expense of the monarchy. For example, in 1560 Frederik found it convenient to transfer his brother Magnus's domains to the island of Øsel, in exchange for relinquishing control over Holstein. Roberts, *Early Vasas,* pp. 119, 164.

14. Jakob Ulfeld (died 1593) was a Danish diplomat and the author of *Hodoeporicon Ruthenicum* (The Muscovite Legation). Because Denmark was confined to its one enclave, the island of Øsel, to strengthen his position King Frederik dispatched missions to Russia in 1571, 1575 and 1578 to secure Ivan's cooperation against Sweden. According to Hugh Graham, as the embassy of 1578 which Ulfeld headed illustrates, the Danes were poorly received and suffered harsh treatment. Ulfeld exceeded his instructions and actually ceded some Danish-controlled territory. King Frederik refused to ratify the treaty that Ulfeld negotiated and brought the envoy to trial. Convicted, his career ended, Ulfeld retired to his estate and composed the *Hodoeporicon* as part of an effort to justify his

conduct to the new king Christian IV. For a detailed description of Ulfeld's work, see MERSH, Volume 40, pp. 178-182.

CHAPTER III

1. In 1552 Muscovite armies conquered the khanate of Kazan, a momentous moment in Muscovite history because for the first time Russians conquered Tatars. Although the Kazan khanate was very weak compared to the Tatars who conquered the Russians in 1240, the symbolism was great and the fact that Moscow was the instrument of that conquest served to solidify its leadership of the Russian land. When Ivan's generals took Kazan they used artillery and a newly formed corps of musketeers to supplement his usual armies. The Russians now gained control of the river routes flowing from the Urals to the Volga, thus opening the way into Siberia. See Lincoln, *Conquest of a Continent*, p. 30 and Dmytryshyn, pp. xxxv-xxxvi.

2. The actual conquest of Astrakhan took place in 1554. Soloviev notes that the Nogay khan Izmail killed his brother Yusuf and many other Nogay leaders and wrote to Ivan in February 1555 claiming complete control over the Nogay Horde and asking that the tsar grant him the right to trade freely in Kazan, Astrakhan and Moscow. See Volume 10, pp. 38-46.

3. Yediger and his brother Bekbulat, sons of Kasim, were the rulers of the Siberian khanate at the time of the 1555 mission to Ivan. Yediger apparently hoped to find a new ally in Ivan against his enemies. His effort was to no avail when in 1563 he and his brother were deposed and killed by Kuchum, son of Murtaza, ruler of the Uzbeks. Yediger and Bekbulat were descendants of Taibuga whose family had engaged in a long-standing feud with the descendants of Sheiban, grandson of Chinghis Khan. Kuchum was a Sheibanid. See Armstrong, p. 2.

4. According to Lincoln (p. 35), furs were worth their weight in gold in Western Europe, making the Siberian pelts an extremely valuable commodity. Armstrong (p. 3) writes that the definitive English work on the subject is R.H. Fisher's *The Russian Fur Trade, 1550-1700* (Berkeley, 1943).

5. Soloviev uses the term doroga here which is the Tatar term for tax collector or financial agent. It raises an interesting question of the degree to which Tatar terminology was being incorporated into Muscovite ranks since this term refers to Ivan's appointee, Kurov, not a Tatar agent.

6. Skrynnikov (*Sibirskaia ekspeditsiia*, p. 91) maintains that the Shibansk prince was Khan Kuchum.

7. This again may refer to Kuchum, with whom Yediger was at war until Kuchum deposed and killed him in 1563. For a detailed discussion of Kuchum's career see Armstrong, p. 2.

8. Kuchum was the khan of Sibir, an area to which Lincoln (p. 38) refers as the sister state to the khanate of Kazan. Although the Muscovites were aware of its existence, Lincoln notes that they knew little or nothing about the khanate of Sibir, including the extent of its military strength or resources. Lincoln writes that

while the Tatars of Kazan fought Muscovy, the Tatars of Sibir faced a whole series of other enemies who assassinated several of Sibir's khans in the early sixteenth century. Lincoln claims that Ivan was taking advantage of this chaos when he demanded thirty thousand pelts as the tribute to which Soloviev refers. It was Kuchum Khan who with the help of Bukhara brought to an end the internecine feuding of the 1560s, defeating Yediger Taigubid in 1563. After paying Ivan a last tribute in 1570, Kuchum prepared for war, attacking Stroganov outposts while fully aware of the 1571 attack on Moscow mounted by the Crimean Tatars, supported by the Ottoman empire. This alliance was natural since Kuchum had introduced Islam forcibly to the Siberian Tatars. He carried on this struggle even after his defeat at the hands of Yermak in 1582, when he abandoned his capital at Kashlyk, which Soloviev calls Sibir. In 1585 Kuchum's forces actually destroyed a detachment of Yermak's forces, and he continued to oppose the Russians until 1598. That year Kuchum was defeated in battle by the Russian military governor Voeikov. Kuchum then fled to the Nogay Horde, where he was put to death. See also Skrynnikov, pp. 92-93 and MERSH, Volume 18, p. 143.

9. According to Armstrong, "Ivan IV's ambassador, Tret'yak Chebukov or Chubukov, who had arrived in 1572 to receive the tribute, and had been welcomed by Kuchum, was killed on Kuchum's orders when on his way back to Moscow." (p. 2) It was at this same time that Kuchum's nephew Mahmet-kul attacked Russian territory across the Urals.

10. This phrase refers to the Urals.

11. Here Soloviev is referring to the Time of Troubles (1598-1613) during which there were major disputes over succession to the Muscovite throne, leading to chaos, civil war and a Polish invasion. In 1606 the boyar Prince Vasily Ivanovich Shuisky was proclaimed tsar after an aristocratic coup in Moscow that killed False Dmitry, the first pretender to the throne. Shuisky's rule was marked by constant rebellion by the lesser service nobility and the invasion of a Polish army led by yet another pretender, the second False Dmitry, also claiming to be the son of Ivan IV. Shuisky was defeated in 1610 after four years of civil war and instability when the Poles took Moscow and attempted to place Wladyslaw, son of King Sigismund III, on the throne. It would appear that the letter from Stroganov to Shuisky, to which Soloviev refers, coincides with the tsar's efforts to raise money to fight the Poles (see Volume 15, Chapter II, Note 22). Shuisky's defeat began the final stages of the Time of Troubles, during which the service nobility reclaimed Moscow from the Poles, defeating them in 1612 and proclaiming Michael Romanov as tsar at the Assembly of the Land in February 1613. Shuisky's brief reign marks the beginning of the end of boyar power in Muscovy and the growing strength of the service nobility as the mainstay of the Russian state. See Crummey, pp. 205-233, for a short but insightful discussion of the Time of Troubles. S.F. Platonov, *Time of Troubles*. Translated and edited by John T. Alexander, gives English readers access to a classical treatment of the subject, while Skrynnikov, *The Time of Troubles. Russia in Crisis, 1604-1618*, is the most recent comprehensive account of this era. See also Volumes 14-15 of this series.

12. Vasily the Dark, or Vasily II, grand prince of Moscow, 1425-1462, was involved in a long civil war during much of his reign. Soloviev is referring to Vasily's capture and imprisonment by the Golden Horde in 1445 when Khan Ulug Mehmet sent his sons Mamutek and Yusuf on a raid into Muscovy. Vasily had trouble mobilizing forces and met with a disastrous defeat at Suzdal on July 6. He was taken prisoner for over four months, during which time his rival, his first cousin Dmitry Shemiaka of Galich, tried to assume the grand-princely throne. Since Shemiaka, whose claim was based on his being the son of Yury of Galich, Vasily I's brother and Vasily II's uncle, did not take full advantage of this opportunity, Ulug Mahmet apparently decided to return Vasily II to Moscow, but only after payment of a large ransom. The reference here is to this ransom. The following year, as the civil war raged on, Shemiaka once again captured Vasily and blinded him, which is how he received his epithet "the Dark." Shemiaka's conduct as grand prince was such that he eventually earned the enmity of most of the princes and towns and within a year, in December 1446, he found himself outcast and on the run, with Vasily back on the Muscovite throne. See Crummey, Formation, pp. 73-75, and Volume 5 of this series.

13. Vasily III, grand prince of Moscow, 1505-1533.

14. According to Lincoln (p. 37) the charter of 1558 leased one and a quarter million acres to Grigory Stroganov. For the text, see Armstrong, pp. 281-284 and Dmytryshyn, et. al., pp. 3-6.

15. The term namestnik, viceregent or lord lieutenant refers to the tsar's appointed local administrator for major towns and adjacent territories. The term volostitel denotes a similar position in a rural district. See Pushkarev, pp. 66 and 181.

16. The Russian term used here is tiun which Pushkarev defines as agents who performed various economic, administrative, and judicial functions. In Muscovy they also were stewards, bailiffs, and judges as well as assistants and deputies of the provincial administrators, the namestnik and volostotitel. See pp. 157-58.

17. Soloviev is paraphrasing this document. According to the Dmytryshyn translation, page 5, the passage reads "If any person in another town has a complaint against Grigorii, such person is to secure an official warrant, on the basis of which both plaintiff and defendent [sic!] will appear before our Treasury officials in Moscow by the Feast of the Annunciation in the same year." The term upravnye gramoty is translated as official warrants by Dmytryshyn. The term judicial official or pristav does not appear in the Dmytryshyn translation.

18. Lincoln (p. 37) notes that once Yakov received rights to land along the Chusovaia river the Stroganovs controlled land equivalent to two-thirds of sixteenth-century England. In short, the Stroganovs had become the largest private landholders in Russia.

19. This section refers to raids engineered by Kuchum Khan on Stroganov lands in alliance with neighboring tribal groups. According to Armstrong (p. 2) and Lincoln (p. 34). Kuchum was determined to stop Russian encroachment

across the Urals. The Stroganov frontier settlements held close to ten thousand freemen and five thousand serfs in 1570. These settlers built blockhouses and stockades to protect their homes and fields and were prepared to fight off any attack against them. The attack described here occurred in July 1572 when Kuchum sent his allies on raids against the Stroganov settlements, where they killed eighty-seven Russians. Armstrong notes that the raiders were the Cheremiss who revolted against the Russians, pillaging settlements along the Kama and Chusovaya rivers. See Dmytryshyn, pp. 9-10 for the complete text of Ivan's 1572 letter.

20. Mahmet-Kul was Kuchum Khan's nephew. The force he led was larger than in the previous year, and massacred not only Russians, but also natives who had allied themselves with the Russians. See Lincoln, p. 39 and Armstrong, p. 2.

21. When the Stroganovs petitioned Ivan to permit them to invade Kuchum's territory for their counterattack against the Tatars they were favored by good timing. Their petition reached Moscow shortly after Ivan learned that his envoys were murdered by Kuchum's forces, inclining the tsar in their favor. Ivan extended the charters to include Siberia. Lincoln, p. 39. For the text of Ivan's reply, see Dmytryshyn, pp. 7-8.

22. The text uses the phrase "how many puds...." For the English text of Ivan's 1574 grant to the Stroganovs see Dmytryshyn, pp. 9-12.

23. See Volume 9, pp. 134-137 for descriptions of cossack activities during Vasily III's reign.

24. The Don Cossacks, like their fellow Zaporozhian (meaning "beyond the rapids") Cossacks, were descendants of runaway peasants and other fugitives who fled the increasingly limited conditions and escalating taxes in areas controlled by Muscovy, Poland and Lithuania to places beyond the reach of authority. The steppe area between the expanding borders of Muscovy and the area under control of the Crimean Tatars provided these fugitives with a kind of no-man's land where they could live freely. In this area they organized themselves into loose bands, electing their own leaders and earning a precarious living either by brigandage or by hiring themselves out to whichever military employer could pay the most. The cossacks were renowned as fierce fighters and great horsemen who roamed the steppe at will, in great contrast to the increasingly burdened peasant populations.

25. The Nogay Horde was extremely important to Moscow for a wide variety of reasons. The Nogay, nomadic horsemen of Turkic origin, supplied Moscow with horses and their trading camps were spread near the city as they pursued this profitable trade. Muscovite diplomacy was aimed at keeping the Nogay from alliance with the Crimean Tatars and prior to its conquest with the khanate of Kazan. After 1558 the Nogay were under much closer Muscovite supervision, but they continued to use the possibility of an alliance with the Crimean Tatars as a wedge in their diplomacy with Ivan. In the conflicts resulting from the competition for control of the steppe the Nogay offered themselves as soldiers for both sides, Moscow and the Tatars. See Volume 10, Chapter I, especially pp. 35-38 for Soloviev's discussion of the "Nogay nomads."

26. After the conquest of Kazan, and even prior to that event, the Crimean khanate was the largest and most powerful of the successors to the Golden Horde, which it even defeated in 1505. At various times throughout Ivan's reign the Crimean Tatars raided Muscovy's borders, invading and attacking Moscow as late as 1571, and posed such an ongoing threat to Moscow's southern border that skeleton military forces had to be stationed in the area at all times. The Crimean Tatars remained a thorn in Russia's side well into the eighteenth century, until the incorporation of the Crimea into the Russian empire in 1783 during the reign of Catherine II.

27. When Russian armies were about to close in on various Tatar leaders they fled to the safety of Azov where, surrounded by the Crimean Tatars on one side and the Astrakhan Tatars on the other, Muscovy could not reach them. As such, Azov was an asylum for the enemies of Moscow.

28. The text never explains clearly whether Levon But was the Muscovite courier to the Crimea or the Crimean courier sent to Moscow. It would appear that he was from Moscow based on Soloviev's reference to him as the "Russian courier" at this point in the text. Unfortunately, it is not entirely clear why Soloviev placed this episode in the narrative between the complaints of the Nogay prince, except to establish that Muscovite officials and their entourages also were subject to cossack attacks.

29. Perekop refers to the isthmus between the Black Sea and the Sea of Azov that attaches the Crimean peninsula to the mainland. It is also often used to refer to the Crimea in general.

30. This accusation must pertain to a raid on Astrakhan prior to Moscow's conquest in 1554-1556, and may be contemporaneous to the 1549 complaint of Yusuf Nogay.

31. Soloviev is referring to Novosiltsev's mission to Constantinople in 1570. Ivan sent his envoy on the pretext of congratulating the new sultan, Selim II, on his accession to the throne and to remind him of Moscow's good relations with his predecessors, especially emphasizing that Muslims suffered no penalties in the lands Moscow had conquered from the Tatars. See Volume 10, p. 185.

32. Ataman was a title held by elected cossack military commanders. At the head of the Don Cossack Host stood a voiskovoi ataman, or military chief and each cossack military unit, settlement, or embassy usually was headed by its own ataman. See Pushkarev, p. 2.

33. The Russian term is priboru which means service by contract. According to Pushkarev, in Muscovy people who served on the basis of a contract were called pribornye servitors. Such contracted personnel included the cossacks. They were recruited for government service by contract and occupied an intermediate position between the higher-class service men such as the "children of the boyars," the deti boiarskie or lesser boyars, and the masses of obligated people. See Pushkarev, p. 102.

34. The phrase used is v rtakh, literally "on our mouths."

35. Namely, that the Russian cossack leader had a Tatar name, while the Tatar cossack leader had a Slav name.

36. This is another reference to Kuchum Khan.

37. As Lincoln (p. 42) describes it, Nikita and Maxim spent twenty thousand rubles outfitting Yermak with the best weapons they could buy. While Kuchum Khan's armies fought with bows, arrows and spears, Yermak's force was equipped with matchlock muskets, sabers, pikes and several small cannon. "Divided into companies of fifty, each with a supply of rye flour, cracked buckwheat, salt, gunpowder and lead, and with three priests and a runaway monk to give them spiritual comfort, Ermak's force set out in a flotilla of the high-sided boats that centuries spent on the rivers of southern Russia had taught them to build."

38. According to Skrynnikov (Sibirskaia ekspeditsiia, pp. 47-49) there is some controversy over the identity of the Pelym prince, whom Skrynnikov identifies as Ablegirim. The Pelym principality was one of the largest in Siberia, in existence since the late fifteenth century. It was apparently this Ablegirim who attacked Perm in an assault so bloody that after 1584 it was commemorated by a march to the graves of the victims.

39. In his letter to Nikita Stroganov Ivan wrote that Semeon and Maksim had asked him to send fighting men from Perm to help them against the Pelym prince because Nikita refused to join them in their fight and to send soldiers to their aid. Ivan ordered Nikita to send as many men as necessary to fight the Voguls and to stand as one with his uncle and cousin. Soloviev's comment that Nikita did not live in harmony with his relatives is likely based on this document. See Armstrong, p. 292 or Dmytryshyn, p. 13 for the text.

40. Soloviev is not using the document in full, for the complete text in English see Dmytryshyn, pp. 24-25. This letter is dated November 16, 1582.

41. As they sailed down the Tura, apparently the Tatars shot arrows at Yermak's boats, to no effect because their high-sided boats acted as shields.

42. According to Lincoln, Sibir was called Isker by the Tatars. It may also have been called Kashlyk. It was situated near present-day Tobolsk, and the area became the site of the primary Russian presence in Siberia during the seventeenth century.

43. After his capture, which the Stroganov Chronicle dates to spring, 1583, Yermak sent Mahmet-Kul to Moscow, where the Tatar commander pledged his loyalty to the Russians at Ivan's deathbed. See Dmytryshyn, pp. 19-20. Soloviev follows the Stroganov Chronicle in recounting the story of Yermak in Siberia. See Dmytryshyn (pp. 14-23) for excerpts translated from the Stroganov Chronicle which closely follow the passages that Soloviev paraphrases in relating the activities of Yermak and his cossacks.

44. In the original Sol' Bol'shaia and Sol' Malaia.

45. Although the Stroganov Chronicle (Dmytryshyn, p. 20) reports that Yermak and the Volga atamans and cossacks went to Moscow from Siberia to report to Ivan on their successful conquest, Soloviev does not accept this version.

Apparently Yermak's messenger to Ivan was Ataman Ivan Koltso. It was Koltso who brought Yermak the gifts from the tsar which included the chain mail that Yermak wore to his death. Upon returning to Yermak in 1583 Koltso was sent to defend a local chieftain against attacks by marauding Nogay. Koltso and his men were ambushed and slain during this expedition. See MERSH, Volume 17, pp. 131-132.

46. Lincoln (p. 43) describes the content of the tribute which Yermak sent to Ivan noting that "at a time when a prime sable pelt sold for ten times what a peasant family could earn in a year and a black fox fetched up to ten times the price of a sable, Ermak's cossacks carried the pelts of twenty-four hundred prime sable, eight hundred black fox, and two thousand beaver."

47. Ivan sent Yermak a long coat of fine chain mail emblazoned with the double-headed eagle which formed the Muscovite crest. See Lincoln, p. 43.

48. For the English text of this letter see, Dmytryshyn, p. 26. Dmytryshyn relies on G.F. Muller, *Istoriia Sibiri* (Moscow-Leningrad, 1937) for the text of this letter. Soloviev was probably paraphrasing or condensing the content based on text similar to that in Muller (originally published in the eighteenth century).

49. Yermak's fate is the story of folk legends. The Stroganov Chronicle (see Dmytryshyn, pp.20-22 and Lincoln, pp. 43-46) relates how the cossacks suffered privations as they ran low on supplies during their second Siberian winter. Moreover Kuchum's Tatars constantly attacked them, succeeding in decreasing their already small numbers. When during the summer of 1584 there was still no new supply of food, arms or reinforcements, it was clear that the cossacks had little chance of surviving a third Siberian winter. Ironically, the tsar's musketeers finally reached Yermak's camp in November 1584, actually making conditions even worse since the cossacks lacked adequate supplies for their small force, let alone the reinforcements. Lincoln quotes the chronicler as saying that many died, and they were forced to cannibalism to survive. Ivan's commander, Prince Semeon Bolkhovsky, was among the many Muscovites and cossacks who perished. (Dmytryshyn, p. 20) While the cossacks and musketeers starved and died of scurvy, the Tatar attacks continued to diminish their numbers even further. During the summer of 1585, as another Muscovite expedition searched for Yermak's forces, on August 5 a Tatar force ambushed the cossacks. Taken by surprise since in their exhaustion they had failed to post sentries, most of Yermak's men fell in the Tatar assault.Yermak escaped and raced to the river, where he leaped from the high bank to one of his boats. Misjudging the distance, he lost his footing and fell into the deep water where the coat of mail sent to him by Ivan pulled him down, drowning him. The remainder of Yermak's forces, now leaderless, began their withdrawal to the Urals in attempt to retain their booty. Armstrong (p. 16) in discussing Yermak as folk-hero notes that one of the many songs immortalizing Yermak's deeds has him leaping from boat to boat when he slipped, broke his head and was killed. Armstrong then that adds according to some cossack legends Yermak drowned because of the weight of his armor, a gift from the tsar. As Lincoln writes, "The gateway that Ermak's 'conquest' had opened into Siberia

never closed..." for by 1586 Boris Godunov, regent for Tsar Fedor Ivanovich, sent another force to establish the Russian presence in Siberia, building forts all along the river routes Yermak had followed in his conquest.

CHAPTER IV

1. Anastasia Yurievna-Zakharina (of the family later known as Romanov), Ivan's first wife, whom he married in 1547, was said to be the great love of his life. Anastasia bore Ivan six children, three girls and three boys. The three girls did not survive whereas the eldest of her three sons, Dmitry, to whom Ivan demanded that the boyars pledge their loyalty in 1560, died shortly thereafter. Their second son was the ill-fated Ivan Ivanovich killed by his father in 1581, and their third son Fedor, the simple-minded one, reigned as tsar from 1584 to 1598. Anastasia died unexpectedly in 1560, and Ivan later blamed her death on a conspiracy against him. See MERSH, Volume 31, p. 148.

2. This may be a reference to Katarzyna Jagiellonka who married Duke John Vasa, the future King John III of Sweden (1568-1594). When the current king Erik XIV imprisoned John and his Polish bride in 1562, Ivan demanded that Katarzyna be sent to him. See above Chapter II, section "Ivan's Relations with Sweden."

3. Ivan's second wife Maria, formerly Kucheney, daughter of the Cherkess chieftain Temriuk, married Ivan in 1561. Her brother became Prince Cherkassky, a leading figure in the oprichnina (crown estates). After Maria's death in 1569 Ivan again suspected poisoning, as in the death of his first wife Anastasia, and he executed a number of people he thought might have been connected with the plot. For details, see Volume 10, Chapter IV, Note 25.

4. These remarks most likely refer to Ivan's alliance with the Cherkess (Circassians) who in 1560-1561 combined with Muscovite forces to attack the Crimea, causing concern both in Poland and the Ottoman empire. By marrying Maria, Ivan both cemented the alliance and entered into a formalized, church endorsed relationship rather than a sinful one with a beautiful Cherkess princess. In the text, Soloviev uses the word "nravstennom otnoshenii" or literally a moral relationship. This is an instance of rather Victorian language on his part. In effect Ivan conquered the Cherkess without spilling blood. Zimin notes that to seal the alliance, as early as 1558 Temriuk sent his son Salnuk to Moscow where he received the name Michael at his conversion to Christianity and as Prince Michael Cherkassky became one of Ivan's most trusted henchmen. See A.A. Zimin, *Oprichnina Ivana Groznogo*, p. 68.

5. Ivan married Marfa Vasilievna Sobakina on October 28, 1571. Apparently to induce fertility the bride's mother gave her some kind of potion, causing the girl to become ill. She died within three weeks of the wedding, on November 14. See Volume 10, Chapter III, Note 83.

6. This statement pertaining to the ruined and fragmented state of Christendom may well refer to the conflicts pervading Europe as a consequence

of the Reformation, the Council of Trent and the religious wars endemic in Europe.

7. According to Eve Levin, choosing to remain "in the world" for the sake of underage children was a common reason for asking permission to remarry. "A second marriage," she writes, "was appropriate for persons who were not capable of mature restraint...," a factor certainly appropriate to Ivan IV! The Orthodox church held serious objections to more than one marriage. In Levin's view the church's stand on remarriage was governed by the often-repeated formula of Gregory the Great, "The first marriage is law; the second, dispensation; the third, transgression; the fourth, dishonor: this is a swinish life." Eve Levin, *Sex and Society in the World of the Orthodox Slavs, 900-1700* (Cornell, 1989), pp. 107, 113.

8. This passage describes Ivan's penance. In stating that he must stay with the catachumens the church fathers assigned him to a section of the church originally preserved for those seeking conversion to Orthodoxy who were not yet baptized into the faith, and thus not entitled to communion. By the sixteenth century this was a part of the church for those not entitled to take communion, still recalling the place of those not yet baptized. It has been suggested that exclusion from the building proper is the reason why from the sixteenth and seventeenth centuries Russian Orthodox churches have porches.

9. When an ordinary person wanted to enter even into a second marriage, let alone a fourth, he was expected to do penance, including a lengthy deprival of the right to take communion. In this case the petitioner was the tsar, thus his penance was relatively short, only a year. Levin, pp. 108-109.

10. The "Virgin bread" is what is left from the whole loaf after the small proskury, the part actually sanctified in the eucharist, is taken out. The rest of the loaf is dedicated to Mary. This is a variant of the antidoron, the bread which is blessed but not consecrated, and distributed to the faithful at the end of the eucharistic service in the Orthodox church. My thanks to Eve Levin for her assistance in defining this term.

11. This term probably refers to mead specially blessed on major saints' days and distributed to the faithful. Eve Levin has found a possible clue contained in the travel account of Giles Fletcher (1591)."At every brewing their manner is likewise to bring a dish of their wort to the priest within the church; which, being hallowed by him, is poured into the brewing and so giveth it such a virtue as when they drink of it they are seldom sober. The like they do with the first fruit of their corn in harvest." Giles Fletcher, *Of the Rus Commonwealth.* Edited by Albert J. Schmidt (Cornell, 1966), p. 141.

12. This passage actually describes the kind of activities from which Ivan was prohibited because of his fourth marriage.

13. Levin writes (pp. 111-112) "If third marriages were little better than legitimized adultery, fourth marriages were scandalous. The venerable St. Basil declared that fourth marriages were a greater insult to God's law than simple fornication.... Most Slavic writers forbade fourth marriages outright. Those who entered into fourth marriages were to be denied participation in any ecclesiastical rites

until they had separated from their illicit spouses." Nevertheless because Gregory the Great included fourth marriages in his formula some texts did permit them, but with very long periods of penance. The Orthodox church also had an established tradition of forbidding a fifth marriage.

14. Soloviev actually expands on this point in a note, quoting at least two contemporary sources. He uses a notation from the Obikhodnik (account book) of the Joseph of Volokolamsk monastery, which noted a donation from Anna Vasilchikova (but no title) of one hundred rubles. He also points out that according to the chronology of the period Vasilisa Melentieva is referred to as widow. Her former husband was stabbed by an oprichnik, and in 1577 the tsar ordered her to a convent because of some offense. Eve Levin believes the reason why neither of the "concubines" were referred to as tsaritsas in contemporary accounts was that it would have granted legitimacy to forbidden marriages. Nevertheless both women were treated as if they were his consorts. See Levin, pp. 106-114, 128.

15. Ivan's final marriage to Maria Nagaia produced a son, Dmitry, who was still a baby at the time of his father's death in 1584. Since his eldest son Ivan Ivanovich died at his father's hand in 1581, Ivan was succeeded by his son Fedor whose brother-in-law Boris Godunov became the de facto ruler of Muscovy. Dmitry was sent with his mother and her family to Uglich where they lived under the supervision of Moscow agents headed by Mikhail Bitiagovsky. In 1591 Dmitry mysteriously died and rumors attributed the boy's death to a conspiracy by agents of Boris Godunov. An investigation of the death headed by Prince Vasily Ivanovich Shuisky exonerated Godunov, claiming that Dmitry accidentally cut his throat with a knife during an attack of epilepsy. Neither the Nagoy family, the people of Uglich nor popular opinion were satisfied with the verdict, and the populace put Bitiagovsky and other Godunov agents to death. Godunov forced Maria Nagaia to take the veil, exiled many of her relatives and executed many of the inhabitants of Uglich in retaliation for their actions. Rumors that the boy actually survived formed the basis of the claims of False Dmitry during the interregnum following Fedor's death in 1598. See Volume 13 of this series and S.F. Platonov, *Boris Godunov. Tsar of Russia.* Trans. by L. Rex Pyles. (Gulf Breeze, Fla.: Academic International Press, 1973).

16. In his translation of Possevino, Hugh Graham (p. 146) notes that "Tsarevich Ivan led a kind of 'war-party,' which demanded strenuous efforts be made to relieve Pskov, hold Livonia and drive back the Poles. By this time Ivan was totally committed to ending the war by negotiation and whatever concessions to Batory [sic] were necessary. The Tsarevich's overt opposition to this view made Ivan so angry that he struck his son down. The incident took place on November 14, 1581, and by November 19 the Tsarevich was dead."

17. "It will prove worthwhile," wrote Possevino, "to say something concerning young Ivan's death, both because the event itself was of consequence and because it had a great deal to do with causing the Prince to listen to what we had to say with more graciousness than he might otherwise have done. There is strong

evidence that the Grand Prince of Muscovy slew his own son in the fortress called Aleksandrovskaia Sloboda. One of the interpreters assigned to me had been in the young prince's service at the time. He was among those who looked into the cause of his death and gave me the more probable account of it. Decent women of means customarily wear three garments, which may be heavy or light depending on the weather, and those who wear only one garment are not considered to be of good repute. Tsarevich Ivan's third wife was attired in only one garment because she was pregnant and not expecting anyone to approach her. It chanced that the Grand Prince came on her resting on a bench. She immediately rose, but he flew into a rage, boxed her ears, And hit her with the staff he was carrying. The following night she was delivered of a stillborn child. Meanwhile the Tsarevich had rushed up to his father, but when he sought to prevent the Grand Prince's beating his wife he brought down his father's wrath upon himself, and was mortally wounded by a blow on the head near the temple from the same staff. Before this happened, the son in a rage had taken his father severely to task, saying: 'You thrust my first wife into a nunnery for no good reason; you did the same thing to my second, and now you strike my third, causing the son in her womb to perish.' After wounding his son the father began to grieve and hastily summoned physicians from Moscow, together with Andrey Shchelkalov and Nikita Romanov, to make sure that every possible remedy was tried. However, the Tsarevich died five days later and was transported to Moscow amidst universal mourning. His father followed the bier, and as the cortege approached the city he actually went on foot, while nobles dressed in mourning, bore the coffin aloft on the tips of their fingers. They were still in mourning, deliberately making themselves look untidy, on our return. They had let their hair grow long, a sign of mourning, and were not wearing the little cap which is a mark of nobility.... The Prince summoned his Senate and declared that his own sins had caused the Tsarevich's death.... Each night grief (or madness) would drive the Prince from his bed, to scratch the walls of his chamber with his nails and utter piercing sighs.... After the death of the Tsarevich the Prince wept copiously, dressed in a most unbecoming way.... His whole kingdom, but particularly the court, presented the same appearance and observed the same sad rituals. The Prince laid aside his diadem and other bright adornment.... He transmitted large sums of money to all his monasteries to pray for the salvation of his son's soul." *Moscovia*, pp. 12-14. Possevino's account is by far the more widely accepted of the two versions recounted here. Clearly the Pskov chronicle has a very particular point of view, or even an ax to grind.

18. It would appear that here too Soloviev is quoting Possevino, who describes exactly such a incident. See *Moscovia*, p. 13. Clearly the reaction of the boyars is reminiscent of 1560 when a similar plea by Ivan preceded the period known as the oprichnina.

19. Ivan took monastic vows because the monastic state was considered more pious than the lay. The monastic vows administered on the deathbed were the higher level, the skhima, which monks took in order to die at the highest level of

piety. Traditionally the initial letter of the monastic name chosen corresponded to that of the secular name. Thus Ivan became Iona, in anglicized form Jonas.

20. Ivan III is often referred to as Ivan the Great to distinguish him from his more notorious grandson.

21. The term "North Russian" refers to Vladimir, Suzdal and Moscow and is used in contrast to Kievan Rus, or "South Russian."

22. Sophia Paleologus, niece of the last Byzantine emperor, was Ivan III's second wife and the mother of Vasily III, Ivan IV's father. For Soloviev's discussion, see Volume 9 of this series.

23. This reference is confusing. Soloviev probably means the Byzantine emperor Constantine IX Monomachos (reigned 1042-1055), whose daughter married Vsevolod, the third surviving son of Yaroslav the Wise. Their son Vladimir, who ruled Kiev in 1113-1125, adopted the surname of his maternal grandfather but of course was never styled "tsar," merely "grand prince." There is a legend that the Byzantine emperor sent Vladimir the imperial regalia in order to prevent him attacking imperial territories. Vladimir Monomakh is associated with the period during which Kiev attained its greatest political influence. Despite the relatively short duration of his rule Monomakh was successful in subduing both domestic and foreign enemies. He also is said to have received the imperial insignia from his grandfather, hence the title Monomakh. The crown with which the grand princes of Moscow were crowned was called shapka Monomakha or the Cap of Monomakh, an indication of the veneration which Monomakh continued to receive centuries after his death.

24. These statements refer to two separate doctrines which developed in the wake of the fall of Constantinople. The first of these is "Moscow as the Third Rome" originally declared during the reign of Ivan III but clearly in common use by the reign of his grandson. This doctrine propounded the succession of Moscow as a third Rome following the fall of Constantinople (the second Rome). There exist a variety of sources which elaborate this idea, beginning in late fifteenth-century Novgorod with the *Tale of the White Cowl.* The most famous elaboration of this doctrine is contained in the Pskov abbot Filofey's letter to Grand Prince Vasily III's vicegerent. Crummey (*Formation,* p. 136) quotes him as writing "all Christian states are drowned because of the unbelievers. Only the sovereign of our realm alone stands by the Grace of Christ." "Thus," Crummey continues, "now that Rome and Byzantium had fallen into apostasy, the ruler of Muscovy had become... 'the only tsar for Christians in the whole world'... and his capital, Moscow, the center of Christendom. At the climax of his work, Philotheus [sic] encapsulated his theories in a slogan of striking power: 'two Romes have fallen, the Third stands and there shall be no Fourth.'"

The connection to Augustus Caesar and Vladimir Monomakh is established in the sixteenth-century legend of one Prus, the brother of Augustus, who founded a dynasty on the banks of the Vistula which became known as Prussia. Hugh Graham (*Moscovia,* pp. 148-149) quotes the monk Spiridon-Savva as containing a succinct formulation of the story. Graham quotes from R.P. Dmitrieva, *Skazanie o kniaz'iakh vladimirskikh* (Tale of the Princes of Vladimir) (Moscow and Leningrad, 1955), pp. 161-162. "Augustus began to distribute the whole world. He set up his brother... Prus on the banks of the river Vistula... Prus ruled a long time... and to this day the land is called 'Prussian,' after his name." Next came the link with Novgorod and Kiev, the axis of the first Russian state, which always was considered a part of the grand princes' territory, in spite of the fact that Poland-Lithuania controlled the territory the Kievan state formerly had occupied. "And at the time a certain Voeivoda in Novgorod called Gostomysl' was at the end of his life; he called those ruling with him in Novgorod and said: 'I give you some advice; send to the Prussian land and summon a prince from among those dwelling there which are of the line of Augustus, the Roman tsar.' They went to the Prussian land and found there a certain prince named Riurik, who was descended from the Roman Tsar Augustus, and entreated him in the name of all the people of Novgorod. Prince Riurik came to them in Novgorod and brought his brothers with him, Truvor and Sineus and Grand Prince Riurik ruled it. Grand Prince Vladimir who brought Christianity to Kiev... was said to be fourth in line of descent from Riurik, and the Byzantine Emperor Constantine IX Monomachos was supposed to have given the Imperial insignia (that Ivan used in his own coronation in 1547) to his grandson Vladimir Monomakh, eighth in line from Riurik." Muscovite boyars, in conversation with Lithuanian envoys in 1563, told essentially the same story. They explained that Riurik was of the fourteenth generation after Prus. See Volume 10, p. 154.

25. Among the most famous in Ivan's correspondence with Kurbsky is his description of the viciousness with which he was treated as a child by the rival boyar factions. When his father Vasily III died in 1533 Ivan was only three years old. His mother Elena Glinskaia was named regent on his behalf. During the next five years the most influential boyars were Mikhail Glinsky and Dmitry Fedorovich Belsky, in whose care Vasily III had left his son. Very quickly the struggles among the various boyar factions developed, and within a year Glinsky was arrested. After Elena Glinskaia's death in 1538 the factional rivalry grew even more vicious, and even if we take Ivan's descriptions with a certain amount of skepticism, unquestionably his youth was surrounded by intrigue and chaos. Until Ivan assumed the throne in 1547 the various factions, led by the Glinsky and Belsky families on the one side, and the Shuisky family, which dominated the boyar council on the other, struggled for control. Ivan relates a variety of humiliating and frightening experiences, including how the rival factions searched his bedroom seeking someone who had taken refuge there, and how as a young boy he was badly treated by the rival noblemen who went so far as to put their feet up on his bed when discussing matters in his presence. See Volume 9, Chapters IV and V for Soloviev's retelling of the period.

26. Here Soloviev is probably referring to the *Povest' vremennykh let*, in English known as the Primary Chronicle.

27. Precedence or mestnichestvo was a system regulating the service positions of members of the high aristocracy. The boyars and princes formed a hierarchical

ladder and their claim to service positions was based on their place on this ladder. These places were determined by the official Genealogical Directory (gosudarev rodoslovets) prepared for the tsar and the lists of crown and army officials (razriadnye knigi). The tsar was expected to choose his councillors and to appoint high officials of his army and administration based on these registers. The system understandably led to many disputes. According to Vernadsky, the grand princes formed the top class, the original Moscow boyar families were considered the second group, next came the descendants of lesser princes, etc. Within each family distinctions between genealogically senior and junior members were strictly observed. See Pushkarev, p. 60.

28. Sylvester probably moved to Moscow from Novgorod sometime in the 1530s where he became a priest at the Annunciation cathedral. Even prior to Ivan's assumption of power from the boyars in 1545-1546 Soloviev believes that Sylvester had achieved a certain recognition. During Ivan's early years as tsar he was one of his most influential counsellors. Ivan's other significant adviser during this era was the lord Alexis Adashev. See Volume 9, pp. 220-225. See also R.G. Skrynnikov, *Ivan the Terrible*. Translated and edited by Hugh F. Graham (Gulf Breeze, FL: Academic International Press, 1981).

29. Soloviev quotes pieces of the correspondence between Ivan and Kurbsky and sometimes without complete consistency (see Note 30 below). For a complete translation see *The Correspondence between Prince A.M. Kurbsky and Tsar Ivan IV of Russia, 1564-1579*. Translated and edited by J.L.I. Fennell (Cambridge, 1963). The passage quoted here is found in Ivan's second letter to Kurbsky, p. 191. In comparing the Russian in Soloviev to the old Russian in Fennell we find that there are some important differences. Soloviev writes in modern Russian, moreover where the document source in Fennell uses the word opalialsia (put into disgrace), Soloviev uses the word gnevalsia (to become angered). Fennell's translation of this passage reads…"are you corrupt or am I, in that I wished to rule you and you did not wish to be under my power, and that for this I inflicted disgrace upon you? Or are you corrupt, in that not only did you [not] wish to be obedient and subordinate to me, but you even ruled over me, and took all my power from me… in word I was sovereign, but in fact I ruled nothing."

30. Fennell, letter 1 from Ivan to Kurbsky, pp. 139-141.

31. Ivan returned to Moscow first by boat up the Volga to Nizhny Novgorod. He was escorted by cavalry riding along the banks as far as Vasilsursk. This is the explanation of the reference to being imprisoned in a boat and escorted by a second-rate or worthless detachment of horsemen. See Volume 10, Chapter I, p. 26. There are no such derogatory remarks in Soloviev's recounting of the return to Moscow, these are only Ivan's in his correspondence with Kurbsky (See Fennell, p. 93). The martyrs are Sylvester and Adashev whom Kurbsky claimed were unjustly punished for treason by Ivan when the tsar ignored their saintly deeds and listened to the ill-founded charges of his wife Anastasia's brothers, the future Romanovs. Kurbsky emerges as the main defender of Sylvester and Adashev, yet Soloviev tends to discount his claims (Volume 10, Chapter III, p. 102), writing

that Ivan never denied his cruel behavior, only attempted to justify it while Kurbsky tried to exculpate himself from all fault. Consequently, Soloviev tends to accept Ivan's account as the more reliable version of events. Similarly, in this section of his history, Soloviev continues in the same vein. Curiously, although it would appear that Soloviev is using the same passage from Ivan's letter to Kurbsky, the Russian language differs slightly, although both sections use quotations. In Volume 10, Chapter III, p.103, the translation reads "with a small number of followers," which in Russian in (Soloviev's original Volume V, Chapter 4) is "s malym chislom liudei" whereas in this section of the text (Soloviev's Volume VI, Chapter 7), the Russian reads "s nichtozhnym otriadom" which can be translated as "with a paltry [cavalry] detachment " The Fennell text cited above uses the wording (s maleishimi liudi) similar to, but not exactly that of the Soloviev, Volume V, chapter 4.

32. Fennell's translation reads slightly differently but has the same intent. His notes are helpful in understanding what Ivan meant because if we follow Soloviev's and the original text the literal meaning is not always correct. The most important example is in the words there *were more than fifteen thousand not with us at that time.* The Russian apparently could read "There were not more than fifteen thousand with us." Fennell notes that according to sources such as the *Poslaniia Ivana Groznogo* (Edited by D.S. Likhachev and Ya. S. Lur'e. (Moscow-Leningrad: Academy of Sciences, 1951) between 120,000 and 150,000 men participated in the Kazan Campaign of 1552 and that many servicemen from Novgorod failed to make an appearance. Ivan could well be alluding to this group in his letter to Kurbsky (pp. 114-115).

33. According to Paul Bushkovitch three known heresies existed during the era influenced by Sylvester and Adashev. The most obscure of these was that of Matvey Bashkin, who was accused by Ivan Viskovaty, secretary of the Chancellery for Foreign Affairs, of disbelief in the Trinity. He was imprisoned and possibly executed. By his surname, Bushkovitch surmises that Bashkin was a member of the lesser nobility, in Russian a syn boiarskii. See Paul Bushkovitch, *Religion and Society in Russia. The Sixteenth and Seventeenth Centuries* (New York, 1992), pp. 26, 41.

34. Artemy, archimandrite of the Trinity-St. Sergius monastery, was one of the other heretics. The last was Feodosy Kosoy, a slave. All three were arrested and tried in 1553-1554. Artemy, according to Bushkovitch (p. 26), was the most important of the three, and was accused of disbelief in the Trinity, opposition to the persecution of the Judaizers and praise of the Latin faith. Artemy eventually escaped to Lithuania where he defended the Trinity against "real anti-Trinitarians" in Poland. Feodosy Kosoy was accused of denial of the Trinity, and when he made his escape to Poland he actually joined the Polish Arians who were anti-Trinitarians.

35. Matiusha is the diminutive of Matvey, and therefore refers to Bashkin.

36. In early 1571, while Ivan's armies were occupied in the West, Khan Devlet-Girey of the Crimea raided Moscow with a large force of Tatar horsemen.

They occupied the outskirts of Moscow, and fire broke out in the occupied areas. According to Crummey (*Formation*, p. 171) the disaster completed Ivan's disillusionment with the oprichnina and the following year, when the Crimean khan tried to repeat his raid, he was met by a large force which repelled his attack.

37. Vsevolod III, grand prince of Vladimir 1176-1212, was the youngest son of Yury Dolgoruky (1120-1157), the first of the Kievan princes to make the area around Vladimir and Suzdal a major Russian center. Vsevolod, known as "Big Nest," was actually the first of the princes in the North to take the title of grand prince officially. According to Fennell "Vsevolod's reign was marked by an increase of his authority as ruler of Vladimir, both internationally and among his southern relatives, but also by a significant increase in territory." John Fennell, *The Crisis of Medieval Russia, 1200-1304* (London, 1983), p. 4.

38. This refers to Ivan III's famous "Stand on the Ugra" of 1480 which actually was a "stand-off" on the Ugra. Both the Muscovite and Tatar armies retreated rather than engage in battle. This event marked the end of Tatar rule over Muscovy, for Ivan III discontinued tribute payments to the Tatars.

39. Ivan Semeonovich Peresvetov migrated to Moscow from Lithuania and wrote *Legend of Mohammed the Sultan* and the *Petition* which he presented to Ivan in 1549. The former deals with the Turkish conquest of Constantinople in 1453. Sultan Mohammed, in contrast to the last Byzantine emperor Constantine, was stern but just. Constantine was humane and gentle, but imposed on by his magnates, leading to the final ruin of the empire. Peresvetov's writings are notable in that they clearly emanate from a secular milieu, innocent of church rhetoric. His ideology corresponded closely to the politics of Sylvester and Adashev. He suggested a variety of reforms to benefit the service nobility as opposed to the old boyar aristocracy. These included the creation of a standing army of musketeers. Peresvetov drew attention to external and domestic dangers, presumably including the entrenched boyar aristocracy. He was a strong proponent of Ivan's aggressive policies against Kazan and Astrakhan. After his appearance in Muscovy there are few biographical details about him. See MERSH, Volume 51, pp. 145-146.

40. Here Soloviev is referring to Metropolitan Philip, born Fedor Stepanovich Kolychev (1507-1569). The Kolychevs were an old boyar family in Muscovite service. Because his family was connected to the appanage house of Staritsa which led a revolt against the regency of Elena Glinskaia, Philip became a monk. By 1548 he was head of the Solovetsk monastery, and in 1566 Ivan appointed him metropolitan of Moscow. According to Soloviev, Philip originally accepted the position on condition that Ivan abolish the oprichnina. Soloviev presents Philip's story within the context that the church made every effort to support the Muscovite autocracy until the grand princes "entered their final struggle with the remnants of antiquity, the cluster of princes and retainers." Each of the metropolitans of Moscow, Makary, Afanasy, German and Philip, attempted to intercede for the intended victims of Ivan's wrath. When Ivan grew angry at Philip for putting conditions on accepting the position, Philip gave in, accepting that his "duty lay not

in opposing the tsar's will but in soothing his anger at every possible opportunity." Despite Philip's written promise not to intervene in the oprichnina, he did not renounce his right to intercede. Because of this effort, which Soloviev recounts in all its drama, Philip was dragged in disgrace from the Dormition cathedral and exiled to the Otroch monastery in Tver. In 1569, when Ivan passed through Tver on his way to punish Novgorod and Pskov, he sent Maliuta Skuratov, his most trusted henchman, to ask Philip for his blessing. When Philip refused, Maliuta Skuratov strangled him. "Thus," writes Soloviev, "fell unconquered a great shepherd of the Russian church, a martyr to the sacred custom of intercession." See Volume 10, pp. 127-128, 215, and Michael Florinsky, *Russia. A History and Interpretation* (New York, 1966), p. 184.

41. See Note 15, above.

42. The term used is samozvantstvo, the abstract noun derived from samozvanets, meaning "pretender." There were those who believed that Dmitry Ivanovich had never really died. During the Time of Troubles (1598-1613) there were two False Dmitrys who claimed the Muscovite throne. The first of these appeared as a claimant to the throne in 1603. The Polish government immediately recognized him as the legitimate heir to Ivan IV although Boris Godunov, who was elected tsar in 1598, claimed that the pretender was a monk by the name of Grigory (Grishka) Otrepiev. The pretender did invade Muscovy in 1604 but was not very successful until Boris died in April 1605. At that point the boyar families opposed to the Godunovs "recognized" False Dmitry and supported his efforts to oust the Godunovs. Grishka Otrepiev entered Moscow in June and was crowned in July 1605 then, within six months, the first False Dmitry rapidly lost popularity and power. His decision to marry a Polish woman (Marina) without her conversion to Orthodoxy convinced the Muscovite population of his heresy, and he was deposed in favor of Prince Vasily Ivanovich Shuisky in May 1606. The fate of the first False Dmitry did not deter yet another, who appeared to claim his throne in June 1607. Historians do not know the identity of this second pretender, who generally is referred to as the brigand of Tushino, and served as a figure head to justify the Polish invasion of Muscovy. The Polish "Tsaritsa Marina" recognized him as her husband who allegedly survived the May 1606 massacre in Moscow when over two thousand Poles and Lithuanians were slaughtered during the upset of the first pretender. The second pretender's army was composed of Poles and Lithuanians, and Russians opposed to the Shuisky regime. These nobles expediently allied themselves with the pretender's Polish backers to dethrone Shuisky, at the cost of seeing an invasion of Russia by the Swedes in the North and the Poles from the West. By the summer of 1610 Moscow had no tsar, only "pretenders" in the view of S.F. Platonov, thus allowing the Polish armies to march to Moscow and capture the city. See, Platonov, *The Time of Troubles*. See also Volumes 14-15 of this series.

43. The era from the death of Fedor Ivanovich in 1598 until the assumption of the Muscovite throne by Michael Romanov in 1613 is referred to as the "Time

of Troubles." During these fifteen years Muscovy was wracked by civil war, invaded and conquered by Poland, saddled with a False Dmitry and finally rescued by armies of the service nobility who defeated the Poles in 1612. In an effort to restore stability the Assembly of the Land of 1613 elected Michael Romanov tsar and grand prince of Moscow, thus inaugurating three centuries of Romanov rule.

44. The Shuisky in question here is probably Prince Ivan Vasilievich Shuisky, a powerful boyar during Ivan's youth whom Ivan regarded as responsible for the lawlessness and terror felt throughout Muscovy and in the Muscovite court itself. In his correspondence with Kurbsky (letter 1, Fennell pp. 75-77) Ivan wrote that Shuisky and his confederates deprived Ivan and his brother of food and clothing, treating them as "foreigners and beggars." In the most vivid passage Ivan describes Shuisky as sitting "on a bench, chin in hand, resting his leg on our father's bed." Soloviev notes that this conduct by Shuisky and his fellow boyars indicated how little respect they had for the very young boy. He never forgot their slights and at age thirteen in December 1543 Ivan arrested Prince Andrei Shuisky, president of the boyar council, thus depriving the Shuisky faction of their power over his life. See Volume 9, pp. 213-214.

45. In the early 1950s a special commission from the Ministry of Culture opened the sarcophagus of Ivan IV in the Moscow Kremlin's Archangel cathedral. The tsar's bones were examined by anthropologists and finally the archeologist and anatomic sculptor M.M. Gerasimov reconstructed Ivan's face. In his discussion of how he reconstructed Ivan's face and body Gerasimov wrote that Ivan was a tall man, almost six feet in height, "well developed in his youth, but towards the end of his life apparently very fat.... " He also suffered from polyarthritis and was often in great pain. Moreover he must have suffered from severe metabolic disturbances occurring thanks to his "way of life." His early senility and death were due in part to lack of regular exercise, immoderate indulgence in alcohol and overeating. There was also mercury in his body, attributable to his use of a mercury ointment to relieve the pain in his limbs. The physical examination of his body revealed a very unusual development of his teeth, which Gerasimov thinks made his mouth droop. "The skeleton proves that Ivan must have been stoutly built, and... towards the end of his life, fat....The most revealing portrait was that of the face without any hair. It seemed to hide nothing—the form of the low forehead, the peculiarities of the supraorbital area, the size and outline of the symmetrical orbits conditioned the external specific appearance of the eyes. The mouth with its drooping corners and expression of disgust was determined by the shape of this dentition. The face was hard, commanding, undoubtedly clever but cruel and unpleasing with pendulous nose and clumsy chin. The lower lip was indicated by the occlusion of the teeth and the face was set off by a powerful neck and a massive, well-filled torso." M.M. Gerasimov, *The Face Finder* (Philadelphia, 1971), pp. 184-188.

46. The argamak is a breed of race horse found in Central Asia and valued greatly in Eastern Europe.

APPENDICES

1. Nikolai Mikhailovich Karamzin (1766-1826) was an historian, writer and publicist. He was associated with the Masonic circle of Novikov and achieved prominence as a litterateur and journalist. In addition to writing histories Karamzin often translated belles-lettres into Russian, and was Russia's leading sentimental novelist during the 1790s as well. In 1803 Karamzin was appointed official Russian historiographer. Edward Thaden writes of him "It would also be incorrect to deny that Karamzin had merits as a historical thinker. The distinction he made between the monarchy of Kiev Rus and the autocracy of Muscovite Russia and his careful and detailed study of the gradual emergence of the unified Muscovite state from the political fragmentation of the appanage system provided a solid foundation for the work of the dominant State school of historians in Russia during the second part of the eighteenth century." MERSH, Volume 16, pp. 9-12.

2. According to Skrynnikov (*Sibirskaia ekspeditsiia*, Chapter I) the *Stroganov Chronicle* was based on a compilation of writings at the Stroganov offices. It is one of several chronicles which tell the story of Yermak's expedition. Skrynnikov carefully examined the texts of the available chronicles to determine their origins and their political leanings. Ironically the Yesipov and Stroganov chronicles probably are based on the same source. The Stroganov chronicle emphasizes the role of the Stroganov family as agents of Moscow in sending the cossacks into Siberia. Whether he was aware of this or not, Soloviev naturally would have tended to look for validation in this viewpoint.

3. P.I. Nebolsin, *Pokorenie Sibiri* (Conquest of Siberia) (St. Petersburg, 1849).

4. Apparently Nebolsin's reference to the anonymous chronicle is actually to the Remezov Chronicle which Armstrong explains was composed by a Tobolsk boyar's son, Semen Ulyanovich Remezov. When the chronicle was found in Tobolsk in 1734 by G.F. Müller, whose *Opisanie Sibirskago Tsarstva* (St. Petersburg, 1750) was the first narrative of the history of Siberia. Müller evidently determined the authorship of this chronicle. According to Armstrong there is a letter code in the last paragraph which reads "'written by Semen Remezov' followed by the names of his four sons Leontey, Semen, Ivan and Peter in the genitive case." It is not clear why Nebolsin insists on calling it the anonymous chronicle. See Armstrong, p. 27.

5. Moscow Archives of the Ministry of Foreign Affairs, Polish Matters, No. 18. The modern citation is TsGADA, fond 79. Relations between Russia and Poland, Volume 18.

6. *The Diary of Stefan Bathory's Final Campaign against Russia (the Siege of Pskov) and the Diplomatic Correspondence of that Period, Relating Primarily to the Conclusion of the Polish Peace (1581-1582)*. Published by M. Koialovich. St. Petersburg, 1867.

INDEX

THE EDITOR AND TRANSLATOR

Although formally a specialist in modern Russia, Alexandra S. Korros always has been particularly interested in Russian medieval history. During her years as a graduate student at Columbia University she studied with Michael Cherniavsky and Andrej Kaminski, learning that medieval Russia's history was as exciting and complex as any series of events preceding the 1917 revolutions.

After receiving her A.B. from Cornell University, Korros earned her M.A. and Ph.D degrees from Columbia, completing her dissertation under the direction of Leopold Haimson, Marc Raeff, and Cherniavsky. Her fascination with medieval Russia began in her second year of graduate school when Michael Cherniavsky arrived as an adjunct professor at Columbia. Cherniavsky's colloquia introduced students to new ways of thinking about the past. His provocative and original teaching style, relying heavily on the same texts Soloviev used to compose his history, taught her to read all sources carefully and critically.

During her varied career Korros has worked as an archival indexer and instructor in Zionist history at the Ben Gurion Research Institute and Archives in Israel, and as a university administrator at Miami University in Ohio where she also taught Russian history. She was a Research Associate at the Center for the Study of the American Jewish Experience of the Hebrew Union College, Jewish Institute of Religion in Cincinnati, Ohio. For the past fifteen years she has taught at Xavier University in Cincinnati where she is Professor of History. A versatile historian, Alexandra Korros has published in American Jewish history, and Russian Jewish history, as well as her first love, Russian history.

FROM ACADEMIC INTERNATIONAL PRESS*

THE RUSSIAN SERIES

*Request catalogs. Sample pages, tables of contents, more on line at www.ai-press.com